George Clarke's

HOME BIBLE

George Clarke's

HOME BIBLE

WEIDENFELD & NICOLSON

George Clarke is an architect and creative director of his architectural practice clarke: desai, property development company dreamspaces and design and build company CDS Build. He is a writer, TV presenter – *Build a New Life* three series for Five), *The Home Show* (two series, a third in preparation for Channel 4) and *Restoration Man* (Channel 4) – and a postgraduate lecturer. He also writes three monthly columns for *Grand Designs Magazine*, *Real Homes* and *Your Home*. He is married with three children.

To my family - Catri, George, Emilio and Iona x

Contents

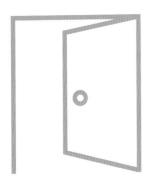  

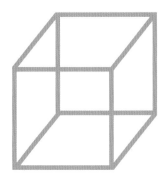

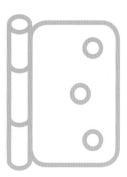

Introduction

'The house is a nest for dreaming, a shelter for imagining ...'

Gaston Bachelard, French philosopher

Since I was a young boy, I've been fascinated by buildings. I would take the bus to nearby towns and cities like Sunderland, Durham or Newcastle to sketch the beautiful architecture that affected the everyday lives of people in the Northeast. From my humble bedroom, I would read books about spectacular buildings that had transformed civilisations in faraway places. I would imagine myself walking through the streets of ancient Rome, climbing to the top of an Egyptian pyramid or scaling the dizzy heights of the Great Wall of China. Since deciding to become an architect at the age of 12, I absorbed myself in hundreds of buildings and dreamed of visiting them all one day. To this day I've only managed to see a tiny fraction of those I've studied; many of them I doubt I'll ever see. I don't mind this at all, for they exist in my mind as such beautiful structures and magical spaces that I'm worried I may be disappointed by the reality of them. I'm happy to dream.

The home I grew up in. It may not be much but it was everything to me… It still is.

My student home: the typical Tyneside flat in Byker, Newcastle.

The first flat I lived in as a student in London.

The home that got me dreaming

But, there is one very real building that meant more to me than any of the architectural wonders I dreamt of as a kid. That building was our family home. Our new home sat in the middle of a revolutionary new town, where everything – from the dazzling town centre, shops, schools, libraries, offices, swimming baths to the public transportation system, road network and enough housing for over 100,000 people – was built in only five years between 1972 and 1977. What was once arable farmland and home only to pigs and sheep became Washington New Town, the jewel in the crown of the Local Development Corporation. It was the realisation of a new philosophy in town planning. I was a human guinea pig thrown into a new social and urban experiment, and I loved it.

Our 1970s home was very simple, brick-built and two storeys high. It had a single-pitched, gently sloping roof that I later learned is called a 'mono-pitched roof'. We were on the end of a terraced row, with three other terraces surrounding us to form a small pedestrianised square in the middle. Here, I could play with my three sisters and my friends in complete safety, away from the roads and cars.

The plan of the house was very good. Downstairs there was a small loo, a cupboard to hang coats, a small but cleverly planned kitchen, and then a decent-sized space to the rear that was used as a combined living and dining room. This room had a huge window giving views out and, alongside it, a standard single door providing access to the small back garden.

Upstairs there were four very small bedrooms with modern full-width windows that, up until the age of about 12, I had to stand on my tiptoes or on my bed to see out of. We had one bathroom, which was a miserable space with no windows or natural light at all, and no shower aside from one of those rubber hoses with a plastic showerhead on the end, which could fit onto the hot and cold bath taps to use in the bath. There was no fire in the house because it had an all-singing, all-dancing central heating system, with combi-boiler and gleaming radiators had been installed in every room to keep us warm. It was a hopeless system! I can't remember the number of times we needed to light a scrunched-up bit of *The Sunderland Echo* to reignite the pilot light in the boiler. Even though this was a new-build house, the building regulations were so poor there wasn't a single piece of thermal insulation in the floors, walls or roof. No matter how much heat we pumped into the place, it soon escaped to warm the cold Northeastern air. It must have cost my Mam and Dad a small fortune to run.

Small but efficient

All of the rooms were small, but the design was very efficient. There was very little wasted space and no pointless corridors. Every single square inch of that house was useful and served a purpose.

To this day I can remember every single part of that house. You spend so much time in your home that its geography becomes part of your subconscious. So much so that if I wandered the house at night, either on boring visits to the loo or more exciting and covert adventures without my parents knowing (on Christmas Eve to see if the presents had arrived), I could navigate my way around perfectly in the dark. I could feel every change of surface along the way and find every step with ease on the staircase – even managing to avoid the only squeaky floorboard mid-flight. I could accurately reach for every door handle and open it at just the right speed to avoid making a single noise. The map of your home – the very essence of its built form and the design of the space that surrounds you – becomes a fundamental part of your being.

Today, our little council house would be referred to as an 'affordable home'. This simple building, built on a shoestring, was the container of all my dreams and the absolute centre of my world for over 15 years. I will never forget that the home in which I raise my kids will not only be remembered by them, but will become part of them for the rest of their lives.

There's no place like home

Our homes are very special places, and they grow to reflect us. I truly believe that there is 'no place like home'. As the 1970s home in which I grew up was for me, your home is *the* most important piece of architecture in your life.

Our homes not only serve the very simple function of protecting us from the elements, but they are powerful containers of intimate spaces that tell a story about our own very unique way of life. A home is constructed using some very basic elements to form walls, floors and roofs; their purpose, when brought together, is to create something that allows us to store all of our personal belongings and live in comfort. That something is *space*.

I moved to Hampstead. The shop beneath us was a handy wine shop when I lived there.

Next, I rented a room in this house in Primrose Hill for a short time.

And then I moved in with my girlfriend, Catri, who soon became my wife.

The concept of space

Space is, without a doubt, the very essence of architecture. It's very difficult to describe what it actually is, as it isn't something that we can necessarily smell, taste, hear or touch. However, it is certainly something that we can see, and spaces that are well designed can stimulate incredible emotions and feelings. Just think about the most beautiful buildings you have visited in your lifetime. Yes, the architectural style and the selection of materials most certainly add to the experience, but if you are able to look beyond these structural elements it is often the atmosphere and quality of the space that lifts your heart.

My job as an architect is to make space work, to create homes that truly reflect the needs of the people who live in them. Although there are many newly built houses in Britain today, the vast majority of us live in older houses that have been around for years and years. Beautiful as they may be, they don't really reflect the way that we live in the 21st century. The layout of the rooms may have been very well designed for the generation for which they were built, but most houses don't suit the needs of our society today. There is nothing more rewarding than redesigning an existing home that not only looks beautiful, but also works.

The meaning of home

I feel that during the biggest boom years the housing market has ever seen since the 1990s, we have lost sight of what 'home' actually means. In fact, the word 'home' has often been replaced with the word 'property', meaning something different altogether. The phenomenal rise in house values meant that we were completely infatuated with how much our 'properties' were worth rather than thinking what a 'home' could do for the emotional wellbeing and happiness of our families.

But when recessions return, which they do regularly, the economic climate makes us look at our houses differently. We have begun to think about our families' 'needs' in a home, rather than our 'wants'. We all love to watch extraordinary modern houses being built on eye-watering budgets, but what about the vast majority of us who don't necessarily want, or can't necessarily afford, such over-indulgent designs? What of those of us who would love to take a more affordable budget and transform the ordinary house in which we already live into something truly special?

Why move house time and time again, just to climb the property ladder? You are throwing hard-earned money down the drain on stamp duty, legal fees and estate agent's fees, and that's money you can never get back. During a recession it's time to stay where you are and improve what you've got.

Efficiency does not depend on what the interior of a home actually looks like, but on how the spaces are organised within it. I had absolutely no idea at the time, but this simplicity of design and the efficient planning would have an enormous effect on my life and the way I would design in the future.

Creating something special

Through the work I do in my office, and in making *The Home Show*, I know that good design and efficient planning can make an ordinary house into a beautiful home on even the smallest budget. It breaks my heart to see people spending the money they've worked so hard to earn having work done on their homes that hasn't been either designed or considered properly. It is a complete waste of time, energy and money. I want to show you how to avoid doing this.

So what is it that we want from a home? For years I've asked people what they consider to be their most important need when they think of home. I've been given a wide range of answers, from people wanting their homes to be 'beautiful', 'light' and 'ecological' to 'practical' or 'with stunning views'; however, the answer I hear more than any other is that people want their home to be *'comfortable'*.

Comfort is a very simple human need, and yet it never fails to amaze me that, in all of my years of architectural study, the word 'comfort' has only been used on a couple of occasions. You would expect comfort to play a massive role in home architecture and appear constantly within academic lectures and debates; however, the truth is that the word has been relegated to fairly uninspiring technical design lectures about heating and ventilation systems. Architects felt uncomfortable with comfort. They believed that cosy and comfortable architecture couldn't possibly be radical and contemporary. But it *can*. We want comfort in our homes, realised through efficient planning and good design appropriate for the needs of 21st-century society. It's important that we rediscover the beauty of comfort.

I want this book to be an inspirational guide, one you can return to time and time again – a guide that will help you to avoid the many common pitfalls into which people stumble when refurbishing their homes. I want to share with you all of my experience, knowledge and the tricks of the trade that I've learned since starting my apprenticeship at an architect's practice at the tender age of 16, and subsequently redesigning hundreds of homes across Britain.

This book will open up your mind and show you the exciting opportunities that exist in many perfectly average homes across Britain and how making the simplest changes at the lowest cost can have the most incredible effect on transforming a space. With this bible at your fingertips to guide you every step of the way on the journey of home improvement, you will discover that the house you live in right now could be the home of your dreams.

Happy reading, designing and building … good luck!

How often I hear people exploring the inside of well-designed public buildings and saying to their friends: 'What a beautiful space.' Why shouldn't we say the same for our very ordinary domestic homes?

Section 1

My home story

'Home is where the heart is ...' John McLeod

I'm going to share my home with you. This was a big decision for me and my family, because it reveals our hidden world. Our home is a very special, personal and – until now – a very private place that I hold very dear to my heart. Other than close family and friends, very few people have been into my home and it has never been published in any other book, magazine or column. I've briefly discussed it in lectures and presentations, but you are the first to see it in so much detail.

The reason I've decided to welcome you into our home is because it is the best example I can ever use to show you all of the decisions I had to make to change a very ordinary and unloved Edwardian house into a unique family home. This was an ambitious refurbishment for a fairly typical semi-detached house, so some of these decisions were quite radical; however, when it came to the detail of the redesign, the majority of the decisions were small: moving a wall 30 centimetres one way, or a bedroom door several centimetres the other. Irrespective of its finished style, it captures so many of my philosophies about what a home should be.

I want my home to show you the intimate values of inside space. Making a series of spaces work to suit the specific needs of your family will transform your lives forever, and I'm here to show you how.

My home and building history

When we leave home and fly the nest of comfort, safety and general pampering by our parents, many of us move out to rent a room in a small flat. My first such room was on the first floor of a traditional Victorian Tyneside flat near the Byker Wall in Tyneside, and I shared it with two other architecture students. Thankfully, the room was nearly double the size of the one I had at my parents' house, so I could fit in a bed, my drawing board, a radio and CD player, and some pretty dodgy clothes. This was the beginning of life as a flat-hopper. I also slept on a few sofas, floors and spare bedrooms in Primrose Hill and Hampstead (among other places), until I settled down and moved in with my girlfriend (now my wife, Catri) in a flat near Hyde Park.

My architectural practice had been established for some time and we made the decision to get married and start a family. Being at the top of a Georgian apartment block with no lift wasn't ideal when I was entering into the world of baby buggies and pushbikes, so we started to look for a house. We needed to move further out of the area to be able to afford a bigger place, but that was fine with us.

At the starting block

For all of my life, I had vowed never to buy a finished house that was ready to move into; I knew I'd always want to rip out someone else's style and taste and do my own thing. Why pay money for a finished place, when I'd change it anyway? A good estate-agent friend of mine called to say that a rundown place had come onto the market. An elderly couple had passed away and their family had decided to sell it on. It was a very tall, five-storey, very skinny Victorian house, with lots of stairs. It was *huge*, and from the outside looked like my dream home. Inside, the layout and the size of the rooms were pretty good, so we wouldn't need to move many internal walls. However, the condition of the place was appalling. There was no kitchen, toilets or bathrooms in there at all, and everything would have to be done from scratch, from top to bottom.

I'm telling you the story of this particular property because I did something that I have promised myself I will *never* do again. It's something that I want you all to learn from, so you'll never make the same mistake yourselves.

top left and right The day we viewed the house with the agent; and the scaffolding goes up for the new roof.

bottom left and right The internal spaces are stripped bare; and the finished family home…brought back to life.

The truth is that Catri and I completely overstretched ourselves. I was young and naïve, and committed to a place that not only cost a small fortune to buy, but would cost another small fortune to refurbish. We didn't have enough money but we spent the next three years doing up every room – bit by bit, whenever we had a few spare pennies. My stress levels were going through our leaking roof and there were a lot of sleepless nights.

During the build, we somehow managed to have our two boys – Georgie and Emilio – who seemed very content being raised on a permanent building site, surrounded by chippies, brickies, plumbers, painters and decorators. Where most kids play with a few blocks of Lego and toy tool sets, ours were doing the real thing. The builders made great childcare assistants, the boys were happy as Larry, and I managed to keep the costs down with a bit of cheap labour paid in jelly babies.

Joking aside, as the refurbishment works were nearing completion I began to notice two major things. First, the financial pressure to buy and refurbish such a big house was no fun at all, and we weren't enjoying the process. In fact, it was so unsettling that it created a huge barrier that really prevented us from falling in love with the house. Secondly, and far more importantly, I had begun to realise that even though we had spent a great deal of money doing up a huge house, it simply didn't work.

I'll never make either of these mistakes again. I'd been so seduced by the grandeur of the place – and so desperate not to lose out on what seemed to be a great opportunity – that when I bought it I really hadn't thought about the way the house worked and whether it was right for us.

The kids never went to their bedrooms, as they were right at the top of the house; the living room was on the first floor, miles away from the kitchen and dining room; and the garden was north-facing, which the kids hated because it never got a single ray of sunshine. Worst of all, we were sick and tired of constantly having to run up and down the seven flights of stairs.

The day the house was finished, and without telling Catri, I called my mate the estate agent to get him round to value it. I sold it three weeks later without a single regret. The lesson is simple: when you go and visit a potential property on the market, *really* think about how the spaces work, to be sure there is an opportunity to get the home you really want. And whatever you do, do not overstretch yourself financially. It's just not worth it.

opposite The house was completely impractical for us. We were constantly running up and down flights of stairs, the kids never wanted to be in their rooms and the garden never saw even a glimpse of sun.

The house that never really became our home

Kids bedroom

Kids bedroom

Master bedroom

Living room

Kitchen/dining room

Self-contained flat

Downscaling

With a young family, we made the wise decision to reduce our burden of debt and downscale. We gave up the idea of a statement home and began to look for something that would become a practical and comfortable home. We camped out in a rental flat and began the hunt for a more sensible property – one that we could afford and enjoy doing up. Lesson learned.

Only a few hundred metres from our old place, a very ordinary and unimpressive semi-detached house had come onto the market. It was Edwardian in style, but had been stripped of so many of its period features that it was a desperately sad house. The original clay roof tiles had been replaced with ugly, man-made copies; the old timber sliding-sash windows had long gone, thick metal-framed windows had taken their place. Over its 100-year history the interior had been knocked around so many times – and walls reconfigured in such bizarre locations – that the spaces had lost all of their character and identity. It was a mess, but I loved it.

This house was built around 1910, as part of a West London residential housing estate. Apart from a few minor variations in style, the design and layout of every house on the estate is roughly the same. The house was two storeys high, and built of London red bricks, with a bay window to the front, and a hipped roof. Although it had four small bedrooms, it was only around 1500 square feet (or about 455 square metres), which was less than half the size of the property we'd just sold. This would be a big downscale for us!

Large-scale five-storey town house...

A home with a history

When speaking to the owner, I got the impression that the house had been in his family since the day it was built. He was a lovely guy – a retired engineer, who was obviously a bit of a DIY enthusiast because he'd had a go at every part of the house over the years. Like most DIY boys, there was no real master plan to his work; he just randomly tinkered with electrics, plumbing, and fixtures and fittings, when change was necessary. He'd reached the point where the general arrangement of the spaces and the building's services were not only outdated, but all over the place. He was so passionate about all the work he had done to the place that, when we first met him, it took him over three hours to talk us through every single electrical circuit, pipe run and joist position. I was so absorbed in this man and his storytelling that my car had been towed away!

His father had lived in it before him and, at one point, the two floors had been split into two separate flats to generate a bit of extra income when they didn't need so much space. So they'd obviously bashed around all the electrics and plumbing again. It was knocked back into one single dwelling and, although he and his wife had moved away some time ago, the place had become home to his daughter. Soon to be married, she was ready to move on with her new husband, so the family was ready to sell.

While it may not have seemed a gem to some prospective buyers, we felt lucky to find it. We wanted to put a smile back on the face of this house again and make it into a home. I couldn't wait to get started.

I love old buildings because they tell us stories about the past. They have qualities that a new-build home takes generations to possess.

...............and just down the road.................…..... a two-storey small-scale Edwardian house.

Before ...!

My home profile

The layout of our new house was very typical of most semi-detached Edwardian houses but, because it had been knocked around a lot, there were some odd routes and spaces.

As you walked through the front door and into the hallway, you were greeted with a staircase on your left-hand side and a long corridor running from the front to the back of the house. Getting into the existing living room was nothing short of bizarre: you walked past the staircase, turned left under the stairs, turned again through a dark corridor, past a small door to a study/office, and then through the living room door! Why you couldn't just enter the living room straight off the entrance hallway was beyond me. The nicest part of the living room, however difficult it was to reach, was the original bay window.

Only five metres wide?

Although it was in its original position, the staircase also didn't feel right. The overall width of the house is only 5 metres, which sounds fine in theory, but by the time you take off the space for the two runs of corridor and the staircase, plus the width of the dividing walls, the remaining study room is only 2 metres wide. Having 3 of 5 metres taken up by corridors and a staircase seemed like a complete waste to me!

In all of the rooms, the brick chimney breasts were still in place; however, none of the fires worked or they had been stripped out. These large brick projections made the spaces feel narrow.

An impractical layout

The ground-floor toilet was in a sensible location, as all of the drainage in the house came down in the corner of the side yard; but the space itself was depressing. If you sat on the loo, you had the hot radiator burning your left knee, while you sweated from the heat coming from the tumble dryer on your right, or the hot-water tank directly in front of you. I won't even *bother* going into the general style of the room and its finish …

Outside the toilet door was the darkest part of the house. There was no natural light at all, and the corridor lights had to be switched on constantly just to see where you were going. It was a poor atmosphere, environmentally unfriendly, and an expensive addition to our electric bill.

opposite The dark and dingy entrance hall; the unmodernised living room; the depressing kitchen; and the architecturally desperate loo.

The kitchen was far too small for a family home, and incredibly dark. Light only entered the space through a small window and side-access door. The kitchen units were badly arranged; for example, there was a washing machine in the most ridiculous location – squeezed into the corner with such poor accessibility there was a risk you could burn yourself on your cooker each time you had to load and unload the machine.

After walking through the kitchen you entered the separate dining room at the very back of the house. This was a reasonably sized room with access out to the back garden through an old set of aluminium sliding doors. But the room was never really used by the family, and there was no strong connection with the kitchen. The kitchen was for cooking and the dining room was for eating, with no other social interaction or activity happening in these spaces.

Outside, the garden was a good size; I didn't want anything bigger as no one in my family is a keen gardener. The side yard, however, was purely a dumping ground for rubbish bags and lawnmowers, and a complete waste of space.

Too much circulation space makes for an inefficient plan. The best plans reduce circulation space and maximise liveable space. These diagrams show the ratio of liveable space to inefficient space.

Used space

Poorly used space

Inefficient space

Ground floor plan

First floor plan

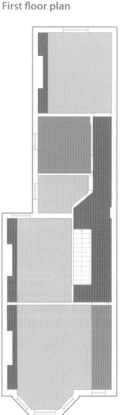

Moving upstairs

Upstairs, the layout was very straightforward and ordinary. The master bedroom was at the front of the house, facing west, with the lovely bay window. As a space, the staircase and landing were pretty good, as they were lit by a very small skylight in the roof, but the staircase position still annoyed me. Alongside the staircase was bedroom number two. This was a very simple room, but with a redundant chimney breast wasting much-needed space.

In the centre of the plan was the family bathroom. The location for this made sense, as it was situated over the ground-floor loo, keeping drainage runs to a minimum. But again, the room itself was outdated and completely depressing. There was no separate shower cubicle, so you had to stand in the bath using a hose connected to the hot- and cold-water taps. What's more, because showering took place right next to the side window, the owners had installed rippled glass, so the neighbours couldn't see in. I hate this stuff! Although people can't see you, it cuts down the light and you can't see out of the window, making the room even more claustrophobic. This is simply bad planning. And if that wasn't bad enough, you had to have a fight with an old plastic shower curtain while taking your shower. I hate shower curtains!

Alongside the bathroom was bedroom three – the worst bedroom in this house. You couldn't fit a double bed in there and, even with a single bed, it was a struggle to fit in any wardrobe space. If you managed to achieve this feat, there would certainly be no room left for an occupant!

At the back of the house, the fourth bedroom wasn't too bad, and it provided views over the back garden. Again, however, the unused fire and chimney breast had no other use than being a good spot to keep a wastepaper basket.

The loft provided storage, lots of hot and cold water pipes running everywhere, and a couple of huge water tanks to give a head of pressure to the bathroom beneath.

This house was a design disaster, but it got my creative juices flowing and I could see possibilities everywhere. The most important thing, however, was to get it right for my family and the way we live.

My family profile

When we bought the house we had two very small boys: Georgie was nearly four, and Emilio was nearly two. Catri was also pregnant with our third child. It's amazing how we all decide to do refurbishment work to our homes at the worst time – either just before or after a new baby is born. Maybe it all comes down to the nesting thing.

The boys liked to share a room, so with a new baby coming we would need a minimum of three bedrooms. As they grew older, they'd undoubtedly all want their own spaces, and because we often have family and friends to stay, it was clear that we could do with five bedrooms. This, however, would probably have to wait!

We are a very sociable family and we love to interact as much as possible in the living, kitchen and dining areas of a home. I like spaces to be as open and light as possible, but I'm not always a fan of open-plan living, where kitchen-dining spaces are in your living room. Don't get me wrong: they are wonderful spaces architecturally, but if your kids want to watch TV while you are cooking and chatting with friends in the kitchen area, your voices tend to enter into a volume war with the TV. I prefer an element of division and control.

I love homes to be as modern as possible, but not minimal. Design and style have to be of the highest quality, and spaces have to work perfectly. After a number of moves, I decided that I wanted this house to be a home for life. So what basic ingredients did *we* need to make the perfect home for *our* family?

- 3 bedrooms (short term)
- 5 bedrooms (medium–long term)
- Living room (spacious)
- Fire (real)
- Combined kitchen-dining room (big, light)
- Utility room (self-contained)
- Home office (quiet)
- Garden (green, nice)
- Storage (lots!)
- Wardrobes (integrated)
- Natural light (every room)
- Artificial lighting (designed, integrated, dimmable)
- Style (modern, practical, durable, comfortable)
- Water (soft, hot and cold, high pressure)
- Heating (no radiators)
- Materials (quality)
- Ecology (insulation)
- Furniture (beautiful)

And after ...!

The redesign

'The reality of the building does not consist in the roof and walls, but in the space within to be lived in.' Lao-Tse: Chinese philosopher, born c. 640BC

Designing a new home from scratch is relatively easy. You have a plot of land with very few constraints and you create a vision for it. Radically redesigning an existing home that has all of its elements in the wrong position, and spaces that don't work, is like playing with a sliding puzzle. To complete the puzzle, you have to push, slide and reconfigure all of the pieces into the small gaps available – testing every avenue of opportunity until all of the individual squares are rearranged perfectly, to reveal the completed picture. Reconfiguring houses is no different. Through the process of drawing, all of the building elements, such as walls, stairs, floors, roofs, windows and doors, have to be pushed, pulled and manipulated in all different directions – over and over again, until the final plan is created. It can be very difficult – move a wall one way to make one space work, but the space on the other side may not feel right. So you move it again.

When I'm redesigning a home I sit down with the existing plans of the old structure, a black pen and a large roll of tracing paper. I quickly sketch, producing overlay after overlay, testing idea after idea, pushing around the elements of the architectural puzzle until all of the rooms become the right spaces to live in. This is architecture.

Redesigning every single element of my home was a challenge. There were so many things wrong with the existing spaces that nearly every internal element had to move. It would have been much easier to demolish the entire building and start again, but we lived in a conservation area, so demolition wasn't an option.

The following drawings show you the key moves I made to make the house work.

top left and right The staircase moves to the side to create a larger living space; the glass roofed kitchen makes the space bigger and lighter.

bottom left and right Losing the corridor creates a more open plan and spacious living room; and our master bedroom.

My new home

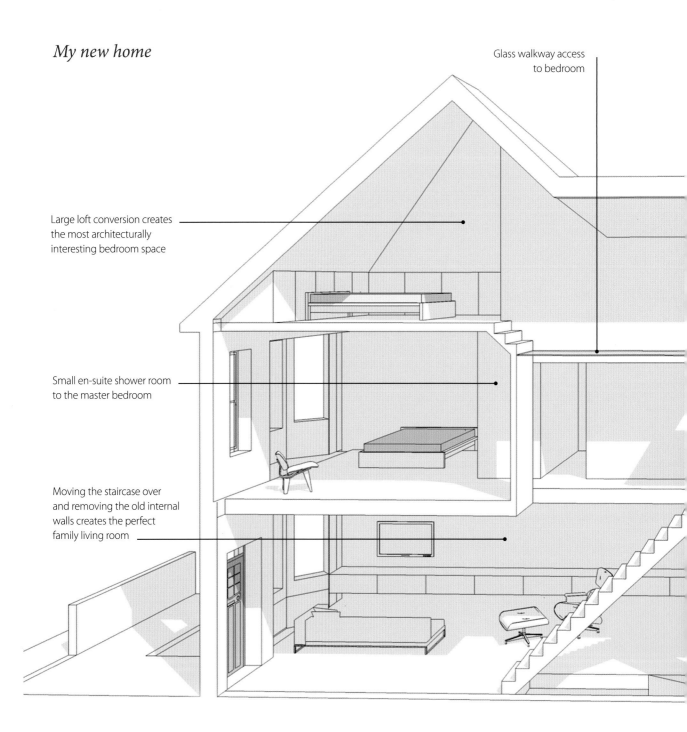

Glass walkway access to bedroom

Large loft conversion creates the most architecturally interesting bedroom space

Small en-suite shower room to the master bedroom

Moving the staircase over and removing the old internal walls creates the perfect family living room

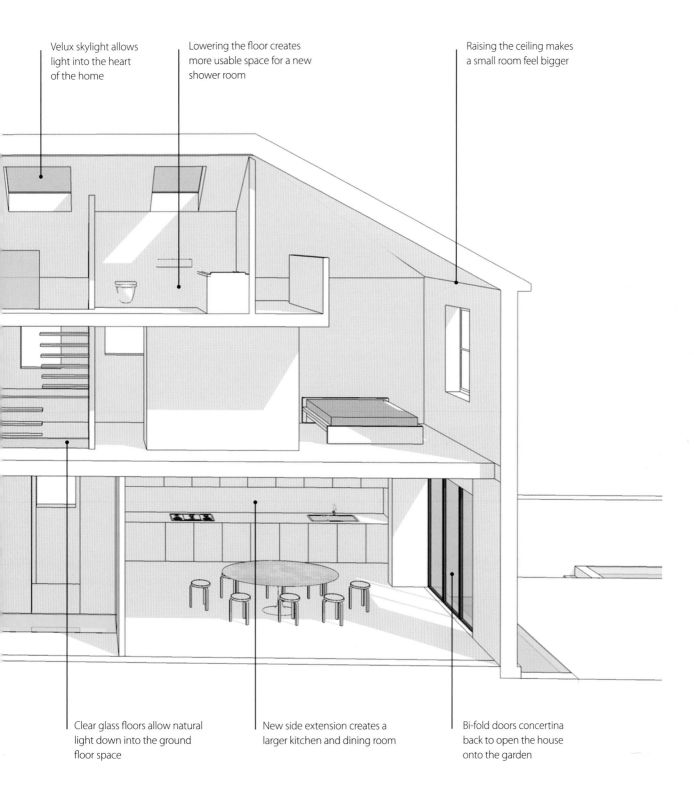

Velux skylight allows light into the heart of the home

Lowering the floor creates more usable space for a new shower room

Raising the ceiling makes a small room feel bigger

Clear glass floors allow natural light down into the ground floor space

New side extension creates a larger kitchen and dining room

Bi-fold doors concertina back to open the house onto the garden

Downstairs (ground floor)

1. Move the staircase from the middle of the plan to the sidewall to create a much wider living space.
2. Create new storage space under the staircase.
3. Remove all of the walls that form the existing living room and study.
4. The dark corridor space running the length of the house is lost. A new route is created through a larger living space.
5. If you circulate through a room to get to another you must arrange your furniture at design stage to make sure the routes and the space work.
6. Create a larger ground-floor toilet and a new utility room.
7. Relocate the water tanks and boiler up into the roof space. The ground-floor spaces are too important to be taken up by tanks and boilers.
8. To get light into the darkest part of the plan, install a glass floor in the ceiling of the small corridor to get light from the skylight above.
9. Create built-in storage to the side of the corridor opposite the toilet door.
10. Demolish the wall between the existing kitchen and dining room to make a combined space.
11. I still need a bigger kitchen and dining area. Build a new side extension, right out to the boundary wall to create a bigger space.
12. Keep a small outside yard to store rubbish from the kitchen, and it maintains external side access to the front of the house.
13. Create a larger opening to the back of the house to give a better connection to the garden.
14. Design a canopy over the doors so that I can have the doors open in the summer, even when it's raining.

above The living room and study were knocked through to create a beautiful light living room.

below The bi-fold doors onto the garden really give a sense of extra space.

Ground floor plan

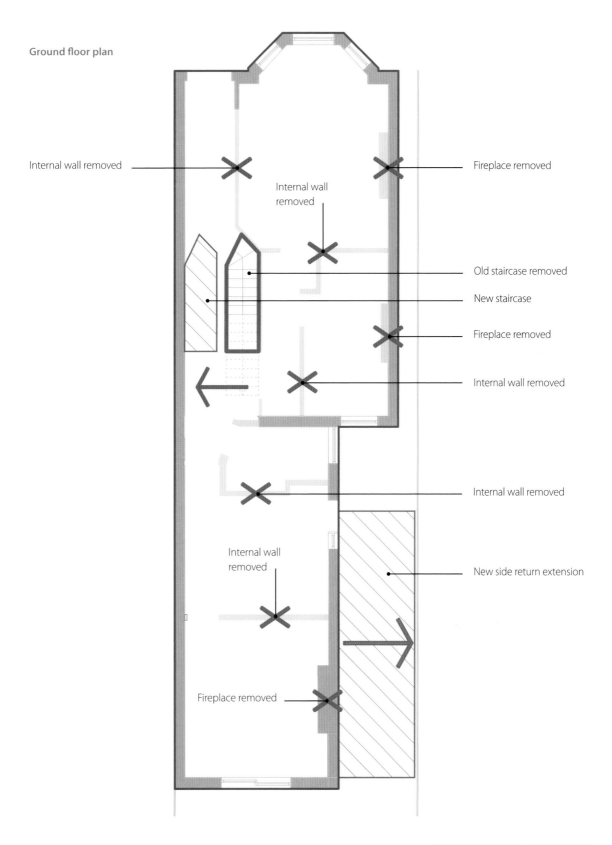

Internal wall removed

Internal wall removed

Fireplace removed

Old staircase removed

New staircase

Fireplace removed

Internal wall removed

Internal wall removed

Internal wall removed

New side return extension

Fireplace removed

above The open riser staircase and the glass panels let the light bounce around.

Upstairs (first floor)

1 The staircase is moved to the sidewall.
2 The new glass floor provides a view down to the ground floor.
3 The flat ceiling is removed and a new, larger skylight is installed in the sloping roof. You are flooded with light.
4 The old bathroom is removed to make way for the new staircase to the loft. The old bathroom window is opened up and made central to the new staircase.
5 The door to the master bedroom moves over. This frees up much-needed wall space for wardrobes.
6 The redundant chimney breast is removed from the master bedroom; the bed can go up against this wall and a wider room is created.
7 The wall between the master bedroom and bedroom two is removed to make way for a new en-suite shower room. I'm basically stealing 40cm from each space.
8 The chimney breast is removed to form bedroom two.
9 Bedroom three is made into the new family bathroom. The bathroom is given a much wider window.
10 The old bedroom four now becomes bedroom three. The chimney breast is removed and the flat ceiling is opened up to follow the slope of the roof, to give greater height.
11 A mezzanine sleeping deck is built in at high level and accessed by a ladder. The sleeping deck allows the space beneath to be used as a home office.

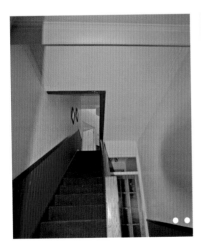

Wall and old staircase position

Staircase moves over mid-build

The finished staircase

First floor plan

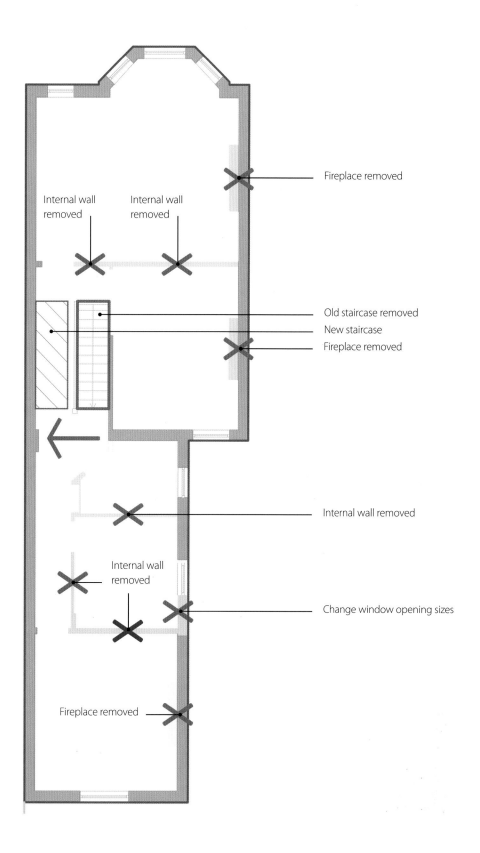

Fireplace removed

Internal wall removed

Internal wall removed

Old staircase removed

New staircase

Fireplace removed

Internal wall removed

Internal wall removed

Change window opening sizes

Fireplace removed

Loft Conversion (second floor)

1 The new stairs up to the loft conversion are open-riser, to let in as much light as possible.
2 The loft floor level has been lowered in the corridor areas to provide more room in the loft space. This allows a shower room to be installed near the top of the stairs.
3 The lowered floor is built-in frosted glass, which makes the floor thin and light. A solid floor would make the floor very thick and would make the space feel claustrophobic.
4 A few steps up take you back to the original loft level and into the new loft bedroom.
5 As I have a hipped roof, rather than a gabled roof, there is not as much space as I would like; but, it's enough. I couldn't change the roof profile at all, as the house is in a conservation area.
6 The hipped roof also meant I could not install a large dormer window. Instead, there are two simple Velux skylights.

bottom left and right Not your ordinary loft conversion stair. The kids love it; and the kids' loft bedroom is a world of angles, shapes and light.

Loft space before

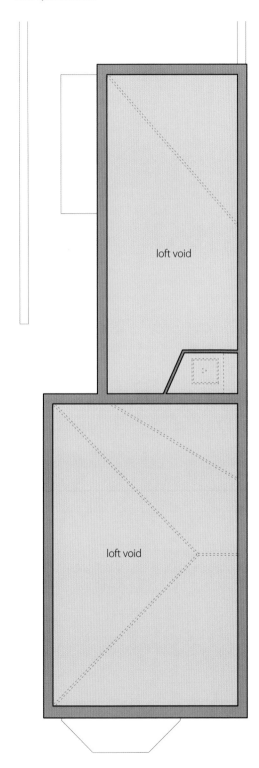

loft void

loft void

Loft space after

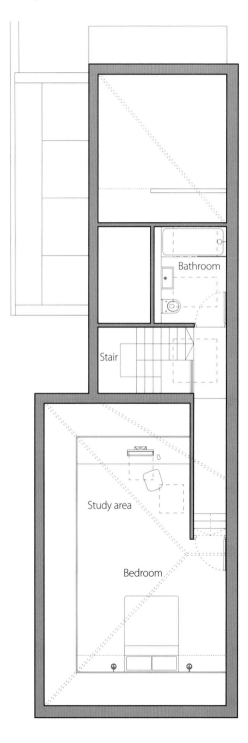

Bathroom

Stair

Study area

Bedroom

Ground floor plan before

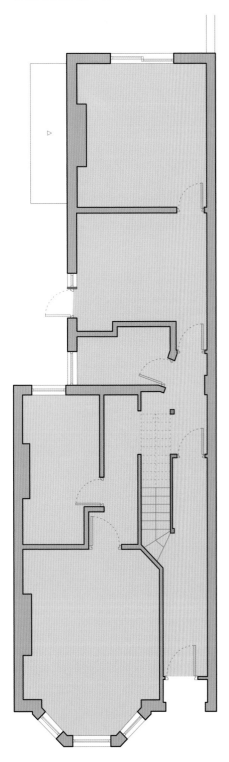

Ground floor plan after

Kitchen

Dining area

WC/Utility

Storage

Storage

Living room

First floor plan before

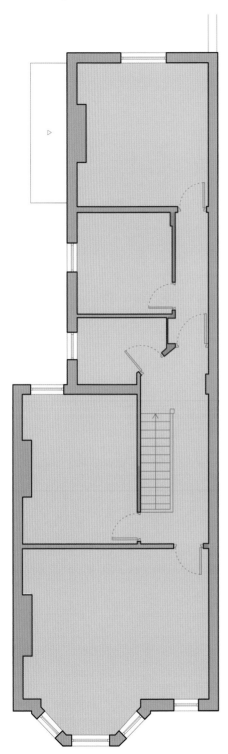

First floor plan after

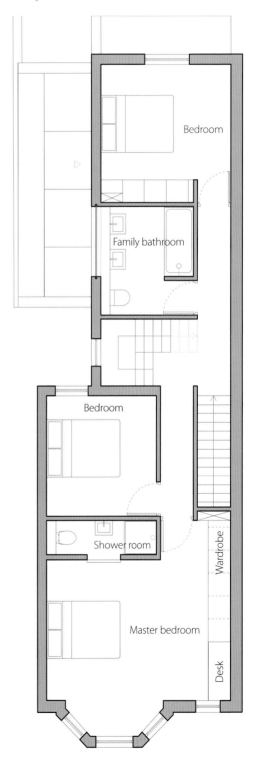

Bedroom

Family bathroom

Bedroom

Shower room

Wardrobe

Master bedroom

Desk

Ground floor plan

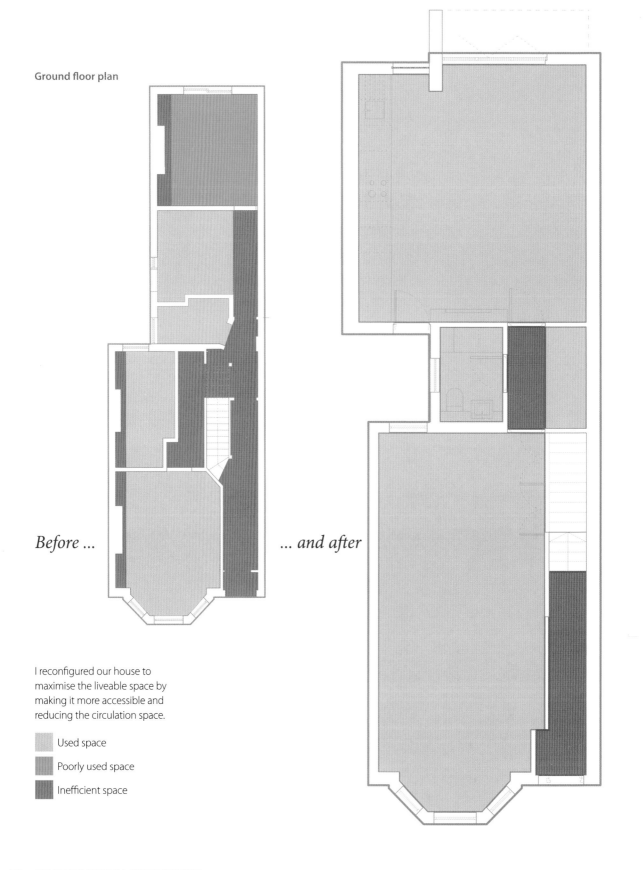

Before ...

... and after

I reconfigured our house to maximise the liveable space by making it more accessible and reducing the circulation space.

Used space

Poorly used space

Inefficient space

First floor plan

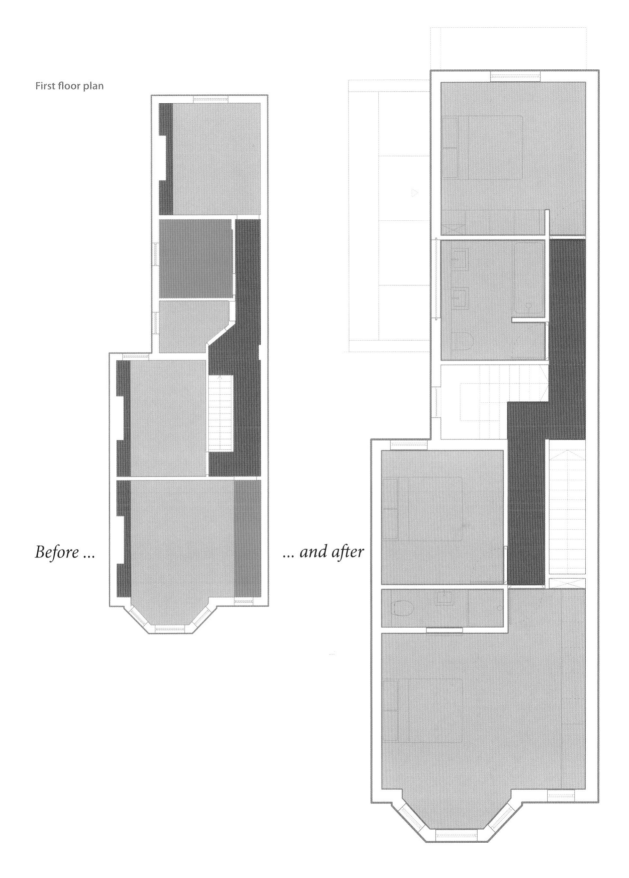

Before ...

... and after

The build

The building process is incredibly difficult, mainly because there are so many different trades and people involved. At the top of the pile is you, the client, followed by a site foreman and then a full team of builders who will work on site: electricians, joiners, plumbers, plasterers, brick layers, kitchen-fitters, floor-layers, tilers ... the list is practically endless. Someone needs to position themselves in order to manage every member of that team.

I've been working on building sites since the age of 16, so I took the decision to manage everybody from the very beginning to the very end of the project. I wanted to oversee every element of my build because of what my home means to me, and also because I could save some money in the process. But it was daunting; because of my other commitments, there was a good chance that I wouldn't be on site as often as I needed to be. That's a crucial element of successful project management; everyone from the tradesmen upwards needs to know where to find you, and fast.

During my build, I broke the first rule of home renovation: *Never go on holiday and leave the builders on their own.* If you are responsible for project-managing the work, you need to be there or two things happen. First, the pace slows down on the build (your builders will deny this until they are blue in the face but, like they do in all small companies, staff go into mini-holiday mode while the boss is away). Secondly, the team starts making 'executive decisions' in your absence, changing important design details that cost money to put right.

It goes without saying that you do have to put them right because my second rule of home renovation is: *Never compromise.* It's your home and you will be living in it for many years after the builders have moved on. Compromises and someone else's executive decisions will drive you mad when you have to look at them every day.

Project management is a full-time job, so if you've already got one, be prepared. Most importantly, get some help and support because you're going to need it.

A builder that is highly recommended, with a track record of reliability and good-quality workmanship, is worth his weight in gold. And, yes, they do exist!

Managing the build

The management of any building project is the key to its success. There's no doubt about it: if you manage it badly, the build is going to cost you a lot more money, take a lot more time and be a lot more stressful. The building process is all about communication – keeping everybody happy, organised and well informed of everything that needs to be done in order for the entire team to realise the perfect refurbishment.

Having made the decision to project manage my own home, I allocated a site foreman with whom I'd worked for many years on site. His job would be to keep control of the project, making sure that we had all the right labour and materials on site for the house to be built. With such a busy TV and office schedule, I knew there was a risk that I'd be away from the site for longer periods than I'd hoped. Away from site, however, I could keep on top of all of the paperwork to ensure that the project was on time and on budget. Project management is really a full-time job, and my schedule was unforgiving. This meant that there were many late nights, weekends and long hours fitted into my daily routine to keep on top of it all.

TO MANAGE A PROJECT PROPERLY AWAY FROM THE SITE:
1 Monitor all of the building costs every week. Whenever an invoice comes in, make sure it's paid for and then filed away. Figures should be put on to a spreadsheet immediately to make sure you know the running costs at any point in time throughout the building project.
2 Make sure the project programme and the schedule are being met so that the guys are doing their work efficiently – and in a timely manner. You'll need to know who's doing what and when.
3 Stay in contact with the site foreman to make sure you have the right trades on site at the right time.
4 Make sure the specification of *all* of the products and materials is crystal clear. Ensure that they are ordered in time and delivered to the site as and when they are needed. You don't want all of your products and materials turning up at the beginning of the job and getting in the way of all the guys on site, who need some space to do their work.
5 Push as hard as possible for a good trade discount, to get the best deal on everything you need. Visit a few building merchants to find out what's on offer.
6 Think about creating your own building materials account with your local building merchants. I organised one at the outset of the project, which meant that I qualified for all trade discounts. It also made it easier for the site foreman to order all the materials he needed.

Tip Building merchants are an important part of the community and can give you much of the advice you need to move forward with any home-building project. If you are stuck for good tradesmen, your local building merchant can supply you with recommendations you can trust.

Cramped kitchen and dining rooms ...

... into light open space.

Becoming your own contractor

Because of all of the experience I have had in the building game, I was, in effect, the main contractor. Everything from the materials to the labour was done at cost, and nobody else was making a profit on the project. This allowed me to stretch my budget that much further, but it definitely meant more work for me.

I had a responsibility to arrange the site professionally, taking care of everything from health and safety requirements to building and contract insurance – and even public liability insurance to protect everybody on site. Being your own contractor isn't something you should enter into lightly, but if you're confident and if you've had experience doing it before, then it's a really exciting way of running the job. Working in such a hands-on way means that you can make decisions as you go, and really take control of the fine details.

The demolition game

Once the project was set up, we could begin the stripping out. The stripping out of the build is incredibly exciting. By stripping the home naked of old furniture and carpets, getting rid of old wallpaper and light fittings, pulling out old ceilings, breaking out walls, you can create a blank canvas of space before rebuilding your dream home.

In my home, we cleared out as much as possible, which was a major transformation of a very ordinary Edwardian home. There was very little in the old house that was really worth keeping; all of the period features had already gone. I had major plans for the house – changing all of the services, and the positions of the walls and staircases – so everything had to go, apart from the surrounding brick walls. That meant removing all of the internal walls and floors, and taking off all the old concrete roof tiles. We left the roof timbers in place, but away went the electrics, the plumbing and all of the light switches until just a shell was left.

This was an incredibly radical step, but because the old building was in such a state of disrepair, there really was nothing worth keeping. Moreover, this was a house in which I planned to stay for a very long time, so I wanted everything in it to be brand new, fully covered and guaranteed.

Stripping out isn't cheap; every single skip cost me £250 to be dropped off, filled and taken away again. My skip bills alone were nearly £10,000, and that doesn't include the huge amount of labour that was needed to bag everything up and fill the skips. This is one thing worth considering as so many people forget about the very basic costs of doing a major refurbishment project – at their peril! Everything from the skips and plastic bags to the brushes required to sweep up the site have to be paid for from your own pocket.

When you plan changes in your own home, make sure your design ambitions are based on a very clear and realistic budget, or you're in trouble!

opposite The master bedroom was gutted – electrics, the internal wall, chimney breast, the switches all went. In fact, the only things to remain in place were the roof timbers.

The finished house

I love my home. Turning what was an average, 1910 Edwardian
semi into something unique, and designed with our family needs in
mind, has been a tremendous achievement and a fantastic exercise
in creativity. As an architect, there is nothing more rewarding than
transforming the ordinary into something truly extraordinary. From
the outside, the house represents a great restoration project; on the
inside, I have created a very different and modern interior world.
When people visit the house they are truly shocked by the difference
between what they see outside and what they discover when they
walk through that front door.

It's not just the architectural transformation that makes this home
something special. It is the fact that the spaces and the way that they
are arranged inside absolutely suit the way that my family and I live.
Every single square inch of available space has been redesigned and
maximised, to create what is for me the perfect family home. A home
cannot be a successful piece of design if it achieves architectural
success as a piece of modern design, but then fails to be practical
and functional as a family dwelling. The best homes are those that
achieve the perfect balance of being a stunning piece of architecture,
while being functionally and practically designed to create a series
of exciting spaces. The design has to work for *living*, providing
comfortable living spaces, efficient kitchens, much-needed utility
rooms, good-sized bedrooms, functional bathrooms, and as much
integrated storage as possible. Thankfully, my home does all of these
things.

Family living

The complete refurbishment was very substantial and we knew
that we would need a reasonable budget. This was a house that we
planned to live in for many years to come and it was, therefore,
something in which I was more than happy to invest. We are lucky
to live in a good area, which means that there was no risk of over-
investing in the property. Making changes to create a dynamic and
practical living space was important to me, but it was also essential
that I got the standard, quality and finish that would last a long time.
I didn't plan on replacing any fixtures or fittings for years.

On the ground floor, the large living room is perfect for us.
Designed as two separate zones, there is a TV-seating area close to
the bay window, and then – towards the back of the space – an area
that is soft and cosy, with a real fireplace, a smart area to sit, and lots

For me, the greatest challenge was always to get as much light as possible into the centre of the house, and I achieved this by opening up the rooms, creating a stunning glass floor that allows us to receive light from the sky all the way down to the ground floor, and creating a light metal staircase up to the loft.

of my books. Under the stairs, there is tons of integrated storage, which is essential to modern living with children in the house. Through a small corridor on the ground floor, there is a utility toilet on one side, more storage on the other and, above the corridor, one of the most exciting architectural moves of this very simple piece of domestic architecture: a clear glass floor that allows you to look all the way up through the house, from the ground floor to the first floor, right up to the loft level and through the roof to the sky above. This made what was a very boxy house into something truly special and three-dimensional – and flooded with natural light.

Straight ahead is the open-plan kitchen and dining area. Unless you live in an enormous house, I think separate formal dining rooms are a complete waste of space. For my family, it was all about kitchen and dining, with some extra seating in the same zone. This is, in effect, a separate living space, which is, for me, essential in a family home. When your kids are sitting watching a DVD in the living room, you can be in the kitchen making lots of noise without disturbing them! A major part of any refurbishment is controlling the space in an elegant way, to suit the way you live.

When you walk up the stairs to the first floor, you are standing in one of the most exciting spaces in the house. What was once a miserable hallway is floored in glass, allowing you to look down to the ground floor. Above is frosted glass, giving access to the loft via a metal staircase with open risers. I went for a metal staircase with thin stairs to allow as much light as possible into the house, through the side window. For me, the greatest challenge was always to get as much light as possible into the centre of the house.

From here, there is the main family bathroom, a bedroom at the rear of the house, and then two further bedrooms, one of which is my master bedroom. Up at loft level, there is a separate en-suite shower room and the main loft conversion. None of the spaces in the house are too big, and none are too small. The balance, scale and size of these rooms suit the way that we live perfectly, and will do for many years to come. That's why it's absolutely critical to make all of these important decisions at the design stage; you don't want to get it wrong when you're on site.

opposite The kitchen became the heart of the home.

above left and right The glass floors are one of my favourite aspects of the design – the place is flooded with natural light.

Lighting

Lighting in any home is incredibly important. Natural daylight brings architecture to life during the day; however, it's the very clever use of artificial lighting that brings architecture of any description to life at night. In fact, no matter how well you've redesigned the spaces, if you get the design of artificial lighting wrong in your home, they will never be enjoyed to their maximum effect when the sun goes down.

When thinking about your lighting scheme, the key word you should never forget is *flexibility*. Being able to adjust and control the different lighting levels throughout the spaces in your home gives you the flexibility to change the atmosphere, the ambience and the mood. I don't think it makes any difference whether your style of lighting is modern or traditional; what does matter is that you get it right. In my own home there are very different types of lighting to do a multitude of very particular jobs.

Making use of technology

While you can obviously stick to the very simple light switch, with hang-down pendant light fitting, it's worth taking a look at the lighting technology that now exists. Some of these new products can definitely provide you with a greater level of flexibility and control. There is a danger that some of these products are so technologically advanced and complicated that it's often difficult to know how to use them. Some of them however, are straightforward and worth considering.

In my home, I went for a lighting-control system called 'i Light', which allows me to create different scenes and lighting levels in each space, at the touch of a button. If you can't afford this type of system and are looking for a more affordable option, then simply change all of the standard switches in your house to dimmers. Dimmers are great: simply push the button and twist the dial to adjust the lighting level in any space.

If you have many different light fittings in any particular room, there is a danger that you need banks and banks of light switches on the walls to give you individual control of each light. For example, in a kitchen you may need lighting under the units, over the dining table or around seating areas. Having to pay for separate dimmers, all on separate switches and all with separate cables, can prove quite costly. So, if you have lots of light fittings, and you want lots of flexibility and control each individual light, then something like the I Light or the Lutron system would be perfect for you.

The benefit of the new intelligent lighting systems is that they allow you to have full flexibility with your lighting, to create scenes without ruining the look of your interior. There is no large, unsightly bank of light or dimmer switches, simply a single switch that controls the whole lot.

i Light panel

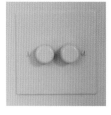

Standard dimmer

Heating thermostat

Kitchen lighting

In our house, kitchen lighting is the most important by a long way, as this is the room that we use the most. In the kitchen itself, we have recessed downlights under each wall unit, providing task lighting just where we need it. Just above the kitchen units, there are some very fancy, architectural recessed lights at a high level, which shine a softer light on to the kitchen units.

We had to install a big steel beam to create the new kitchen extension, and this offered the perfect location to install seven architectural feature lights that beam up at high level. They aren't critical to the space, but when they are turned on they pick out the glass skylight and shine a more gentle light onto the main units.

In the main dining space, there are two pendant light fittings. I'm a huge fan of George Nelson's classic architectural lightshades, and we have two of these in the dining space – one over the dining table and another slightly closer to the seating area. We then have a row of recessed directional downlights, which shine light down on to the art wall, where we display all of our family pictures. And if that's not enough, we have a couple of 5-amp lamp sockets placed in key positions near to the picture-display wall, to provide softer light in the corner of the room.

this page Task lighting above the counter. The glass splash back also reflects light outwards.

Tip Flexibility is the key with a kitchen lighting system and you need the ability to dim the lighting levels to suit the atmosphere you want to create at different times of the day. You need:

- good 'task' lighting so you can prepare and cook food safely;
- good 'ambient' lighting so you can avoid shadows in the space; and
- 'feature' light to create the right atmosphere and pick out any strong architectural features in your new kitchen space.

I think we achieved all that and more in our new kitchen.

Bad lighting can ruin a space, no matter how well you design the rooms and get them to work.

Top lighting tips to remember

- Use recessed downlights to define clear routes through your home.
- Use directional lights to illuminate feature walls and artwork.
- Use hang-down pendant lights over very particular zones in the house, such as your dining table.
- Use task lighting in very specific areas – under your kitchen unit to help while you are cooking, or over your bathroom mirrors in order to shave or do make-up.
- Place 5-amp light sockets in the corners of most rooms, and alongside your beds in the bedrooms, so that lamps can be added and controlled in the corner of each space.
- Really go to town on architectural feature lighting to bring your spaces to life.

Hallway lighting

Many corridors or hallways in homes can feel like very drab, dull spaces – long routes with very little going on in them. Lighting these circulation routes can make them quite exciting spaces to be in. In the first-floor hallway and on the second-floor landing, which gives access to the loft, I've placed a series of recessed architectural feature lights that strongly defines the route from one room to the next. The light from these fittings plays a very important role in lighting up the frosted glass floors and doors within the space. So, what would normally be quite a boring place to be in architecturally becomes an extraordinary piece of architecture, simply by using the right light fittings in the right way.

The gloomy corridor is transformed.

Illuminating the staircase

The new timber staircase that runs between the ground floor and the first floor is illuminated by small recess lights, set at low level to cast light on every other tread as you walk up the stairs.

Bathroom lighting

There are two forms of lighting in the bathrooms. In the ceiling we have recessed downlights, mainly because I don't really like putting pendant lights in small bathrooms – and that's what we've got! Hanging pendants definitely make the space feel smaller. Simple recessed lights in the ceiling void means that the sense of space is much greater.

The second form of light is very simple, very important task lighting over the mirror. This makes it easier for me to shave, and for my wife to put on make-up.

this page The master bedroom en-suite has both recessed downlights for ambient light and a task light over the mirror.

opposite top and bottom The master bedroom has a dimmer operated pendant light and bedside lights for reading; and the uplighters in the room at the back of the house show off the height and angles of the ceiling.

Lighting the bedrooms

All of the bedrooms in our house have simple pendant lights, and these are something I really like. They are all on dimmer switches, not the i Light control. I didn't see the need for i Light controls in the bedrooms, as there aren't that many different forms of lighting or fittings. We've got straightforward dimmer switches – one to control the pendant light in the ceiling and another to control the 5-amp light sockets on either side of the bed. This way, we can control the table reading lights to create just the right amount of light – and the perfect ambience in our bedroom.

In the bedroom-cum-study at the back of the house, I wanted to illuminate the very high ceiling that slopes all the way to the ridge of the roof. I chose a number of uplighters on a dimmer switch, and they really wash the walls with light and illuminate the whole ceiling space. It's a great way to express the best qualities of the architectural space.

Design features in my home

this page My favourite chair: the Eames armchair. There's no better place to relax with a glass of wine and a book.

opposite top left and right The open-riser staircase up to the loft lets the light from the velux above down to the floor below; and the trough sink allows all the kids to line up and brush their teeth at once!

opposite bottom right The wood-burning stove looks beautiful and is incredibly efficient at heating the room.

Refurbishing my home wasn't just about restoring the outside to make it blend back in with the conservation area, and creating a very modern interior inside. It was about creating a place that was not only light and bright, but incredibly comfortable. As I said, 'comfort' isn't a word that many architects use, as it's usually associated with traditional, cosy homes. However, the two shouldn't be mutually exclusive. With good design, there is no reason why comfort and cosiness shouldn't be an important part of a modern, contemporary home.

Statement chairs

One of my favourite design accessories in a home is a series of beautiful chairs. Obviously a chair is something that has to be comfortable – something that has to be fantastic to sit on for long periods of time, especially if you are watching TV or reading. However, I also think chairs should be something beautiful to look at.

One of my favourite chairs in the world is the Eames lounge chair, designed by Charles and Ray Eames, and released in 1956 after years of development. This chair was produced for the Herman Miller furniture company, and it was the first chair that Eames designed for a high-end market. The chair is composed of three curved plywood shelves, which form the most stunning and comfortable shape. I've gone for the classic-looking black leather finish, combined with the Ottoman footstool.

The Eames lounge chair has to be one of the best designed chairs in the world, and well worth the investment. You will be purchasing a chair for life – which you can hand down from generation to generation. In fact, it will become part of your very own family history.

The fireplace

My favourite design feature in my home is the fireplace. Even though modern technology offers us all sorts of amazing ways to keep our homes warm, with under-floor heating, fancy radiators and lots of insulation, having a real fire in the cosiest room in your house is everything. A fireplace creates such a powerful focus in a room.

There is nothing better during wintry months than sitting in my favourite Eames lounge chair, in front of a roaring fire, with a good book and a glass of red wine. It might make me sound like a bit of an old man, but I absolutely love it! My fire is called the 'Balanced Modular Stove System', and it was beautifully designed by Peter Maly. It's a wood-burning stove that can be assembled against the wall in a number of different ways. There are different types of storage elements alongside the main fire, in which you can either store logs or books, or even place integrated drawers or a bench unit. These elements have been fixed to the wall so that they float above the floor with no visual means of support. It not only looks stunningly beautiful, but it also belts out the heat! With the fire on during the winter months, there is absolutely no need for the under-floor heating.

Rugs

Throughout the ground floor of my house, I've gone for an engineered, wide, oak-timber floorboard. I love timber flooring because it ages really well, it's amazingly easy to keep clean, and the kids can fly around it on their little scooters! To soften up this hard flooring in certain areas, I absolutely love to use rugs. Rugs not only provide comfort to certain zones within the house, but they become a fantastic design feature to express the style, colour and feel of a home.

We have a rug to provide a soft area in front of the TV zone, and one in front of the seating area in the kitchen, but my favourite rug of all is the one on which my Eames chair sits in front of the fireplace. This rug is a beautiful, bold handmade rug from Knots Rugs. At 3 metres long and 2.4 metres wide, its design is bright and bold, vivid red, with a slightly off-white abstract floral pattern. It was quite a brave move to go for this, but it has a kind of retro 1950s/early 1960s design feel to it that matches the classic design of the fireplace and the furniture in the rest of the space.

this page left and right Rugs can really define a space. The rug in front of the TV softens the area; and the Knots rug that my armchair sits on is a classic. It is in your face and I love it.

opposite page top The full-height doors allow your eye to flow more easily from one room to the next making it feel that much bigger.

opposite middle and bottom The skirting boards were a really simple addition to the design and prove that small design details really can make a big difference.

Full-height doors

The traditional height of an internal domestic door is normally
2.1 metres. Obviously buying something standard, off the shelf
from a building merchant, makes it more affordable; however, that
2.1-metre door height may just not be appropriate in some homes.
I'm a big fan of full-height doors that run all the way from the floor
to the top of the ceiling. This gives you a greater sense of space when
you look from one room to the next, for the ceiling height in each
room appears to be continuous because there is no need for the
vertical panel above the standard 2.1-metre door, which becomes a
visual barrier between the two spaces.

Full-height doors do call for extra investment because you have to
pay for a specially made door and a specially made frame to house
that door, according to your specific floor-to-ceiling height. But the
investment to make a space feel bigger, brighter and more spacious is
well worth it.

Skirting boards

When carefully considered and brought together throughout a home,
it's all the very small design details that make a big difference to how
a space feels. I didn't want a standard skirting board just stuck on to
the face of the wall in my home. I wanted something far more simple
and minimal. I managed to find a standard plastic section from the
building merchant, which allowed the creation of a simple shadow-
gap detail between the plastered wall and the MDF skirting. This
meant using a laser level during the building process, to ensure that
the plastic shadow-gap detail was placed in a perfect horizontal for
the plasterer. But it leaves a very crisp and simple line for the MDF
skirting board to be fitted beneath, and means that the skirting board
is flush with the plaster above, with the shadow-gap detail formed
between the two.

I used this detail throughout the entire house, running
horizontally between the skirting and the plaster, and then turning
up vertically between the architraves of the doors and the plastered
walls. It also became a detail that I used on all of the joinery,
wardrobes and cupboards. On a practical level, a shadow-gap detail
prevents cracks from appearing at the line where two different
materials (in this case, plaster and MDF) would meet, because it
accommodates all of the shrinkage and expansion in the materials.

My kitchen

The kitchen in my home is incredibly simple. I wanted the design to be beautiful and elegant, but it was also important for me that the kitchen design didn't jump out as a big bold statement. In a similar style to the rest of the house, I like my kitchen to blend in with the whiteness of the surrounding space. Don't get me wrong; I'm not against beautiful bold colours in kitchens, where they can feel like the perfect piece of product design. It's a kind of mid-range kitchen – not in the cheap range and certainly not in the Rolls-Royce category of manufacturers.

Linear space

The layout of the kitchen doesn't really follow the 'golden triangle' rule, which is really the perfect, most efficient layout for a kitchen. I chose a long, linear kitchen, tucked away to one side of the space. If I'd gone for the golden triangle, it would have meant making sacrifices with the dining and seating areas I wanted in this combined space. Similarly, an island simply wouldn't have worked for the sense of space I envisioned. With every kitchen design you have to adapt and sometimes even break the rules according to the space you want and the way you live.

this page My kitchen is long and linear. There is a large double door fridge-freezer, then an area of worktop with a coffee machine and toaster. Moving along to the right is the hob, two ovens and a combined microwave beneath. Next comes the sink and on the far right under the worktop is the dishwasher and bin store.

Working with the height

I was very restricted about how high the kitchen could be because of the boundary wall between my house and the one next door. So, instead of having very tall, full-height kitchen doors, I created wide, low-level units against the wall. I finished them with a gloss (around 30–40 percent; any higher gloss just looks too polished and shiny for me), and used brushed stainless steel handles that are long and very linear, running the full length of the drawer and door units.

My corian worktop

The kitchen worktop was a very important choice, and I went for a thick, white corian top. In my opinion, corian is by far the best kitchen work surface for a domestic home. It's a plastic, resin-based material that is highly durable and super-easy to keep clean. It can be moulded into any shape, and comes in virtually any colour. I went for polished corian, in a similar style to the kitchen units. The top has been moulded over the front edge, so the kitchen worktop looks like it is 80mm thick, when it actually isn't.

In fact, the corian top only measures about 12mm, but by wrapping it around the front edge, the kitchen worktop looks thick, chunky and robust. I set the kitchen worktop height higher than you would normally expect, which may not work for everyone; however, it's great for me because I'm quite tall, so when I'm doing any work in the kitchen it doesn't feel like I'm bending over all the time. A standard worktop is usually 90cm from the finished floor level, and I've set mine at 97cm. Not only is it ideal for the way we live, but it gives the kitchen a strong feel, and provides a great presence in the room.

above Because of our neighbours' right to light, the side extension couldn't be built very high. We built wide, low-level units to make the most of the available space.

Sinks and splashbacks

We went for a simple, stainless-steel sink, and had grooves cast into the corian to create a draining board. We did consider turning up the corian at the back face of the wall to form the splashback, but I thought this was a great opportunity to introduce a new material. We chose a splashback made of frosted glass, which has a beautiful reflective quality to it, and provides the perfect board for us to scribble messages with a water-based pen.

Drawer units

Because storage space is absolutely essential in any kitchen – and we didn't have the room to put in high wall units – we decided on a different solution. In traditional kitchen designs, there is a huge amount of wasted space behind the skirting boards. We bypassed this problem by using drawer units beneath the worktop, so our storage could run all the way down to floor level.

The range of kitchens available on the market today is fantastic. No matter what your budget, there is no longer any excuse for a bad kitchen. Make sure it is well designed, elegantly planned, in a style that suits the surrounding architecture and the way you live, and packed with useful, efficient storage. I am pleased to say that my kitchen has all of that.

Tip You can actually mould corian to form your sinks and drawers, although strongly coloured foods can cause discoloration and staining. While this can be polished out, you'd need to have this done regularly to keep things looking pristine.

this page Our stainless steel sink and frosted glass splashback.

opposite page top and bottom Bags of storage is essential in any kitchen – we maximised ours by using the normally wasted space behind the skirting board; and our kitchen with our new, more traditional, table in place.

My bathrooms

There are three bathrooms and an en-suite in my house, and each plays a slightly different role in the way the house works day-to-day. The most important space is really the main family bathroom, and the layout is very simple, with two main aims. First of all, we kept the drainage as straightforward as possible to keep the cost down. Secondly, the design was created to make best use of the window opening.

The toilet is placed in the corner because this was the easiest place to get the soil-vent pipe into the drainage well at the corner of the house. The sink is positioned right in front of the window, so we get fantastic views across all of the gardens at the side of the house. The bath is flush against the wall between the bathroom and the corridor on the other side. I made a conscious decision not to put a shower in this room; for many, this may seem like madness, but my kids absolutely love taking a bath, and this is a room they will use more than anyone else. Putting in a separate shower would have taken up much more space, and I would have had to make a compromise on either the large sink or the bathroom space available for all of my three kids to be in the bath, dried and changed at the same time. The fact that I was putting two showers elsewhere in the house meant that there wasn't a desperate need for one here.

right I designed the bathroom with the aim of washing and clothing all my kids at one time in mind.

The trough

The sink is the main design feature in this space. As my three kids get older, there is an increasing tendency for them to battle for the sink in the morning. We could have put in two sinks, but that still leaves one short when they appear to need them at the same time! So we came up with the idea of having one huge sink made – 1.7 metres long and 50cm wide, and made out of a single block of Italian travertine – which we call the pig trough.

This may sound extravagant, but I had the sink made to my own design and shipped back from Italy for around £1000. Two or three sinks with individual hot- and cold-water feeds, as well as wastes fitted, would easily come to the same amount of money. And it's completely worth it. The pig trough looks truly beautiful and integrated within the space because it's made from the same travertine stone that we used on the walls and the floor of the bathroom. It's been a huge success with the kids, too; when they were young, and because the pig trough is so big, they often wanted to be bathed in it instead of the tub!

Tiling

The Italian travertine used on the walls and the floors is a beautiful natural material, full of texture and depth. I decided to go for quite an unusually proportioned tile in these spaces. We are so used to seeing bathroom tiles that are 30 by 30cm – or 450 by 450cm – but this tile by Stonell is 90cm long and 30cm wide. This is a very unusual but elegant, long-proportioned tile. And, rather than have them laid in a fairly ordinary gridded pattern, I decided instead to slightly stagger the joints when they were laid. This is quite unusual and it gives a very different quality to the space – a little bit of tension and character to the pattern of the tiles.

Heating my bathroom

The heating of a bathroom space is really important. You should always have a good-sized towel rail to keep all of the family towels fresh and warm. Unless you live in a more traditionally styled house, I can't see the point of having another radiator, which takes up valuable wall space that you desperately need to plan the space well. So if you ever refit your bathroom, always go for under-floor heating.

Where to put the sink?

When I'm designing houses and bathrooms, people always seem torn about where to put the sink. Putting a sink in front of a window means you get a fantastic view while you are brushing your teeth, but then what about a mirror? In my home, I decided to put the mirror on the wall to the right-hand side. It's 1.8 metres long, and 1 metre high, and it's well positioned so you can turn to the side to shave or apply make-up. It makes the bathroom space feel twice as wide – it's practical but at the same time transforms the quality of the architectural space.

A little extra light

Another design trick that I used in this family bathroom – to get natural light that comes from the bathroom window through the space and into the corridor on the other side of the bathroom wall – was to put in a tiny strip of clear glass at a high level above the bath. No one can peer in unless standing on a box (or high on tiptoes), which means that you can use clear glass. It has an amazing effect of making the bathroom feel bigger and more three-dimensional; the ceiling level of the bathroom runs all the way through and out to the corridor, and the clear glass allows more light into the corridor, too! It's these tiny affordable touches that make an ordinary space feel extraordinary.

this page The panel of windows in front of the sink and the pane of glass above the bath combine to make the bathroom really bright and airy.

opposite page top and bottom By lowering the floor on the loft level, we made space for an en-suite shower room on the top floor; and the en-suite to the master bedroom is probably the most efficient use of space you could ever design!

The en-suites

The en-suite shower room to my master bedroom is probably the most efficient en-suite space you could ever design. The room measures 3 metres long and 0.9 metres wide, and there is a sliding door to access the space. Above the loo is a full-height, mirrored storage cupboard which employs the classic trick of making a small space seem much bigger. The sink has been especially made out of the same Italian travertine as the floors and the walls, and the frameless, simple glass shower doors provide a very minimal divide between the shower area and the rest of the en-suite.

The en-suite shower room on the second floor, which is the loft level, was created out of space that didn't really exist before. If I had left the floor joists in the loft at the existing level, there would never have been enough headroom in the roof void to create this additional shower that I really needed. Lowering the floor meant that on the first floor I had to reduce head height in the corridor and the family bathroom, but that's fine.

The toilet is placed in the corner where it is easy to get the soil-vent pipe through the roof void, down through the family bathroom beneath and out to the only manhole and the drainage well at the side of the property. A simple duravit sink is placed alongside the loo, with the shower cubicle placed in the only position it could really be – where the maximum headroom is available within the new space.

The door into this en-suite is quite interesting. I used a frosted-glass door with simple patch fittings – a simple rectangle that only goes up to a certain level before the roof profile starts to slope. This may seem quite unusual, because there is a gap between the top of the glass door and the sloping ceiling above; however, I didn't want the en-suite space to feel like a completely separate, boxy room. You can see the sloping roof running through the first floor hallway and all the way through to the back wall of the en-suite. The panel of glass that divides the en-suite from the hallway is just a simple minimal screen, rather than a solid dividing door. To get as much natural light as possible in to this en-suite I placed a simple Velux skylight in the roof. This very elegant en-suite was created from space that would have previously only been used to store a few suitcases.

The bedrooms

this page All the bedroom floors in my house are carpet – everyone needs a little luxury in the mornings!

opposite page White walls give you the opportunity to personalise the space with photos and pieces of artwork without making the room feel too cluttered.

'Keep it simple' is my philosophy about homes, and it's a phrase I tend to use a lot. Something over-styled, over-designed or over-complicated ends up looking fussy and costing you more.

A blank canvas

The bedroom is painted white, with the simple skirting and shadow-gap detail at low level, running right around the space. The white walls become the blank canvas to allow my personal pictures, artwork and belongings to be displayed. It's these accessories that make a space personal and relevant to you.

A little luxury

On the floors, I decided to use a very thick, very high-quality carpet. Over the last 10 to 15 years, carpet seems to have become very unfashionable in homes, as the trend for timber or laminate flooring has taken over. I'm a huge fan of timber flooring, but it has to be in the right space. Personally, I think carpets are by far the best floor finish to have in a luxurious and cosy bedroom. There is nothing better than climbing out of bed in the morning and having carpet under your feet, rather than a hard floor surface.

To keep something elegant, but at the same time affordable, keep it simple. This is a maxim I've applied throughout all the bedrooms.

It's all in the detail

It's the simple detailing of this space that makes it work. There is a full-height, ceiling-to-floor door as you come in, integrated wardrobe units down one side, a small desk towards the front window, a small seating area within the bay window, and the bed carefully positioned against the outer wall of the house. So, as you lie in bed, you can fully take in the room.

Windows

The old aluminium frames in the master-bedroom bay window were ripped out to make way for double-glazed, timber, sliding-sash windows, which restored a traditional feel to the house. However, rather than using traditional moulded architraves on the inside, I designed a simple box-frame architrave. This not only gave it a more modern feel, but provided a clever way to store the roller blinds.

The roll of the blind is hidden at the top and, as it slides down, it feels like it is integrated within the frame. Because of the design of the blinds, the louvres of the roller blind can open up to allow more light in. As the louvres open, the blind is about 65mm in width; rather than just hanging around and flapping in the space, the blinds feel fully integrated with the design of the window and the wall.

Switches

Even all the light switches and sockets are integrated into the architecture and the space. The dimmer switches, the under-floor-heating thermostat, the light switches for the en-suite, and the telephone points on all the sockets are designed as a flat, sprayed-metal plate.

Wardrobe space

My office call the wardrobes the 'George Clarke Acme Storage Solution'! This makes me laugh! Because money was becoming tight at the end of the build, I couldn't really afford to get fancy wardrobes designed and installed by some of the companies that I would have loved to use. So, I was forced to buy something very standard, to fit into a space that was far from standard.

The budget solution was to buy standard-sized IKEA wardrobe carcasses, fit them in to the space, then design a kind of MDF shell around them to fully integrate them into the room. The floor-to-ceiling height of my bedroom is 2.75 metres; the IKEA carcasses were only 2.3 metres. So, I built a plinth at floor level, and the height of this

this page and opposite Floor to ceiling wardrobes maintain the line of the room and maximise the amount of useable space. This is a standard system adapted to fit.

plinth is exactly the same as the height as the skirting board that runs around the rest of the space. In effect, the shadow-gap detail and the skirting set out everything. I sat the standard 2.3-metre carcasses on top of the skirting plinth, which meant there was still a gap of around 35cm between the top of the wardrobe units and the ceiling. If I left it like that, the gap would have looked messy, and the wardrobes wouldn't have looked as integrated as I had hoped.

My solution? I had the joiners build full-height MDF doors from the top of the skirting board, all the way to ceiling level. This is by far the cheapest and best way to use the most affordable, standard-sized wardrobe units and integrate them into a non-standard-sized space. It might all be a bit cheap and cheerful, but it does the job and it looks great.

All of these simple touches – from the planning of the room to its detailing – produced a bedroom that works. The same design principles were followed throughout every bedroom in the house.

Section 2

Your home profile

'Be grateful for the home you have, knowing that at this moment, all you have is all you need.'

Sarah Ban Breathnach

Every single home – and type of home – in the UK has potential; in fact, bags of it. You may question this statement as you look around your existing home, wondering how the space you have could be transformed into something magnificent and functional. But, it's true. Whether you live in a tiny flat or apartment, a grand detached home, or something in between, it's important to remember that it's not the size that matters, but the way you use your space, and how that space works to fulfil the way your family lives.

That's not to say that all properties don't have their drawbacks and difficulties that must be addressed to get things exactly right; however, there are solutions for *any* space, and plenty of ideas to make them work hard for you. The sooner you get to grips with them, the easier it will be to imagine and then create the house of your dreams.

You don't need to move to live comfortably and efficiently. You simply need to work with what you've got, and embrace some of the tricks of the trade to let in the light, plan an efficient, effective layout, and then transform.

Making the most of your home's potential

If there is one thing that my many years of work as an architect have taught me, it's that every house has promise, and the ability to be a more flexible living space. A little creative thinking (often way outside the box), a firm understanding of a family's needs and the way they operate within their home, and plenty of good, old-fashioned imagination and graft can create something truly extraordinary from the most ordinary, average home.

This view has been compounded by my projects on *The Home Show*, where I've entered homes that are so cluttered, so inefficient and so completely unusable, that the owners' lives have literally ground to a halt. Changing their homes to make them functional again became a hugely liberating experience for these people and they were able to see their space in a completely different way, and use it effectively. That meant living their lives the way they wanted them to be lived, rather than according to the confines of the space in which they truly felt trapped.

A home without a function

Take the home of Mark and Sarah, in Hertford. They lived in a four-bedroom, 1930s detached house in Hertford with their three young daughters – a house that should, on paper, offer them plenty of space. But, the house was failing them. The layout of their home had barely changed in the 70 years since it was built, and the problems started right inside the front door with a cluttered, claustrophobic entrance hall. The dining room was filled to the ceiling with stored goods, and the family had no place to eat. There were similar problems throughout the house, including a kitchen that was inefficient and not remotely suited to the needs of a large family.

The large, south-facing garden held the solution. I created a dedicated playroom for the girls from the former dining room, with the rest of the downstairs space becoming one huge, open-plan kitchen-diner, with a living-room area and a zone for the children to enjoy. This involved creating a large rear extension, opening out onto the garden, with folding doors that drew in the natural light.

The finished home was breathtaking, with the huge rear extension increasing the ground-floor space by almost 50 percent, and completely reconfiguring the layout. The family could now eat together, and cook in comfort in their fantastic, spacious new kitchen; the girls could create as much clutter as they wished in their playroom, and there was plenty of storage to tidy away

family belongings. The family was finally able to relax, too, in the comfortable new living area. I found space for an all-important guest room, a downstairs utility room, a smart new bedroom with en-suite, a large and efficient bathroom, and bigger bedrooms for the girls.

I honestly don't think anyone could have imagined that such a poky, poorly designed space could become something so magnificent.

Growing space

Completely different in terms of space was Simon and Pippa's Brixton home, which looked big from the outside, but was crammed to the rafters inside, with three boys sharing a room, while Mum Pippa took over another to work at home. It was upstairs where this family needed the most help, to make room for their growing boys.

The ground floor got a complete makeover within the family budget, including a brand-new kitchen, and with a little shifting around, the space could be better utilised by family members with different needs.

Upstairs, I created space in the huge bathroom shared by the whole family by shifting an adjoining wall to give an en-suite shower room to the boys' bedroom. The big bathroom was converted into a bedroom, and a mezzanine floor was created on top of the shower to use the extra loft space I discovered. This allowed for four really good bedrooms, but also space for an extra shower, making the daily grind infinitely easier. The top of the stairs, which was all hallway and wasted space, was transformed by moving the walls to create a decent-sized family bathroom, with loads of storage space hidden behind a spacious mirror.

All in all, with a little tweaking, a house that was bursting at the seams suddenly seemed light, spacious and hugely practical for a family of growing boys.

What can you achieve in *your* home?

These are just two examples of how space can be altered, updated and reconfigured to make the most of your property. Every home is different, and every family has its own needs; equally, however, each *type* of home has the potential to work for its owners. It's just a question of looking at the space as a whole, and then getting to work on the details. Let's get started now.

The terraced house

Almost a staple of current-day housing, terraced homes became popular in the 1670s, after the Great Fire of London in 1666 forced architects and city-planners to rethink the housing requirements of the people of London. Terraces filled a very English need for people to have their own homes, preferably on the ground floor and with a garden. The most efficient way to achieve this was through the construction of terraced properties.

That's not to say that terraces were all two-up, two-downs. While there were fairly small terraced homes built for workers (long rows, built back to back to save space, particularly in the north of the country), many of these homes were large and magnificent. The Georgians, for example, came up with the idea of treating a row of houses as if it were a palace front, with the central homes hosting columns under a shared pediment.

Grand terraces

The Georgian fashion for terraces in a uniform plan, around an impressive square or crescent, is still evident in many British towns, such as Bath and Edinburgh. In London, Nicholas Bourbon purchased masses of land all over the city and built standardised terraced houses across it. You can still see many of these today, particularly in the centre of London (St James's Street and Bedford Row are good examples). As a side note, he's the guy who came up with the idea that housing insurance might be a good idea, particularly in light of the devastation caused by the Great Fire. That's one idea that certainly took off!

From here, terraces became the norm for most new housing, a trend that continued well into the 19th century. After this, terraces largely became the domain of the poorer echelon of society, as affluent and socially mobile Brits put their money in suburban semis.

Today, terraces are still built, but they tend to be known as 'town houses' in some locations, even though the principle is similar. What has been lost, however, is the traditional bay window at the front, a beautiful piece of architecture that defines the typical terraced house.

Because of the fairly standard placement of doors and windows, the interior layout of most terraced homes tends to be similar. In some ways that makes them easier to work with, and you are dealing with a known quantity that has been successfully refurbished and reconfigured on countless occasions.

How do you use your home?

The terraced house is one of my favourite types of home. The front of the building is generally well constructed and very smart, with its bay window and brick detailing. This is a kind of decorative architectural screen that hides a simple and functional home beyond, which has been built in a very basic way. All of the services for drainage are generally at the back, freeing up space at the front.

Let's walk the plan to consider the layout qualities of a typical, small terraced house:

Downstairs

1 There is a formal hallway running from the front of the house, all the way back to the kitchen.
2 Under the stairs there is a small toilet.
3 The living room to the left of the hallway is a beautifully proportioned space. The door is hung in such a way that it screens the room and provides a small amount of privacy until it is fully opened and you walk in. The bay window is one of the most distinctive and brilliant features of a typical terraced home, allowing you views in both directions – up and down your street.
4 Behind the living room there is a separate formal dining room. This is a large space, with views out through a sash window to the back garden.
5 At the back of the house is the very functional and utilitarian part of the house – the separate kitchen. This has side access onto the garden.

Upstairs

1 The staircase runs tightly up against the party wall that divides this house from the next-door neighbours.
2 Arriving at the first-floor landing there is a door on your right that gives you access to the family bathroom. This is the only bathroom in the house, but it is in an efficient position for drainage – being directly over the kitchen below.
3 Walking along the landing, there is a second bedroom on your right. This room has an old chimney breast and fireplace. A sash window provides views onto the back garden.
4 Straight ahead of you is the master bedroom. This is a very large bedroom with a chimney breast and fireplace, but the most dominant architectural feature is the front bay window.

The term 'terrace' was used by English architects of the late Georgian period to suggest garden terraces, which sounded much grander and more stylish than 'rows', as uniformly built houses were called in the 16th century.

Plan of existing ground floor space

Plan of existing first floor space

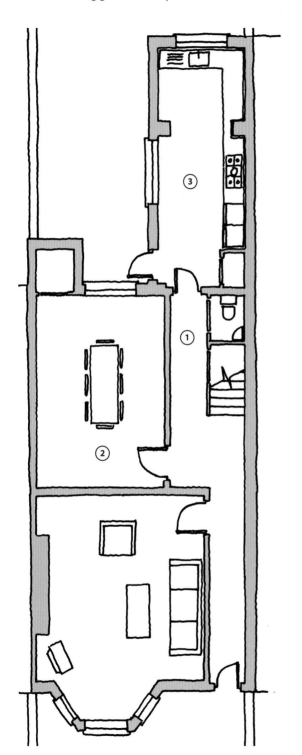

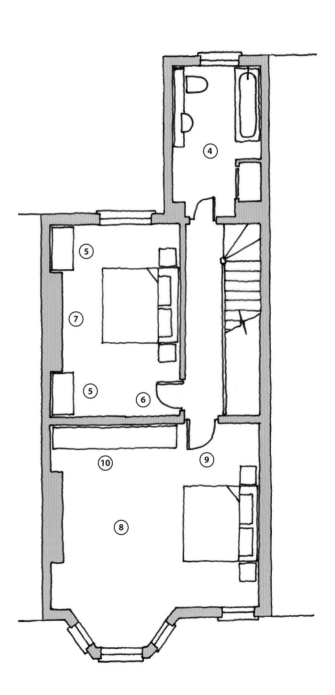

Problems and how to solve them

The existing house has some wonderfully simple, yet effective, qualities, such as the front bay window – and the fact that all of the rooms that require drainage are clustered together, making it very efficient and easy to build. However, the main problems lie in the fact that the rooms are incredibly separate, with very little connection between one space and the next.

The problems

1. As this is such a deep plan – from the front of the house to the back – there is a very long hallway. This is fine at the front of the house, as you will get some natural light coming in from the front door; however, as you walk past the staircase, the hall becomes dark until you reach the kitchen.

2. The dining room is a complete waste of space. I'm not a fan of stuffy, formal dining spaces. This is a large space that will be very rarely used; even when it is used, I can't imagine that it's conducive to the relaxed feeling you want to find in most 21st-century homes. With such a poor kitchen space, this dining room could be put to better use. Other than being features in the room, both the fireplace and the chimney breast are redundant; they serve no place for heating now that we heat our homes centrally. And while I love nothing more than a real fire, the dining room isn't exactly the most obvious place to curl up.

3. The kitchen is seriously utilitarian. Its long and narrow proportions make it very efficient, as you are able to run easily accessible units down one side, but you wouldn't want to spend much time in the space. It's not exactly somewhere you'd choose to hang out in – or do any entertaining. You would use it purely for cooking your food, which you would then take quickly to another room.

4. The family bathroom is in a good position, but there is only one sink and there is no separate shower, meaning that you are forced to shower in the tub.

5. The second bedroom has very little wardrobe storage. Placing full-depth, 60cm wardrobes on either side of the chimney breast is an ugly storage solution, as the wardrobes always project much further than the face of the chimney breast, which looks very messy and awkward.

6. The door to the second bedroom is not in a good position. Because it is located tight up against the side wall, you are unable to put furniture or storage against this wall. That's not to say that people don't do it, but it does mean walking into the side of any unit when you enter the room. It is not a very efficient use of the space.

(7) The fireplace is never really used in second bedrooms like this. It drives me mad when people leave these old fires in place and fail to use them for anything other than displaying a bunch of flowers or a few old logs within the fire itself! What is that all about? If it isn't being used, then get rid of it and free up an important wall against which you can put furniture or storage.

(8) The master bedroom is over-sized for a house of this scale, and it doesn't have an en-suite bathroom.

(9) I don't like the way you enter this room. There is very little privacy when you open a master-bedroom door and the bed is right in front of you.

(10) I don't like the position of the wardrobe in the master bedroom. It throws off the balance and proportion of the room, as the gap on either side of the chimney breast is unequal. This always looks ugly.

My solution

There are so many interesting ways of reconfiguring this house layout. Obviously, any design decisions you make are based on your own personal choices and lifestyle. But, here, I thought I'd show you two new layouts that would work very well for any small family.

Option 1 This approach involves redesigning the house without adding any more physical space.

STRUCTURAL CHANGES

- The major structural change to the ground floor is to remove the wall between the old dining room and the hallway.
- Make an opening in the wall between the living room and the old dining room.
- Demolish the brick storage cupboard to the back of the dining room.
- Create a larger structural opening in the external wall at the back of the old dining room, out onto the terrace.
- Remove the old chimney breast and fireplace in the dining room.
- Reduce the sill level of the side kitchen window, to form a new door opening.
- Upstairs, move the door to the second bedroom by a minimum of 60cm further along the length of the wall.

Plan of proposed ground floor space

Plan of proposed first floor space

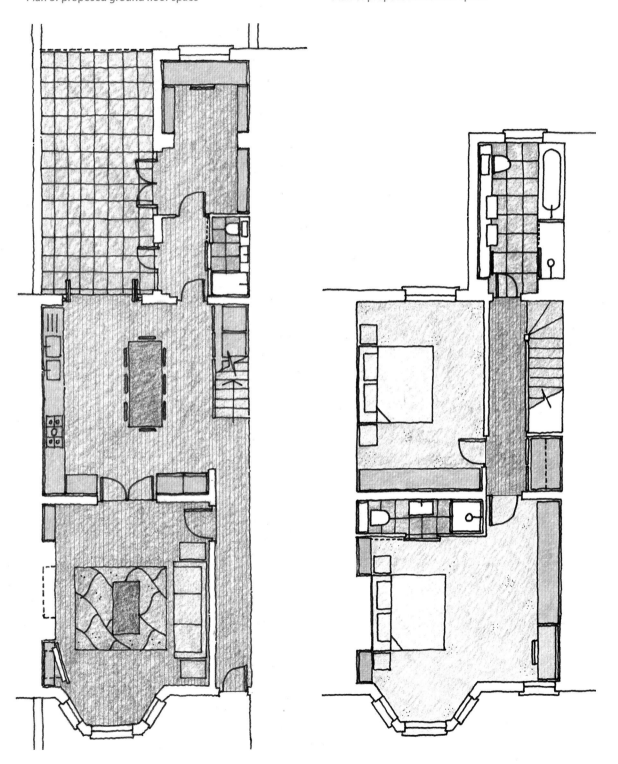

LAYOUT CHANGES
- Keep the living room in the same position.
- Move the kitchen to the heart of the home in the position of the old dining room.
- Provide utility space or additional kitchen storage under the existing staircase.
- Provide a new ground-floor toilet, sink and shower (if required) in part of the old kitchen.
- Provide a study/home-office space to the very back of the house in the old kitchen position. This can be used as a small guest bedroom, if an office is not required.
- Upstairs, the bedrooms remain in the same positions, but an en-suite shower room has been provided for the master bedroom.

THE OVERALL BENEFITS
- The living room has a strong link and connection with the new kitchen-dining area. The double doors can be closed whenever necessary, but there is the flexibility for them to be opened up for a more open space.
- The kitchen-dining room is at the very heart of the home, becoming a much more sociable space.
- By removing the wall between the old dining room and the hallway, the hall floor area now becomes important usable space.
- New bi-fold doors fold back to provide a much larger opening and they allow direct access to the outdoor terrace and garden.
- There is a much larger ground-floor toilet, freeing up important space under the staircase for kitchen storage or utilities.
- The new study/office/guest bedroom will become a great space to work from home, with new double doors giving direct access to the garden.
- Upstairs, there is a refurbished bathroom with two sinks and a separate walk-in shower.
- There is a new storage cupboard over the staircase void.
- Now that the chimney breast has been removed, the second bedroom has a much better position for the bed. There is also more wardrobe storage that has been fully built in.
- The chimney breast remains in place in the master bedroom, as we still require the flue from the working fire in the living room; however, this is boxed in with bedside storage created on either side.
- There is a fantastic new en-suite shower for the master bedroom. This is small, as we don't want to lose too much of the bedroom, but it is functional, efficiently planned and works well.
- There is more built-in wardrobe storage – in a much better position for the room – and there is a small dressing table alongside the front window.

Option 2 This home is crying out for a rear ground-floor extension. Adding this additional space creates more opportunities for the home, so you'll need to completely rethink the design and create a new layout.

Alternative plan of proposed ground floor space

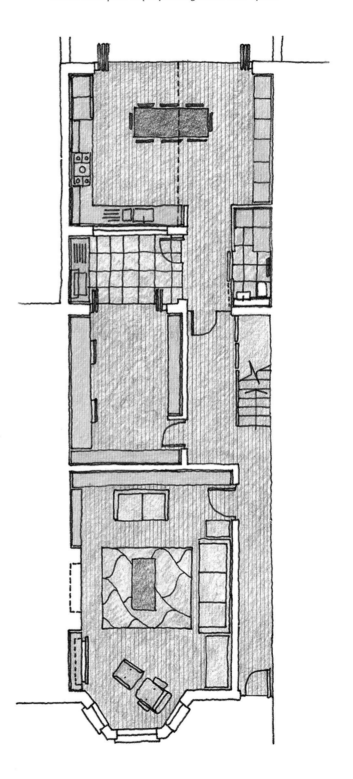

STRUCTURAL CHANGES

- Demolish the side wall and part of the end wall of the kitchen on the ground floor.
- Demolish the brick storage cupboard to the back of the dining room, as in Option 1.
- Create a larger structural opening in the external wall at the back of the old dining room – out onto the terrace, as in Option 1.

LAYOUT CHANGES

- Create a new kitchen and dining-room extension to the rear of the property, and build it full-width.
- Create a new external courtyard between the new extension and the old dining room.
- Create a new study/office in the old dining room.
- Create a new, larger ground-floor toilet and utility room.

Cut-away drawing to show proposed changes to layout of the ground and first floors

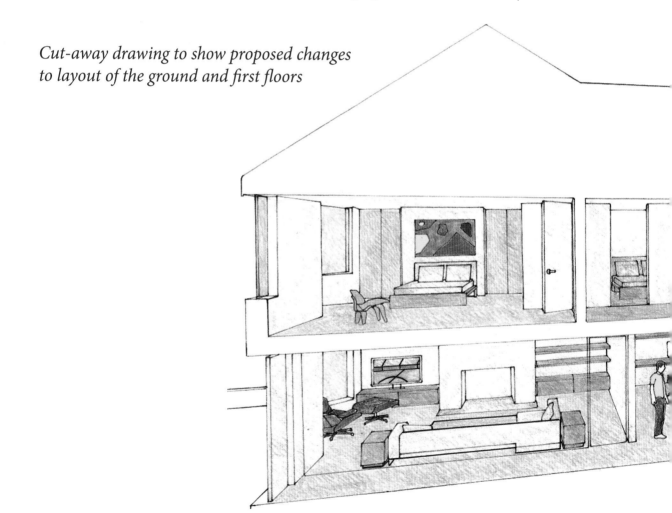

THE OVERALL BENEFITS

- The new kitchen and dining space will transform the way you use the house. It has large bi-fold doors, giving direct access out onto the garden. The extension will be used more than any other part of the home.
- The external courtyard allows you to provide natural ventilation to the back of the kitchen and allows light to get right into the new home-office space. Bi-fold doors from the office also open out onto the small courtyard, making it a great, inspiring place to work.
- A large window in the kitchen wall allows you to see through the courtyard and the kitchen – and out to the garden – from the office.
- With this layout, I wouldn't put in the new double doors to the living room, as you don't really need a connection between the living room and office space.

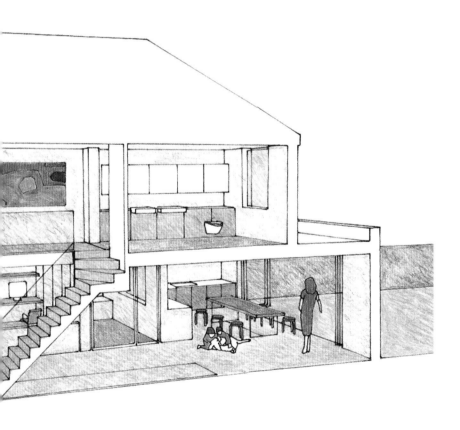

The semi-detached house

The roots of the semi-detached house can be traced back to the 17th century, but it reached the height of its popularity between the two world wars, when more than three million were built in the UK alone. As a result of this building boom, more than a third of the British population now live in a semi-detached house – me included.

Originally, it was an architectural compromise. With the transport revolution in full swing, people were keen to escape the grime and smoke of the cities, and green suburbs were created to appeal to a growing middle class with aspirations towards home ownership. Space was more plentiful here, but detached houses were still too expensive for most people. And so it was that the semi was born as a more affordable alternative. It was easy, quick and cheap to build, and the style became so popular that it is now common all over the world.

The houses go some way to reflecting the changes afoot in British society. Because there was no longer a need to provide rooms for live-in help, the houses were smaller than previously built. In Victorian times, as the suburbs expanded, terraced housing continued for the poorer end of the market, with detached houses for the affluent and semis for the middle ranks. Later on, the inter- and post-war periods saw a massive trend away from building terraces in favour of semi-detached and, for the first time, flats on a major scale.

Suburban bliss

Huge swathes of land bordering towns and cities became devoted to semi-detached housing, with an average of eight to ten built on every acre of land. All were surrounded by green hedges and neatly cut lawns: a cross between country and city living, made possible by cheaper and quicker transport provided by railways, trams and, later on, cars.

Although there are many variations in the style and layout of semi-detached houses, depending on where you live and the exact period it was built, the general principles of the typical plan remain the same.

How do you use your home?

The plan of this semi-detached home is simple and efficient. You might say that it is so efficient that it has very little architectural wonder. It's important to explore the inherent characteristics of your home's plan, to fully understand how the spaces work and don't work for you, before you move on to make any changes.

Let's walk the plan and consider the layout qualities of an average semi-detached house:

Downstairs

1 There is a self-contained traditional hallway, with the staircase in front of you as you enter.
2 Under the stairs is a cupboard that could be used as a small toilet.
3 The sitting room, to the right of the hall, has good proportions and benefits from the beautiful curved bay window giving a view onto the street. There is also a fireplace, which provides a focal point.
4 To the rear, there is a separate formal dining room with double doors opening out onto the back garden.
5 As you walk through the hallway, straight ahead of you is a small separate kitchen.

Upstairs

1 As you reach the top of the stairs there is a small single bedroom to your left, with barely enough space for a bed and a wardrobe.
2 Straight ahead is a good-sized double, with a fireplace that provides a focal point that may or may not be required in a first-floor bedroom.
3 Across the hall and to your right is the master bedroom, whose shape echoes the sitting room below, with a lovely curved bay window. Again, you'll find a fireplace that acts as a central feature on the opposite wall.
4 Tucked in the corner to your far right is a very small family bathroom, which is probably inadequate for the needs of most families living in a three-bedroom house.

If you like to have very separate spaces in which to carry out each individual daily activity, then this layout may suit you perfectly. However, the dramatic developments that have occurred within society over the last 50 years, combined with the changes to family life, mean that this layout is no longer ideal for most of us. It's time for the spaces within the home to change too.

Plan of existing ground floor space

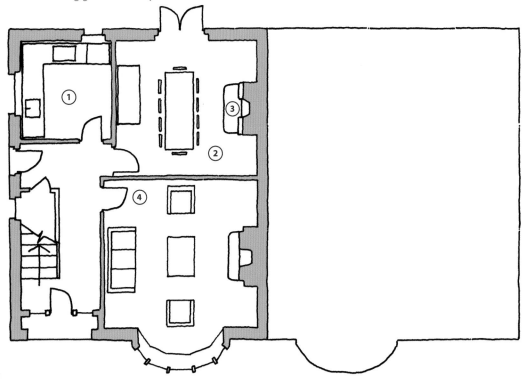

Plan of existing first floor space

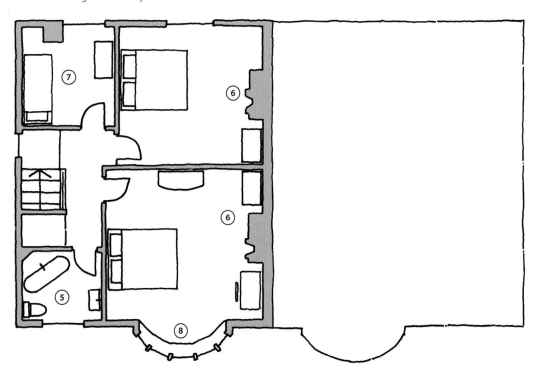

Problems and how to solve them

What works well with these houses is the fact that there are, in effect, two usable spaces to one side of the house – in this instance, the right-hand side of the house – with smaller servicing spaces, such as the staircase, toilets, bathrooms and kitchens to the left-hand side. It's very simple and efficient as a house type, but what I don't like – particularly on the ground floor – is that all of the spaces are very boxy, and have no link or connection with each other. In fact, the spaces just don't flow together at all. For modern-day family living, that can be a mistake.

The problems

(1) The kitchen is probably the worst space in the house. It's a very small room for a family home of this size.

(2) Even just looking at the plan, the dining space feels depressing. When the kitchen is so small and utilitarian, you simply cannot afford to have a large separate dining room that is rarely used.

(3) The fireplace in the dining room is hardly ever in use. If it's an attractive feature, then it could remain in the space; however, I really don't think there is any point in keeping fireplaces like this, if they serve no function. They just waste space on a wall that could have a better use.

(4) The position of the door into the living room is not ideal. It's tight up against the wall, which it makes it difficult to incorporate any built-in storage. Free-standing bookshelves against the wall mean you are looking right at the side of the unit when you walk into the room; what's more, you are unable to make the storage fit the full width of the room because you need to leave an area to be able to open the door and walk in.

(5) Upstairs, the bathroom is far too small and is badly planned.

(6) The fireplaces in the bedrooms are redundant and a waste of space. A fire can be retained in the living room downstairs, but there are other ways of creating the necessary flue up through the building, without having large, dominant brick chimney breasts within the bedrooms.

(7) The small third bedroom is poorly planned and the wardrobe is too close to the window.

(8) There is no en-suite for the master bedroom.

Semi-detached houses were first built in Milton Abbas, Dorset, in 1773. Architects of the newly expanding suburbs were aiming to capture the charm of a country cottage – which goes partway to explaining the rather eclectic collection of features that tend to appear in many suburban semis, such as false beams, weather-boarding, pebble-dashing and lattice windows. Mock Tudor styles were very popular, which explains the regular appearance of the bay window.

My solution

The new layout and changes to the structure of the property will change the entire nature of the house, creating space that will make it more efficient for family use.

STRUCTURAL CHANGES
- The most major change is to remove the wall between the kitchen and dining room, to create one open-plan space.
- Remove the two chimney breasts throughout both levels of the house.
- Make the space that is currently hosting two French doors at the back of the house into a much larger, structural opening. This will require a new steel beam or lintel above this space.
- Create an opening in the wall between the old dining room and the living room.
- Move the structural opening for the living-room door along by a minimum of 60cm clear from the face of the perpendicular wall.
- Remove the wall between the two large bedrooms upstairs. This is likely to be a timber load-bearing wall supporting the ceiling joists above.
- Remove the annoying nib in the smaller third bedroom that ruins the way the space works.

LAYOUT CHANGES
- The layout of the rooms generally remains in the same position.
- Add an en-suite shower room to the master bedroom upstairs.

THE OVERALL BENEFITS
- The new kitchen-dining room becomes the most spectacular room in the house. The kitchen is now an appropriate size for a house of this scale. There is enough room for a breakfast bar.
- The dining area has direct access onto the garden, but in a much more dramatic way.
- Removing the chimney breasts and the fire in the dining room makes the space feel much wider, and there is now room for much-needed low-level storage along the entire length of the wall – possibly with a large TV above.
- There is fully built-in storage on either side of the wall between the dining room and the living room. This can be used for kitchen/dining storage on one side, and storage for books on the other.

Plan of proposed ground floor space

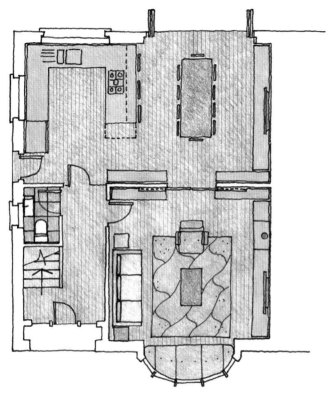

Plan of proposed first floor space

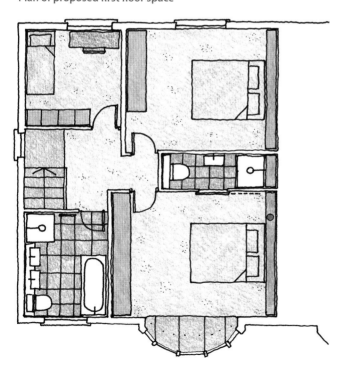

- Creating sliding doors – which ease back into the storage wall – in the wall between the living room and the dining room. When they are open, you'll be able to see from the front of the house, all the way out to the back of the house and into the rear garden. This will make the house feel so much more spacious. More importantly, however, it will allow light to flow through all of the spaces during the day.
- By removing the old fire and chimney breast in the living room, the space feels larger. I would install a new fire that only requires a 20cm flue rising up through the house. The flue can be exposed in the living room, but runs up through boxing-out in the storage wall of the bedroom upstairs. There are now two very small zones in the living room. One is for the TV – which is now aligned with the sofa – and the other is for the fireplace.
- Create a beautiful new window seat in the curved front window. This will be a nice place to sit to look out on the street, but also to look back into the house – and through the living, dining and kitchen spaces.
- Upstairs, the new en-suite shower room makes the master bedroom into a proper suite. The en-suite is small, but very functional and efficient.
- The en-suite allows you to reposition the doors to the bedroom in a better way.
- The beds in both double rooms are positioned against the party wall, which makes the rooms much smarter. Having the doors so close to the bed in the original house wasn't ideal.
- Create a new window seat in the master bedroom, to match the living room downstairs.
- Create storage behind the beds, for books and bedside storage.
- There is now much more usable wardrobe storage in all of the bedrooms – and it is all fully fitted.
- As there is more storage in the bedroom, there isn't much need for the airing cupboard on the first-floor landing. This allows you to make the main family bathroom much bigger, including two sinks as well as a walk-in shower.
- The smaller third bedroom has been replanned to be far more efficient. There is a single bed, built-in storage and room for a desk by the window that overlooks the back garden.

*Cut-away drawing to show proposed changes
to layout of the ground and first floor spaces*

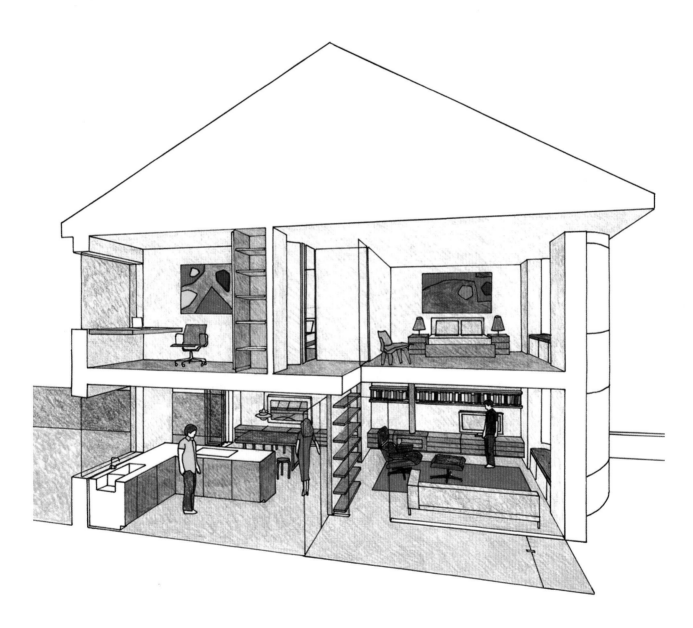

The detached house

The detached home has always been a symbol of affluence, and the country is littered with spectacular villas and manors that were, effectively, single-dwelling homes. Although farmhouses and workers' cottages were 'detached' from their neighbours, they were rarely home to a single family or occupied by their owners.

From the Middle Ages onwards, space in English cities was at such a premium that homes were piled storey upon storey, and as the urban population became increasingly dense, detached homes were considered to be an absolute luxury. These homes became particularly popular after 1810, when architect John Nash built a group of small, beautifully designed detached homes in Bristol and then in London. These developments were hugely influential, and set a benchmark for the aspirational occupants of the urban landscape.

Aspirational owners

As the Victorian suburban belt expanded out around the Georgian terraced homes – and even semi-detached cottages or villas – terraced housing continued to be the norm for the poorer end of the market, with detached homes affordable only to the affluent. By the 1920s, when modern housing estates started to be built, detached homes became increasingly popular, and were marketed as the ultimate in luxury.

The layout of a detached house can vary dramatically depending on the period it was built, the location and the style of the surrounding architecture. There are so many different and unusual designs that it difficult to select one that you could regard as typical.

During the 1970s and 1980s, there was a massive growth in the detached-housing market, and a particular style became quite popular in the suburbs of Britain.

Over the years, developers have tended to become quite lazy, churning out the same house irrespective of the unique site conditions. As potential purchasers, we were left with a standardised, boring architectural lottery. But with a bit of care, thought and design reconfiguration these homes can be made to work.

How do you use your home?

Obviously detached houses can come in all sorts of different styles, shapes and sizes, but I've selected a particular layout of detached house that has common themes with most other forms of this type of housing. By redesigning this particular home, I want to show you the general design principles and changes that can be applied to most other layouts.

Let's walk the plan to understand the arrangement of this typical detached property:

1 There is a large entrance hallway with the main staircase to your left. The hallway gets natural light through the glass panel alongside the front door.
2 There is a separate formal dining room to the right-hand side, which has a large bay window.
3 Beyond the dining room, there is a large living room.
4 Alongside the living room, there is the main kitchen with access through to a utility area, ground-floor toilet, a small storage room and the garage.
5 Access to the garden is via the utility room.

This is a very ordinary house, devoid of any exciting spaces. The plan is an arrangement of rooms that are self-contained, isolated boxes that have no positive connection or relationship to each other. If this is how you choose to live then that's entirely up to you, but I'm sure most of us would want to live in something slightly more inspiring.

Half of all detached homes in Great Britain were built since 1970 while about a sixth were built before 1919.

Plan of existing ground floor space

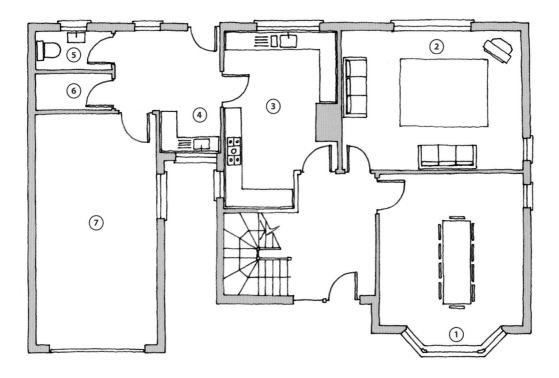

Plan of existing first floor space

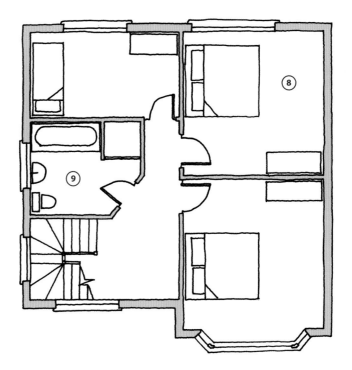

Problems and how to solve them

The very best thing about this house is that all of the rooms are a reasonable size; however, there are areas of very inefficient planning that could be maximised to get even more out of the space available. None of the rooms relate to each other very well at all – and there is a poor connection between the internal spaces and the garden to the rear.

The problems

(1) The formal dining room is awful. This has the potential to be a fantastic space – with views out to the front of the house – but it is currently bland and characterless. As a dining room, it is completely wasted space because it is completely isolated.

(2) The living room is a big space; but, again, this is an isolated room. It has a view of the garden to the rear, but would benefit from having more direct access.

(3) The kitchen is very inefficient. The fact that the units are spread out into two very separate areas is not a workable solution, and the space is even more wasteful because you have to cross diagonally through the room to get from the entrance door to the utility-room door, and out into the garden. This makes the room feel more like a circulation space than a usable kitchen.

(4) The utility room is bizarre. There are five doors off the space, which basically means that there isn't really any usable wall space to install utility units. It is, in effect, a large corridor with a sink in the corner!

(5) The toilet is too far away from all of the living spaces. You've got a long way to go – through many doors and rooms – if you need the loo while dining at the table. Your food would be freezing cold by the time you got back.

(6) The storeroom alongside the toilet is pointless. Once you open the door inwards, there is so little room left, it's hardly worth having.

(7) The garage is absolutely fine and functional, but could be put to better use.

(8) The master bedroom could benefit from an en-suite bathroom.

(9) The layout of the family bathroom could be improved to accommodate two sinks.

My solution

The good news is that there are a host of imaginative changes that could transform this space into something truly special.

STRUCTURAL CHANGES

- Demolish most of the wall between the old dining and living rooms.
- Demolish the central part of the wall that divides the old living room and the kitchen.
- Form a larger structural opening in the wall between the old kitchen and the old utility room.
- Demolish all of the walls that formed the old toilet and storeroom.
- Construct a new corridor link to access new, usable accommodation within the old garage.
- On the first floor, demolish the bedroom wall that separates the two double rooms.
- Construct a more compact garage with a new link incorporating a new utility room.

Plan of proposed ground floor space

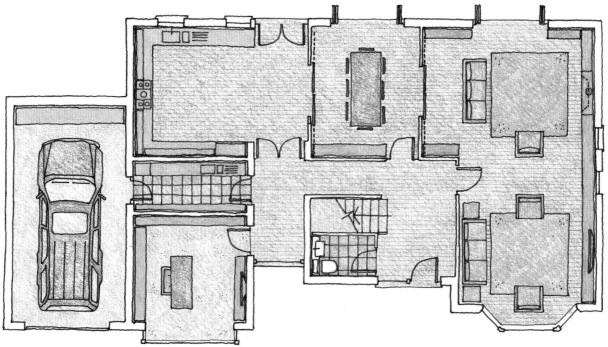

LAYOUT CHANGES

- Mirror the staircase, so that it turns in the opposite direction. This frees up more space to create a larger family bathroom.
- Create a new toilet under the stairs, which is easy to reach from most of the ground-floor rooms.
- Change the old formal dining room into a new living room.
- Knock through the wall to the old living room to create one large reception room and entertaining space.
- Turn the kitchen into the new dining room.
- Create a new corridor link from the hallway, to access the new kitchen, utility room and home office/study.
- Convert the old utility room, toilet, store and part of the garage into a new kitchen.
- Convert the garage into a new, large utility room and home office.
- Build a new garage to the side of the house, if it is required.
- Create a small, but very efficient en-suite shower room to the master bedroom.
- Replan the bedroom spaces to create a more efficient layout and more wardrobe space.

Plan of proposed first floor space

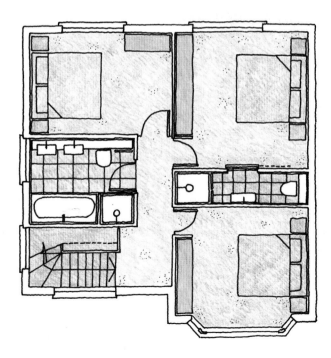

THE OVERALL BENEFITS

- The redesign has created a huge family reception room and living room that is perfect for entertaining. It is designed as two distinct zones. The living room at the front has the bay window, and will be used as the main TV room. The living zone to the rear is more of a relaxing zone where you can chill out by the fire and read a book from the many bookshelves surrounding you. This area has direct access to the garden.
- By opening up the walls between the living room, dining room and kitchen, you can see clearly from one side of the house to the other. This will completely transform your perception of the space. There will be sliding doors designed into these walls so that you can separate the spaces, if you wish. It is this flexibility that allows you to reconfigure the space depending on how you might want to use the rooms at any particular time.
- The dining room is at the very heart of the home, alongside the kitchen, and has direct access out to the garden through bi-fold doors.
- The kitchen is much more efficient – maximising the available space for wall and base units, by wrapping around three walls.
- A new corridor links the rooms, so you don't have to walk through one room to get to another – unless you really want to.
- The new utility room is invaluable for a family home of this size. You have the option of losing a couple of units in the kitchen and having direct access to the utility area from the kitchen space.

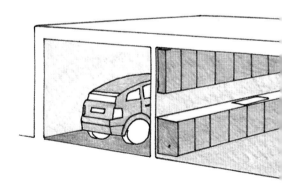

- A new home office/study is a must in most family homes. This could be turned into a guest bedroom, if required.
- Upstairs, the family bathroom has been made substantially bigger.
- An en-suite shower room to the master bedroom makes this an excellent bedroom suite.

Cut-away drawing to show proposed changes to layout of the ground and first floor spaces

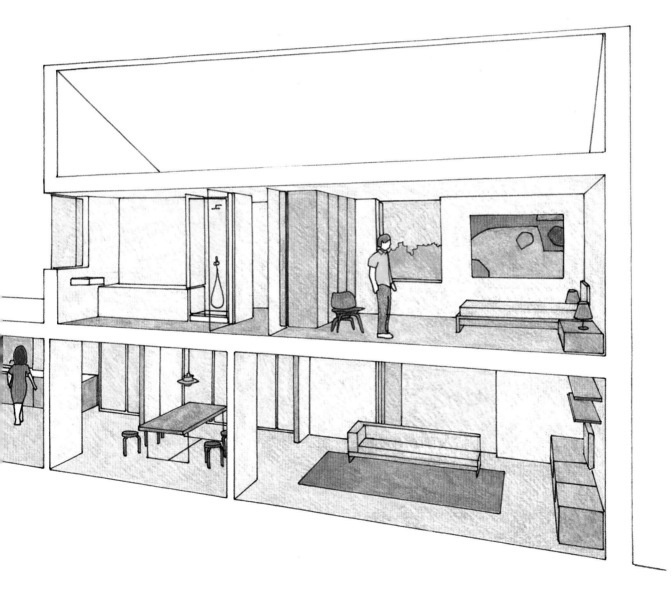

The apartment

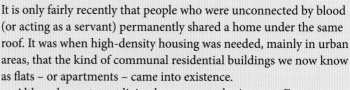

It is only fairly recently that people who were unconnected by blood (or acting as a servant) permanently shared a home under the same roof. It was when high-density housing was needed, mainly in urban areas, that the kind of communal residential buildings we now know as flats – or apartments – came into existence.

Although apartment living became popular in many European cities during the 19th century (and, oddly enough, the 16th century in Scotland), it was slow to catch on in the UK. This type of housing was considered low-class, and it wasn't until 1853 that the first 'high-end' flats were build in Victoria, in London.

Housing for the poor

In Victorian times, apartments or tenements were built for the very poor, and what we now call maisonettes were built for working-class citizens of large industrial towns. The 1920s and 1930s marked a boom in housing for the urban poor, and in the 1940s, just after the war, councils and local authorities began to build blocks of flats that were considered to be wildly innovative and even rather 'posh'. But flats still had a bad name, as large houses that had fallen into disrepair were acquired by disreputable landlords, who divided them up for immigrants and the poor.

In the 1960s, blocks of luxury flats were being built, with the aim of attracting professional people, and they became rather chic for a time. It wasn't until the 1990s that attitudes towards apartment living truly began to change, and trendy apartment blocks were constructed. This, of course, was fed by a booming buy-to-let market.

The standard new-build apartment is designed to a template that can make you feel a bit like a caged animal. If you have purchased one in this category, you probably like the simplicity of it all; if you don't, there is scope for change. However, the apartment or flat that can demand the most work – and probably reap the most rewards – is one of a few in an old home or other type of building, which has been divided up into self-contained units.

These properties do come with a host of problems but there are an equal number of great solutions to set them right and create the beautiful, efficient space you want and need.

How do you use your home?

If there was ever a house type that needs to be totally efficient in every way, it is the domestic apartment. Space is obviously limited, so every square inch has to work very hard to make any apartment a success. There is obviously a lot of variation between one apartment and another, but I've selected a fairly typical one-bedroom apartment that – at face value – doesn't seem too bad. But, once you analyse the space, you realise that it has the potential to do so much more.

Let's walk the plan to understand the layout of a typical apartment or flat:

1. There is a centrally positioned main staircase at the back of the building that leads up to this top-floor flat.
2. The entrance door is on the half-landing, where you then turn and come up the final flight of stairs.
3. Straight ahead of you is the kitchen.
4. To your left, there is the living room.
5. To your right, there is a door that takes you into the main bathroom.
6. Next, there is the door that takes you to the bedroom.

Apartments or flats are the most common type of dwelling in the heart of most cities. The challenge, particularly with small flats, is to strike a balance between making the property feel efficient – with well-organised rooms – and fulfilling the need for our homes to feel light and spacious. Of course, it's also up to you to make sure that you lead an uncluttered life, and don't become a 'hoarder'!

'Should not every apartment in which man dwells be lofty enough to create some obscurity overhead, where flickering shadows may play at evening about the rafters?'
Henry David Thoreau

Plan of existing floor space

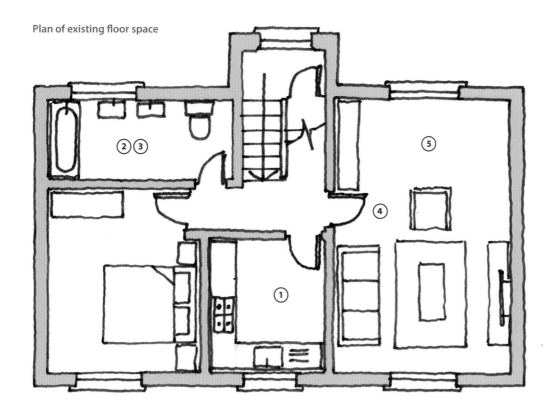

The word 'flat', denoting a suite of rooms in a larger building, stems from the Scottish word flaet, which means a 'floor' or a 'storey'.

Problems and how to solve them

What is great about this apartment is that there is very little circulation space. As the staircase is centrally positioned, it means you don't have to create long corridors to get from one side of the apartment to the other. There is only one small landing, which does its job very well to provide direct access to all of the rooms. However, there is a way of transforming this apartment to be even more efficient, while also looking at the possibility of creating a second study/bedroom – which will have an enormous effect on its value.

The problems

(1) The kitchen is the worst room in this property. It's not a small space in terms of its floor area for this scale of building, but it feels claustrophobic because it is hemmed in on all sides by the enclosing walls.

(2) The bathroom is very long and thin, and you could argue that it's too big for an apartment. You don't really need two sinks in an apartment bathroom.

(3) There is no walk-in shower, which means you always have to shower standing in the tub.

(4) Because the door into the living room is almost in the middle of the space, the room is very inefficient; the door effectively divides the area into two zones. As you walk in, the area to the right works very well, as you can fit in a seating area and a TV quite nicely. However, the space to the left is completely wasted floor space. It doesn't really feel part of the same room, and must be put to better use.

(5) Apartments were generally bad at providing kitchen-dining space. Typically the dining room table would go here, divorced from the kitchen. Modern apartments tend to have better kitchen-dining accomodation.

My solution

It's amazing how few changes need to be made to make this property work harder, and find valuable space to enhance your living arrangements.

STRUCTURAL CHANGES

There are no significant areas of demolition with this proposed scheme, but the relocation of some of the doors is very important. Moving services, such as the electrics and plumbing, is critical.

LAYOUT CHANGES

- The main layout change involves moving the kitchen into the wasted space in the living room. This is incredibly efficient, as it makes this area of the living room usable again.
- By moving the kitchen to a new location, its previous home can be used to create a small second bedroom or study. Creating a second bedroom, no matter how small, will make your estate agent very happy if you come to sell. You will have increased its value.
- Reposition the bed in the main bedroom, so that the opposite wall can be used for full-height and full-width wardrobe storage.

Plan of proposed floor space

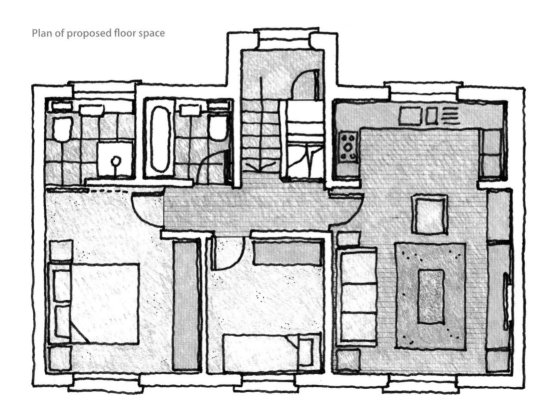

- Split the existing bathroom in two spaces. Create an en-suite shower room off the master bedroom, and a small bathroom alongside it – accessed from the landing.
- There is some space available over the staircase. I've placed a full-height storage cupboard here, for cloak or linen storage.
- Dining space is still not brilliant and a table which folds out to increase capacity will be required.

THE OVERALL BENEFITS
- Placing the kitchen in the redundant part of the living room makes it a far more sociable space – you can now communicate with people in the living room while you're cooking. Obviously, the downside is that if someone wants to watch TV in peace and quiet, while you are banging pans around in the kitchen, it's not ideal! Placing your kitchen here also involves moving all of its services to the back of the building, where the existing services are located. This means that you now have a very simple layout, in which all of the service accommodation – such as the stairs, kitchen and bathrooms – are at the back of the plan, and the bedrooms and living spaces are at the front. Very simple!
- There is more integrated storage throughout the apartment.
- You now have an additional bedroom and an additional bathroom, including an en-suite shower room, which massively increase the value of the property. So, you have created a better place to live and made yourself a few bob on the way. That's win, win!

Cut-away drawing to show proposed changes to layout of apartment

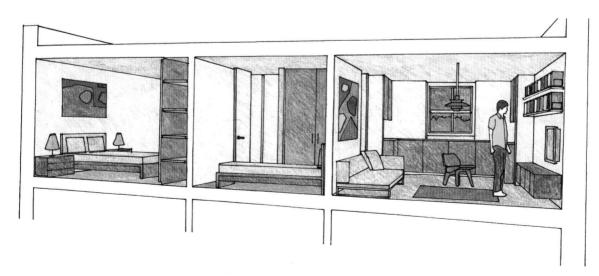

The bungalow

The first bungalow was built in the UK in the 1860s, by a certain Colonel Bragg, who – upon returning from India to Norwood in London – built a lodge in the Indian style and named it 'the bungalow'.

Over the years, the term 'bungalow' was used to describe a variety of different homes, including, strangely enough, large suburban, country houses built in the Arts and Crafts or other Western vernacular style. However, later developers reverted to its original meaning, using 'bungalow' to describe any small building.

Bungalows, as we know them today, became popular in the UK between the two world wars, when a massive number were built – particularly in the coastal areas, occupied by a more elderly population who appreciated the benefits of a property with no stairs. Bungalows were never considered the height of sophisticated living; in fact, in 1927 the *Daily Express* coined the term 'bungaloid', describing 'hideous allotments and bungaloid growth [that] make the approaches to any city repulsive'.

Preferred living space

Things have changed dramatically since that time and, perhaps partly because of our ageing population, bungalows have become the most sought-after properties in the UK, often commanding a premium of up to 20 percent above the price of other homes in the same area.

According to a 2005 survey by the Halifax, bungalows are Britain's happiest homes. A survey of 2000 householders revealed that bungalows 'breed more contentment' than any other type of housing.

The layout and design of bungalows vary enormously across the country, but the general principle is that a bungalow has one floor, with a varying number of rooms, and often a single garage, usually linked to the property. Some bungalows have a second storey with one or two bedrooms (although this is not the norm), usually built into a sloping roof with dormer windows. The typical 1930s bungalow is square in plan, with 1960s ones more likely to be oblong.

With the bungalow constantly reinventing itself, the rise in popularity of the English garden suburb, and the way we are becoming so influenced by American colonial housing, the bungalow will continue to be our favourite type of housing for many years to come.

How do you use your home?

It's not difficult to see why a cheerful bungalow has attracted so much attention, and gained such an amazing degree of popularity. While the layout can be boxy and the space underused, there is enormous potential to open things up to create a home that works efficiently and feels spacious and modern. There tend to be far fewer load-bearing walls in the average bungalow, which means that making dramatic changes is easier – and less expensive – than it might be in older properties, or those with more than one storey.

Let's walk the plan to understand the layout of a typical bungalow:
1   The front entrance hall is spacious, but very boxed in. You are faced with a blank wall straight ahead of you, and a series of doors rather than a welcoming space.
2   To your right is a bathroom. I'm not a fan of bathrooms at the front of the house; no matter how much frosted glass you install, there is a very real sense that your ablutions and everything else are under scrutiny from passers-by.
3   Straight ahead and to the right is a bedroom that is a good size, hosting a double bed and a nice view to the rear; however, the headboard of the bed is right against the kitchen wall, which would not be enormously conducive to a peaceful sanctuary.
4   The kitchen is small and completely self-contained, making it functional but not remotely sociable. You'd also have to transport food to the opposite end of the living area in order to eat it!
5   The long living room is a good space, but with the door in the middle of the room, it's cut in half – and not in a particularly logical way. It's difficult to organise the furniture in this type of space, and the 'zones' don't work. Being long and narrow, this room seems like an extended corridor rather than a useful room.
6   There are stairs up to a loft bathroom, and a useful space. This is definitely something worth exploring to make better use of every square inch of this house.

In bungalow projects I try to open up the kitchen, dining and living spaces to give a greater sense of space and make it into a more sociable home. It's also worth trying to extend, if the spaces still don't feel large enough, or consider the options you have with garage space. Here, there is a good-sized garage that could be linked to the house to create much-needed space, and allow the existing rooms to be used more effectively. Don't underestimate the potential usefulness of loft space either. Although the average bungalow does have most of its living space on one floor – which can be part of its appeal – there's no reason why it can't be adapted to suit the needs of the 21st-century family.

'One may make their house a palace of sham, or they can make it a home, a refuge.'
Mark Twain

The word 'bungalow' originates from the Indian word bangla, *which, in the 19th century, referred to houses built in a Bengali style. These houses, made popular by returning British colonists, were traditionally small, one-storey, thatched houses with a wide veranda.*

Problems and how to solve them

Bungalows are normally very efficiently planned. Being so small, architects were forced to make as much of the space work as effectively as possible. One of the problems in striving for so much 'efficiency' was that the space can feel like a series of tiny little separate boxes strung together. With the refurbishment of a bungalow you need to open up the spaces to make them more exciting without compromising too much on the functional and practical aspects of the home.

Although this existing bungalow plan has a number of good qualities, such as the double-aspect living room and very little circulation space, the rest of the layout leaves a lot to be desired. It is functional in design, but the spaces feel like a bland series of self-contained boxes that do not flow together very well.

The problems

1. First of all, I don't like the way you walk into the entrance hallway and find yourself facing a blank wall. It's depressing.
2. The living room is very long and narrow, and requires change to make it feel more open and less claustrophobic.
3. Access to the living room is smack in the middle of the plan, which makes it difficult to arrange furniture in the space.
4. The dining table is not really in its own defined zone. It is very much a dining table in the living room, which is not ideal.
5. The kitchen is the worst room in the plan. Yes, it has great views over the garden, but it is not a sociable space at all. It is very bland and functional. If you are cooking in the kitchen, you have no connection with anyone else in the house.
6. The bedroom is a good size – it works well if you are entering your later years and you don't want to navigate the stairs. However, for a younger family, this would be better used as much-needed kitchen space. With this bungalow, there is scope to move the ground-floor bedroom upstairs by converting wasted loft-storage space. It is also worth noting that if this were my house, a ground-floor bedroom would only ever be used as a master bedroom. From a security point of view, I would not want my young kids sleeping on the ground floor with me asleep upstairs.

7. There is no need for a bath on the ground floor, as there is a bathroom upstairs in the loft. I also don't like the toilet being right in front of the window that faces onto the street. Even with frosted or distorted glass, you could still see the silhouette of someone on the loo!

8. As the house was built a long time ago, the garage is too small for a modern car and now only works as storage space.

Plan of existing floor space

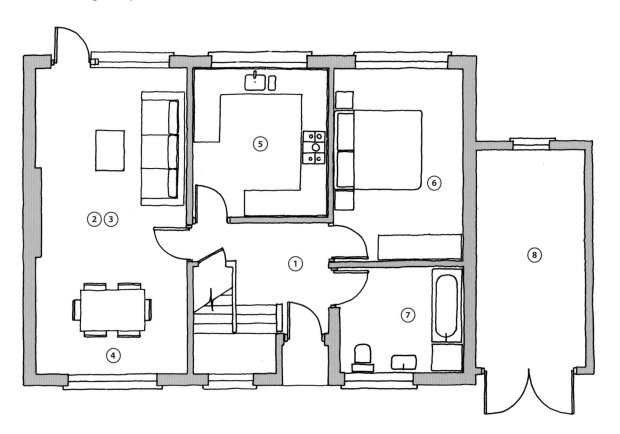

There are obviously many ways to reconfigure this plan depending on your personal needs, but here I've produced a layout that would suit most small families. My aim with this design is to improve the simple functionality of the home, while at the same time forming a series of spaces that flow together – creating architecture that is very exciting for such a small and humble bungalow. Without adding any extra space whatsoever, the result is a sociable and dramatic home that now feels far more efficient and a lot bigger.

My solution

STRUCTURAL CHANGES

- Convert the wasted loft space upstairs to create a new bedroom on the first floor.
- Remove the wall between the existing bedroom and the existing kitchen. This will normally require a steel beam. Taking down walls can seem like a frightening prospect, but it really isn't, if you do it properly.
- Remove the wall between the kitchen and the living room. Again, this may require a beam. A structural engineer can help you with this.
- Break a hole in the wall between the hallway and the old kitchen, to provide new access to the reconfigured spaces.

LAYOUT CHANGES

- Move the ground-floor bedroom upstairs into the partial loft conversion.
- Relocate the kitchen into the space where the ground-floor bedroom was situated, and create more unit space.
- Split the redundant garage space into two, to create a much-needed utility room with direct access from the kitchen. The other half of the old garage remains as storage space for bikes and prams, or whatever, accessed at the front of the house. All new boilers, water tanks and meters can be relocated here to allow more usable space where it is needed in the main house.

Plan of proposed floor space

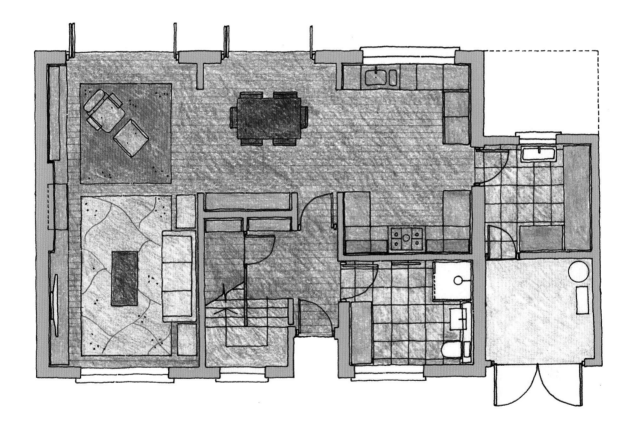

- Create a new dining area in the old kitchen space, away from the main living space. Remove the brickwork beneath the windowsill in the old kitchen to create a larger opening. Install sliding or bi-fold doors to give direct access from the dining area out to the garden.
- Do the same from the living area.
- Redesign the hallway to reduce the corridor space and create a larger cloakroom.
- Install a clear glass-panelled, timber-framed door between the hallway and the dining area. This will allow views all the way through the house and out to the garden, transforming the hall space.
- Redesign the bathroom to create a shower room with increased privacy.

Cut-away drawing to show proposed changes to layout

THE OVERALL BENEFITS

- The spaces have been transformed into a series of linked, but clearly defined, zones.
- The living room will feel bigger as the dining table has been removed – but also because the space has been opened up.
- The plan is more efficient. Where there were once four doors to access all of the separate rooms, there are now only two. This means less square footage turned over to corridors – and a more usable space.
- The kitchen, utility room and shower room are all clustered together, which makes all of the main services and drainage that much easier and cheaper to install and maintain.
- There is more storage space in every new room.

The orientation of your home

'A work of architecture is dependent on the life that fills it – its thoughts and actions, the movement of the sun and the clouds, time itself.' Carl-Viggo Holmebakk

How a piece of architecture sits within the landscape is absolutely everything. The relationship of a building to the natural environment that surrounds it defines its character. The sun rises in the East and sets in the West, and we can accurately define – at any given time of the year – the passage of the sun throughout the day. The weather, however, is something that we cannot always predict and this will also have an effect on the design and style of a building.

The orientation of your home will determine the way that light affects the feeling and ambience of every room. If a room faces north, the quality of the light will be cool and relatively constant. It is a flat light that artists love to paint in, as the direct rays from the sun don't affect you. Alternatively, south-facing rooms are flooded with direct sunlight and have a completely different feeling to them.

It still amazes me how many people visit houses with a view to buying, and spend so much time looking at the bricks and mortar (and the price tag), they forget to look at the way the building faces – and what impact this may have on the way they would use the home. This should be one of the first questions you ask the estate agent: *Which way is this house facing!*

If he says the house faces in the direction you'd like it to – making it capable of creating a mood and atmosphere to suit the way you want to live your life – then by all means go ahead and move on to boring conversations about price, exchange dates and stamp duty.

The front of our own home faces west and the back faces east. We get beautiful sunlight coming into a kitchen-dining room in the morning, which is perfect when we are having breakfast. As the sun moves around to the south, most of the house has only a flat, north-facing light. I quite like this; our home always feels cool in the summer, as it gets very little direct sunlight when the sun is at its highest and hottest. At the end of the day we get wonderful, warm sun-setting light coming into our living room and master bedroom suite upstairs. This suits our way of life perfectly, but it may not suit the needs of others.

So please don't forget: always understand the orientation of your home because it will affect every single design decision you'll make when replanning your home layout.

opposite Once you know what direction your house is facing, you can position the windows to make the most of the natural light.

If you are someone who likes to bear in mind the environmental impact of your lifestyle, then the direction your house faces is even more important as this will affect the ecological qualities of your redesign.

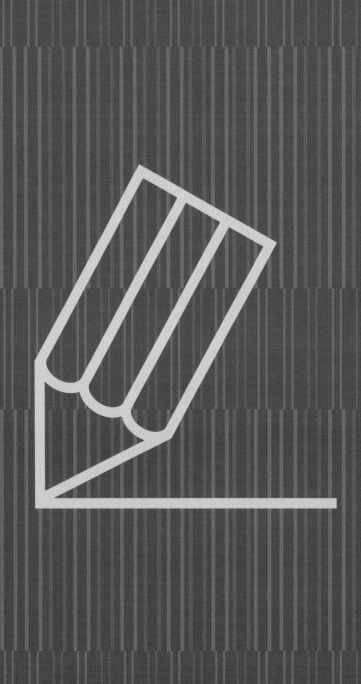

Section 3

How to draw

From a very early age, I loved to draw. I always had a pen in my hand, sketching objects, buildings and spaces around me. Drawing became a part of my everyday life, and to this day it continues to give me such pleasure. I'm incredibly lucky: something that fills me with such joy is now a big part of my job. Drawing is probably the most important element of being an architect. It allows me to communicate my ideas about a space or building to everyone involved in a massively visual way.

Architectural drawing is not just about creating a 'finished' product; it's an organic process, which grows and develops with every stroke of pencil. It's a way of testing and rethinking the different ideas and methods of resolving design problems, as well as finding solutions that aren't immediately evident.

When I am redesigning the layout and spaces of a home, I come up with a variety of different ways to reconfigure the space. It's through the process of drawing that I can quickly see the different layout options and potential design. It's very rare that the first design sketch manages to encapsulate what I'm thinking and solve all of the problems. When I get my ideas down on paper, they seem to flow and present new solutions all on their own.

It is so important that you get the drawing right for your home, well before you start any physical building works. If you get the design right at the outset, it will save you a huge amount of time and money. The last thing you want to do is make changes to the design once the building work has started. Get it down on paper, play with it until you are happy, and then create a final drawing from which everything in your new space will be built.

Freehand drawing

One of the first things you'll hear me ask when I take on a home project is: *Do me a drawing*. Not surprisingly, whenever I make this request of anyone who isn't an architect, or an artist or a draughtsman, I get the same reply: *I can't draw!*

This is absolutely rubbish! If you can lift up a pen and make markings on a piece of paper then, as far as I'm concerned, you can draw.

Think back to when you were a kid. I bet you did drawings of some description every single day – whether you were sketching, drawing airplanes, rockets, dolls, houses, birthday cards for your mum or your favourite cartoon character. Drawing is a fundamental activity in every kid's life, and it was something enjoyable, too, because there was no one there who told us we *couldn't* do it!

The problem is that most of us stopped. Other things in our lives took over, and before we knew it, we gave up drawing for computers, mobile phones and digital cameras. We may also have developed a sneaking suspicion that drawing is for kids, and we weren't actually very good at it. But look at it this way: it isn't a case of you *can't* draw; you simply stopped doing it!

In order to rethink your home and get your ideas across to your architect or builders, it's time to start drawing again.

What you'll need:
- Any sheet of paper will do, but if you want plenty of space to explore your ideas, a big pad of A3 paper will be perfect
- A pencil (or pens, whichever you feel comfortable with)
- A good eraser
- Your imagination
- Don't worry about rulers for your first drawings. The idea is to get your ideas down in a way that everyone can understand, and play with them until you feel you've got them exactly right. That means lots of erasing and ripped-up sheets of paper en route.

above My daughter Iona: All my kids love to draw!

Pictures are a language that everyone understands, and creating drawings helps everyone on the project to visualise exactly what you want your home to be.

Thinking on paper

We now live in an age where the computer drawing – more commonly known as the 'Computer Aided Design' (CAD) drawing – dominates modern architectural practice. There's no doubt that CAD makes an architect's life a lot easier, because we can amend drawings without having to scratch out the ink or use tubs of Tipp-Ex. For me, however, CAD isn't the best design tool with which to start.

The very best way to capture your thoughts on paper and quickly explore your instinctive design ideas is with freehand drawing. A quick sketch is very natural, and it's a hugely enjoyable way to rethink the way spaces work in your home and identify particular problems. This type of drawing doesn't involve a whole lot of detail, nor does it have to be accurate or technically composed. Instead, it's an instinctive response that comes from the way that you *feel* about a space. When you draw in this way, you'll find that ideas literally flow. Never be afraid of drawing; it really is the best and most creative way to express your ideas.

If you look at some of the quick sketches done by some of the most famous architects – Frank Gehry, Norman Foster or Richard Rogers, for example – they often appear to be rough scribbles. In some cases they don't look like anything at all! But that's not the point. These sketches are often seeds of a brilliant idea. Constantly tested, resketched, redesigned and rethought, the scribbles become drawings and, at some point, the final plans of a beautiful building.

'I know I draw without taking my pen off the page. I just keep going and think of my drawings as scribbles. I don't think they mean anything to anybody except to me, and then at the end of the day, the end of the project, they wheel out these little drawings and they're damn close to what the finished building is and it's the drawing.'

Frank Gehry, architect

The playschool house

Remember the drawings you made of houses when you were a kid? The playschool house is the standard house that *everyone* drew when asked to sketch a picture of a home. It was the stereotypical image, too – a square or rectangular elevation, a door in the middle with two sash windows on either side, and then exactly the same sash windows above, on the first floor. There would be a steeply pitched roof and a chimney, too, sometimes with a little bit of smoke rising up to the clouds.

We're all familiar with this image, and it may still be the ideal design for a perfect, chocolate-box home. However, over the last 10 years or so, I've noticed a real change in our thinking – the ideas that constitute what our dream homes would actually look like.

Dare to dream

A few years ago, I created a little test for a group of family, friends and relatives. I asked them to draw their ideal home, and gave them all a pencil and a sheet of A4 paper. Once we got past the *I can't draw* stage, and they were pushed to commit pencil to paper, the results were incredible! Out of over 50 drawings that were done, not one single person – from the youngest kid to the oldest auntie – drew a standard playschool house. Every single house drawn was completely different, and captured a diverse range of amazing architectural ideas.

Take the one drawn by my mam; in a matter of minutes she sketched a single-storey, pavilion-style, modern house with a central courtyard in the middle. It was a very simple but very elegant piece of modern design. I was shocked. It was *beautiful*. When I asked her why she had sketched such a building – something she had never actually seen before – she could very clearly explain her thinking. As she got older, she didn't want to walk up flights of stairs to get to a first floor; secondly, the central courtyard meant that all of her grandkids could play in an outdoor space where they could be completely protected. It was absolutely incredible: those two simple but powerful ideas were the driving force to create the dream home my mam had always wanted.

This process proved to me that absolutely everyone has amazing, unique ideas about what the architecture of their home should be. Everybody can do this, you just need to pick up a pen and draw.

above Emilio's drawing of a house. He wants me to make our home taller! A great idea. Not sure the planners would be happy though!

Watching my kids sitting there for hours on end – seeing them sketching, drawing and colouring, and all of the wonderful and sometimes bizarre thoughts they have in their minds – is, for me, one of the most fascinating and rewarding parts of being a parent.

2-D space planning

Once you've explored your idea, and experimented with the fun of free-thinking and freehand drawing, it's time to test those ideas on a measured, two-dimensional space plan. If you have the original plans supplied by your estate agent, or any old architectural plans, that's a fantastic starting point.

The most important element of this exercise is to ensure that you are drawing to scale. For example, if you are looking to replan your kitchen or your bathroom, the dimensions of the existing space are absolutely critical to replanning the space properly. You need to be entirely sure that the standard elements, such as baths, sinks, toilets, appliances and kitchen units can actually fit accurately into the space you have.

So, make sure your existing plans are to scale. Next, you need to get yourself a scale rule. This is the most important tool you'll need when working out what will fit where in your replanned home. If your ideas won't actually fit in the space you have, it's time to go back to the drawing board.

Starting from scratch

If you don't have any existing plans of your home, it's very simple to produce your own. To create your own plans and begin the process of accurately replanning it, you need the following:
- Sheets of gridded paper. This will not only help you to keep all of your lines straight (most of our houses are square), but will allow you to draw your plans to scale. For example, 1 centimetre on the gridded paper may equal 1 metre of your home's space.
- A decent set of pencils and pens, and an eraser!
- A measuring tape to accurately measure the existing spaces. Make sure it's a minimum of 5 metres in length.
- A decent-sized roll of tracing paper. If you can't find this at your local art-supply shop, then buy a cheap roll of greaseproof paper from your local supermarket. It will do the job just as well!

Your first drawings

A good place to begin is to put together a small library of drawings of all of the standard elements you need to design into your space. Appliance, fixtures-and-fittings and furniture companies quite often provide measured plans of everything they sell. Collecting together the standard sizes from the product catalogues will help you when you are redesigning the spaces. Get them for everything you can find, from kitchen appliances and bathroom fittings to wardrobes and bedroom furniture.

Once you've got your measured, 'to-scale' plans drawn up, the fun begins! Here's what to do:

- To test out many different ideas and configurations, simply place sheets of the tracing or greaseproof paper over your plans and let your pen start doing the work.
- By simply sketching over and over the same space, you can look at rearranging the elements in the space in many different ways.
- You can look at moving the walls or the window positions, or simply moving around the bathroom fittings in the existing space, to find the most efficient and easy-to-build plan.
- Cut out scale drawings of your appliances, fittings and key bits of furniture, and pop them on top to see if your ideas actually work in practice. Move them around until the configuration is just right. When it works, sketch them onto the paper.
- You can place sheets on top of sheets as you investigate different options, and remove the ones that don't work as you go. But keep them to one side; you never know when the seed of an idea will germinate into something new and better!

This process will undoubtedly take time, because there are literally countless ways of redesigning the very same space. But this time is so worth investing; at some point everything will just fall into place and you will be happy in the realisation that you have the design solution absolutely right – on paper, at least!

With any part of architectural design or building game, it's always worth knowing and fully understanding all of the rules before you become brave enough to bend or break them.

opposite You can trace the standard furniture blocks and use them to see how your room will fit together.

Standard scaled furniture blocks

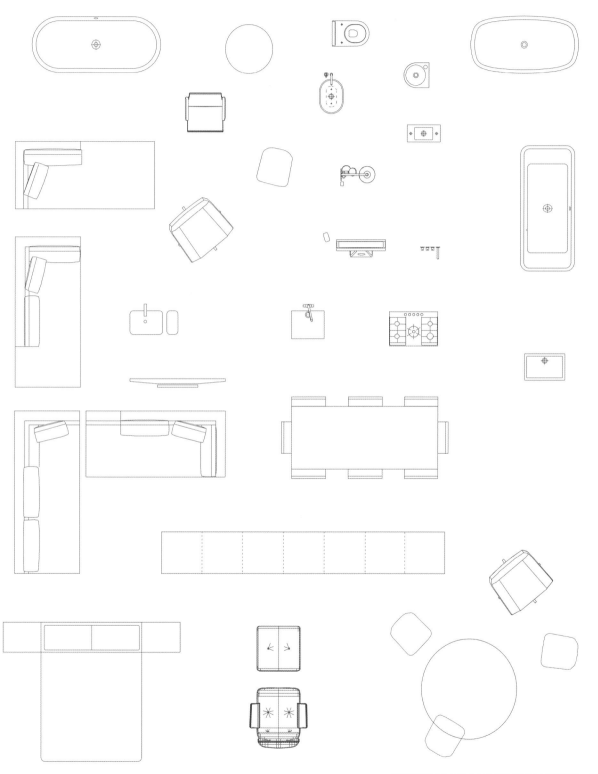

The beauty of the grid

The simple grid has been used for literally hundreds of years to design buildings and whole cities. From the layout of urban metropolises like Manhattan – ruthlessly laid out on a gridded street pattern – to the designs of modern skyscrapers by architects like Mies van der Rohe, grids have been used to strictly and accurately plan buildings and their elevations.

Today, most of our existing homes are designed using a combination of straight lines to form rooms – which are often rectangular or square in plan. In other words, almost everything in architecture is undertaken using some sort of grid. Grids get the scale right and allow us to explore the space with some accuracy.

Drawing to scale

From your point of view, using gridded paper will not only ensure that you get that all-important scale of your existing spaces right, but it will also help you to redesign those spaces in a logical, simple and straightforward manner. Don't get me wrong: I'm not against using curves and organic shapes when you are redesigning your home. Not at all! These exciting forms can transform architecture into something special; however, you need to understand the rules of the grid before you decide to break them.

It's also important to realise that curved spaces are more expensive to build; they can be difficult when it comes to fitting in standard rectangular pieces of furniture or appliances; and, when they are badly designed, curved walls can often make a space very inefficient. So think very carefully before going crazy with wilful shape-making.

There's no reason why you can't achieve something similar with your own home; for a design beginner, the grid makes life simple.

The grid is a beautiful way of keeping your new design scheme well organised, rectilinear and spatially efficient. One of my favourite architects, Alvar Aalto, used the grid in many of his house plans, breaking away in some areas to create exciting, curved forms. My favourite of his house designs is Villa Mairea, in Finland, where he has achieved breathtaking beauty by combining a more formal L-shaped layout with sumptuous curves and stark diagonals.

Simple alignment

Aligning walls and spaces to create very uncomplicated lines and routes through a space keeps the architecture simple and straightforward.

Alignment is a design principle that is a little difficult to describe. It's commonly used by architects when they're going through the process of creating efficient plans. In my design office, you'll often hear people talking about 'aligning walls' to line up with other walls, or having corridors 'line up' with windows to give you a view out in a particular space.

Creating spaces that are balanced and aligned with each other means that they become simple and well organised; in turn, they are efficient and make great use of the space you have. For example, building walls that are randomly staggered – or corridors that bend and weave their way through a space – often creates complicated and in efficient plans that aren't particularly user-friendly, or, more important, easy to build.

As you are sketching over your existing home layouts – particularly if you are using gridded paper to keep an element of control in the creation of the new spaces – you will realise how easy it is to align all of the individual elements to create a balanced plan and elegant spaces.

Creating a floor plan

opposite This plan is really well aligned making it efficient.

If you don't have layouts or plans, accurately measure your space, including windows, doors, storage space, radiators, stairs, electrical and phone outlets, chimney breasts and anything that features in your rooms. You'll only need to do this process once, but you might want to make a few photocopies!

1 Lay a piece of tracing paper over the top and do a rough draft sketch.
2 Now you can arrange the space, moving appliances, fixtures, furniture and even walls to get the look you want. If you like some of the elements, but not all of them, place another piece of tracing paper on top and draw in the ones that work for you.
3 It can be useful to draw a scaled template of each of the main appliances, units, items of furniture or fittings you want in your room. You can then cut them out and move them around until they fit beautifully.
4 Remember to keep things aligned and as simple as possible; not only will your final space flow that much better, but your builders will actually be able to create it!

A typical floor plan ...

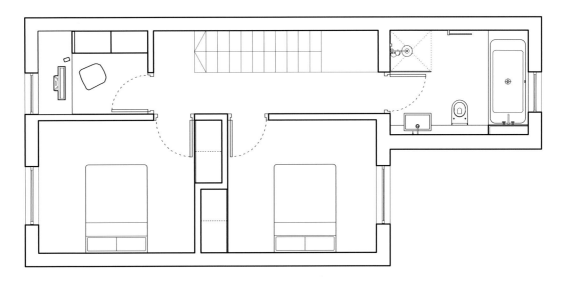

... and showing how the plan is aligned.

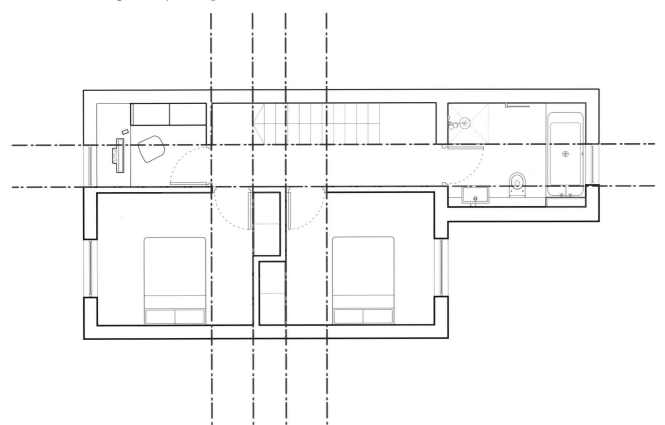

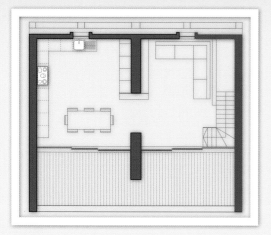

2-D

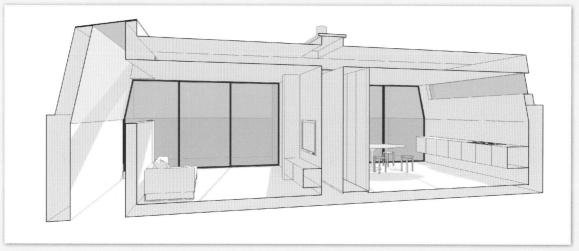

3-D

Built!

3-D drawing

Once you've reacquired the knack of drawing, and have some 2-D sketches under your belt, you are definitely ready to make the leap to 3-D 'perspective' drawings. This is a brave step, and it may seem a little daunting; however, the sooner you throw yourself into it, the more confident you'll become. It's easy, I promise!

I can't tell you how many times I've been asked how I make 3-D drawings so easily. The truth is that it all comes down to hours and hours of practice, combined with an understanding of space. You don't need to worry about producing perfect images; once you get started you'll see how easy it is to get the perspective right and make your drawings come alive.

If you are feeling adventurous, you can create 3-D drawings on your computer. Not only are there plenty of simple programs available for home use, but many furniture manufacturers offer similar services on their websites. This is a great idea if you have the time and inclination, but I love the process of sketching down ideas and working through them on sheet after sheet of paper.

opposite The 2-D floor plan, 3-D CAD and photos of a dynamic studio.

this page On *The Home Show*, I always encourage the whole family to depict their dream home.

Simple perspective techniques

You'll now produce your very first single-point perspective, 3-D drawing. With practice, they will get better and better!

The simplest way to produce a 3-D drawing of a space is by using the 'single-point perspective technique'. The single point is a specific point in a room, on which you train your eye. Once you have chosen and defined this point on your drawing, every single line and angle radiates out from it. Take a look at the example below to see how you can form the proportions of a simple space using single-point perspective. Then have a go yourself, following these simple steps:

1 Decide on the position of the single point. This is the position on which you are going to train your eye; you are always going to look at this point. In effect, it is your 'eye-line', from which you will create the rest of the drawing.

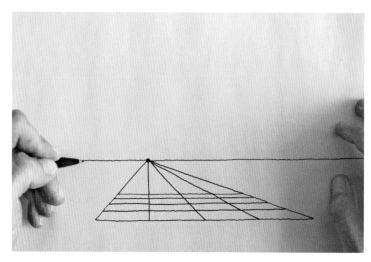

2 Draw the back wall of the space as a flat panel, clearly showing the single point.

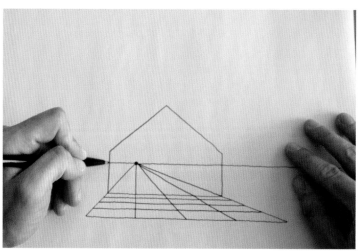

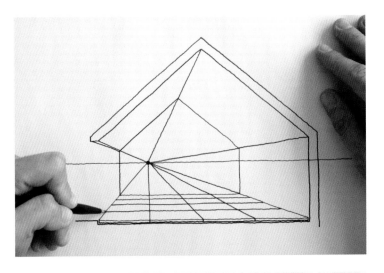

3 Draw the main lines of each floor and wall radiating from the single point.

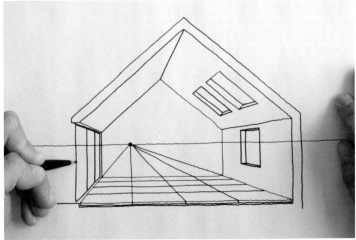

4 Add any windows and doors within the space, again radiating back to the single point.

5 You can then have fun filling in all the details – from floor finishes and light fittings to furniture and, of course, people.

Kids drawing

'Every child is an artist. The problem is how to remain an artist once we grow up.' Pablo Picasso

My kids draw all the time. Not only is it something that gives them a huge amount of enjoyment and fun, but it does serve a purpose – encouraging two very, very important things. First of all, drawing allows them fully to understand the spaces and the environment around them. Spatial awareness is a hugely important part of a child's development and should, therefore, be an important part of their upbringing. It massively improves their observational skills and it allows them to understand and actually *see* the world around them.

Secondly and perhaps far more importantly, drawing allows them to realise their dreams and their imagination on paper. Kids have the most wonderful minds, absolutely packed with great ideas and fascinating images. We keep every single one of my children's drawings, simply because they capture beautiful moments of their childhood.

Never underestimate the power of drawing to encourage kids to understand the built environment around them, the beauty of nature, and the realisation of their own ideas and dreams. On top of all that, sketching and drawing is fantastic family fun. Make sure that you and your kids never lose it.

above Emilio's very own grand design.
left Georgie teaching Iona to draw.
opposite Georgie's happy family home.

Section 4

Space and where to find it

I see myself as a bit of space-hunter! I'm always amazed by how a little bit of reorganisation can make a huge difference.

In order to redesign existing space – or look at ways of adding it – you really need to open up your mind and truly understand the existing space you have. On *The Home Show*, I remove all personal belongings from the house, and spray-paint everything white. This may sound like a dramatic step (and don't do this at home before beginning work unless you want it white in the end!); however, seeing your home stripped back and 'naked' is a hugely interesting process. It can feel quite surreal to see your home without any of your belongings; all that's left behind is a very non-personal space, stripped of any style or personality. Your home becomes anonymous – but it's important that it becomes a blank canvas so that you can really appreciate the space for what it is.

This approach can reveal so many surprises. Some spaces feel bigger, some smaller, and others darker or lighter! It really depends on the success or failure of the spaces you have. Although you may not think it, your brain is very good at understanding the space around you, but you can make the process even easier by encouraging your eyes and brain to gather information about which spaces work, and which don't. A blank canvas opens everything up so that you can easily see what you have – and what you need.

The most important thing is for you to create new spaces that suit you, and your way of life.

Changing your perception of space

I am a huge fan of the legendary American artist Gordon Matta-Clark (1943–1978). He was born in New York and trained in architecture at Cornell University before leaving behind the traditional world of architecture to become an artist. He was fascinated about carving up and manipulating old buildings that were about to be destroyed.

In a very radical and dramatic way, Matta-Clark reconfigured space to such an extent that it changed our perception of existing buildings. He would force his way into abandoned apartment buildings in the Bronx and, using a chainsaw, he would slice up walls and floors, and tear apart the existing structures to reveal a radically transformed piece of architecture. This was off-the-wall stuff – pushing the boundaries of what architecture means – but it had a huge effect on me as a student. This type of reconfiguration of existing built forms is something that I try to undertake in ordinary homes today – albeit in a slightly more restrained way!

Increasing your sense of space

We live in an age in which we all love a greater sense of space in our homes. Most of us don't want to live in tiny, box-like rooms, all with a similar scale, size and proportion. Instead, we like variety in our homes, diverse spaces with plenty of light and a great flow of air. We like rooms to be sized to match our requirements; in other words, we need them to be big enough to host our lifestyles, and smaller when we want to be cosy. The lighting and finishes are then chosen to create an atmosphere appropriate to those rooms.

Many of us adapt our lifestyles to match the layout of our homes, when it can be incredibly easy to match our homes to our lives – and the way we lead them.

opposite top and bottom Artist Gordon Matta- Clark, splitting houses to transform our perception of space; and the same sense of drama is created by an architect.

Knocking down walls

When I walk into a home that's been subdivided so much that it feels like a warren of tiny rooms, I sometimes feel like I am walking into a claustrophobic egg box! Although it can seem like a dramatic gesture, it really is important to open up rooms to make your spaces work. Don't be afraid to knock down a few walls!

I'm not suggesting that you should take a sledgehammer to every internal wall in your house to create a single, open-plan room. That kind of random approach would be bonkers! It would also be seriously dangerous, affecting the structural stability of your home. There are, however, certain walls in a property that you may feel an overwhelming urge to rip down – making two separate, boxy rooms into one elegantly combined working space. But before you get sledgehammer happy, consider the following:

1 Employ the services of a structural engineer to come and check that the wall you want to remove isn't structurally 'load-bearing'.
2 Load-bearing walls can still be removed, but your engineer will need to calculate the size and support of a structural steel beams and its support, which will need to be inserted to maintain the structural integrity of your home. You'll also need to make sure that your builder knows what he's doing when he provides temporary support to remove the old wall and install the engineer's new beam.
3 Before you knock down the wall, make sure you've designed and planned the new layout of the space properly. Drawing is cheaper than building!
4 If your wall is not load-bearing – and your engineer gives you the nod – then go for it.
5 When you have combined two spaces into one, make sure that you've designed all of the 'services', such as the electrics, light switches and sockets. They will need to be integrated to work in your new, single space.
6 Removing a wall that isn't load-bearing may seem straightforward on the face of it, but once it is taken down there will be a lot of work – and lots of different tradesmen involved in getting the space right again.
7 The flooring, ceiling and walls will have to be made good where the old wall was situated.
8 A good plumber will need to isolate and remove any pipework in the wall, and may need to relocate any existing radiators that were fixed to the original wall.

opposite A dark, cramped space can be completely transformed into something light and airy, simply by taking a wall down and avoiding a flat ceiling.

below I love the demolition phase of a build – it is the most radical change you'll make throughout the whole process.

9 If the wall you propose to lose is load-bearing – requiring a new structural beam – try to inset the beam into the ceiling void to avoid any downstands or bulkheads. These always look messy and awkward between two old spaces, unless they are cleverly integrated into the new design.

10 When you get the go-ahead from your structural engineer, and the plumbing, electrics and services are isolated, it's time to plan the new spaces in your integrated room. Once you've done that, you can most certainly get out the sledgehammer and smash away! Happy days!

Think about the balance of the rooms, their size, how they are arranged and how they link together. If you list out all of the problem areas, then you will naturally uncover a list of possible solutions – and places where you can remove walls to create the space you want.

Controlling open-plan design

Fully open-plan spaces, where the living room, kitchen and dining areas are fully integrated into one big space might look fantastic in magazines and architectural journals, but they aren't entirely practical for modern family living. Sure, they look great and are excellent spaces to be in for a short period of time – particularly if you are on holiday or at a weekend retreat where the whole family can come together to spend time in a fun and sociable environment. However, being in a fully open-plan space all the time doesn't really work when you get into the subtleties of private and social space in your average home!

If I have friends over, and I'm cooking in the kitchen, we may have a drink and a good chat that is not necessarily quiet. If my kids are in the next room trying to watch TV, they have to raise the volume over and over again to drown out our booming voices! Similarly, when I sit down to read in the evenings, it's nice to have a little peace and quiet, and not be overwhelmed by the sound of the TV.

I think that combined kitchen and dining spaces work so much better when you have a separate living room or 'snug'. Unless you live in an enormous house and have space to spare, I'm not a fan of the separate formal dining room. These spaces are so rarely used that they are really not worth having.

For me, the ideal family set-up involves avoiding complete open-plan living and going instead for a beautiful, sociable kitchen-dining area, which really does become the heart of the home. The TV and the 'living' space can have their own separate, designated areas.

opposite If planned properly, open-plan kitchen and dining areas can become the centre of the home.

Zoning spaces to make 'open-plan' work

If you do choose to knock down a large number of your existing walls to create one single open-plan kitchen, dining and living space, then getting the design right is more crucial than ever. These three distinctive zones within a house are so important to the success of any home that every single element of the design has to be carefully considered for it to be a success.

This will take a lot of careful thought and clever coordination. In some ways you have to imagine that you have designed the three individual zones so carefully that if you were to reinstate the walls to create three separate rooms again, the spaces themselves would still work. Obviously, you're not going to put walls back up where you've removed them, but once you've carefully coordinated the three distinct zones – with all of their furniture, lighting, electrical switch points and plates, storage systems and circulation spaces – just test your plan by drawing the walls back in again. If the zones work as individual rooms, then you know each one of the zones is going to work perfectly when combined as a single open-plan space.

To create a successful open-plan space that works well for kitchen, dining and living, consider the following:

1 Think of the *exact* tasks that need to be undertaken within the open-plan space, and mark the areas clearly on your new plan. Everything from watching TV, sitting at the dining table, cooking and preparing food, to relaxing by a fireplace and having easy access storage needs to be considered and factored into your plan.

2 Carefully coordinate all of your new electrics within the space; you have to be very specific about light-switch positions, plug sockets, any 5-amp lamp sockets and the position of all light fittings.

3 At design stage, make sure you've carefully positioned all of your furniture to scale on the plan. I've seen so many examples of people creating open-plan spaces without thinking about where the furniture should go in the space. This is always a disaster.

4 You'll need to think about integrated storage locations at design stage, too. In particular, consider low-level storage, mid-level storage or full-height integrated storage. Maximise the available wall space.

5 How is the space going to be heated? If you've removed internal walls where radiators were once positioned, where are you going to cleverly integrate new radiators?

6 With any open-plan space, I personally prefer to avoid radiators altogether, and go for integrated under-floor heating to maximise all of the available wall space.

7 Think carefully about how you move through an open-plan space. There need to be clearly defined circulation routes through the furniture, around the dining area and through the kitchen.

8 Remember that open-plan spaces must be designed and coordinated as a series of clearly defined zones within one single space.

opposite This is my home in Dorset not long after completion.

I always think of an open-plan space as a number of 'zones' – a zone for watching TV, a zone for reading, a zone for sitting by the fire, and so on. This is a much easier way to design the layout in a large space.

Adding space without extending

'Have nothing in your house that you do not know to be useful, or believe to be beautiful.' William Morris, craftsman, designer and poet

Very simple, minor changes can make a massive difference to the feeling and quality of the space within your home. Some of these changes, such as decluttering, don't even require any building work – just a little bit of thought, time and effort. I go into many, many homes across Britain, and I can't tell you how often families complain that they just don't have enough space, when they seem to have mountains of *stuff* everywhere! The truth is that most of this stuff isn't important to the day-to-day running of the home.

There are other, simple changes that you can make to create a home that feels more spacious, lighter and brighter, without physically extending your current home.

1 Declutter! Get rid of all the stuff that you don't actually need. You've got to be incredibly ruthless for this exercise to be worthwhile. Work out the things that you *really* need to keep, as well as the things that definitely have a nostalgic value. Frankly, if it isn't essential, and you haven't used it for years, then get rid of it.

2 The things that you do need to keep should be put into integrated storage. This type of storage can be carefully designed into your space to make a room feel bigger. If you have too many free-standing storage units, the units themselves actually contribute to the feeling of clutter, making your room feel smaller! Fully integrated storage is the best way forward.

3 Try to source clever furniture that contains storage elements within it; for example, footstools, bench seating and under-bed sliding drawers are ideal ways to get the clutter out of sight and free up space in your rooms.

4 Look, too, for clever pieces of furniture that are dual-function. One of my favourites is a writing desk that folds away to become a single bed. In some of my projects, we have integrated-storage 'walls' that look like book shelving. However, when you pull down a huge panel in the centre, a large double bed is revealed! Dual-function furniture is genius, and a fantastic way to save – and make – space.

I can't stand wasteful, unused spaces, such as dark, dingy corridors or wasted loft spaces. Make every single square inch of space work for you, and your inefficient house will become a wonderful home.

opposite Clever storage devices like a door that serves as a bookshelf and under-stair hanging rails help make your room feel bigger by getting the clutter out of sight.

5 Reorganising internal walls gives space to those rooms that really need it, while reducing the amount of space in rooms where it's not so important. You may not mind a smaller, cosy study if it means gaining all-important living space. Sometimes shifting a wall by a matter of inches can suddenly make the puzzle pieces fall into place, and make the spaces either side of the wall work.

6 In first-floor bedrooms and bathrooms, I love to raise ceilings up to roof level. This makes what seem to be small rooms on the plan feel much larger when you are actually in them. High ceiling heights make small rooms feel much bigger.

7 The use of under-floor heating is a space revolution. All of a sudden you can use valuable wall space that was once wasted by having boring radiators lining them.

8 Use clear glass panels in walls and doors. This not only lets more natural light bounce through spaces, but also allows you to see into the next room, giving you a greater sense of three-dimensional space.

9 In some homes (particularly my own!), I've used glass floors. Unlike thick, timber-construction floors, glass floors are very thin, providing a greater sense of physical space. This makes a room feel bigger and brighter because you are allowing in more light.

10 Try to provide access panels for any small areas of roof void, to create valuable storage – ideal for storing things like suitcases, to which you won't need regular access.

11 The old trick of making an internal space flow directly into an outside space is a fantastic way of making the internal rooms feel bigger. The outside garden or courtyard is fully seen within the room and feels a part of it. This is why I love my bi-fold doors.

12 Probably the best way to add room to a space you've already got is to do a loft conversion. You won't need to extend your house – simply use the existing space to the full. By creating an additional room you are also adding value.

opposite I love bi-fold doors. They make rooms feel bigger by making your interior rooms flow out into outdoor spaces. They also bring in tons of light.

Loft conversions

'Up near the roof, all our thoughts are clear.'
Gaston Bachelard, French philosopher

I love lofts! Architecturally, they are often the most unusual and exciting rooms in a home. Just think about walking through the rooms of a fairly ordinary house, where all of the rooms are very box-like, and then entering the very different world of a loft conversion – all of its bizarre roof angles, illuminating skylights and dormer windows with views over the surrounding rooftops and up to the sun and the moon. The converted loft feels like a hideaway and refuge from the rest of the home.

Planning

You are required by law to make a full planning application for any loft conversion. If you live in a conservation area or a listed building, you will also need conservation-area or listed-building consent (see resources section) and these types of properties can have many design restrictions. In a standard planning area, you do have the option to go for planning permission for your loft conversion under 'permitted development rights' rather than submitting a full-planning application (see resources section).

The process of obtaining full planning can take between eight and 12 weeks, and your application has to go through a public consultation period, during which your neighbours have the right to reject your plans. However, by using your permitted development rights, you can extend your home without going through the full planning process *or* the consultation period.

YOUR PERMITTED DEVELOPMENT RIGHTS
The simple rule for permitted development is that you are able to add 10 percent of the overall gross floor area of your home – or no more than 50 cubic meters of volume in an extension. You still have to apply to the council for permission, but it takes a fraction of the time, costs less and your council can't object if your plans comply with permitted development rules! This is a simple fast-track process for loft conversions or, indeed, any extension.

opposite The loft in my house before and after conversion. Most houses with pitched roofs have masses of space in the attic waiting to be used.

Design challenges

(1) Head-height restrictions are the biggest design challenge with a loft. You need to make sure you don't bang your head on the roof going up the staircase – or when you are in the new space.

(2) The position of the new loft staircase is everything. It has an impact on all of the rooms on the floor beneath and also a huge bearing on the quality of the final loft space. Getting the staircase position wrong can be a huge mistake.

(3) Decide upon the purpose of your space. If it's a bedroom – which will add the most value – then the bed is paramount.

(4) How do you get light into the space? Planning policy will affect what you are allowed to do.

(5) Building control now requires steelwork in the floor and often in the roof to comply with the new building regulations. This is costly so design it into your scheme at the very beginning. The steel in the floor will often lift the finished floor level in the loft, putting even more pressure on the available headroom.

(6) The insulation required for you to comply with the building regulations may be thicker than your existing rafters. You may have to increase the thickness of the rafters in order to get the insulation between them and still maintain an air gap between the insulation and the roof tiles.

Loft conversions are a brilliant way to add more space, bring more natural light into your house and, if your budget can stretch far enough, give you a brand new roof that will last you for years and years to come.

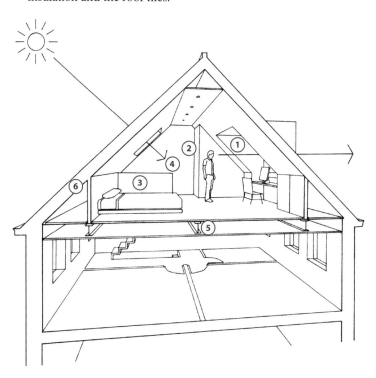

Design solutions

Creating the perfect space in your loft is dependent upon a number of things, but with clever planning and use of the existing space, you can produce something truly special.

The possible solutions to the design challenges you may face when sorting out your loft conversion very much depend on the profile of your existing roof. If you live in a conservation area or a listed building (see resources section), then it is highly unlikely that the planners will allow you to dramatically change the roof profile. In other words, you are stuck with the space you've got. However, if you don't have these restrictions, you can consider the possibility of changing your roof profile – or extending it in order to create a space with a much larger volume. Anything like this will require planning.

The bigger the space you create in your loft, the greater the opportunity to add value. Because your property value is generally calculated on a square-foot basis, the more square footage you add, the more value you add. The ideal loft conversion will be achieved if you can bear the following in mind.

Your staircase

Install a cleverly designed staircase from the first-floor level up to your loft. The staircase needs to be positioned to have a minimal impact on the rooms downstairs while making sure you don't lose too much floor area in the loft bedroom. At the same time, you'll need to be able to get up the stairs comfortably, without banging your head. Balancing all of these constraints is one of the most difficult things to do in a house refurbishment. And I can guarantee you that a compromise will have to be made *somewhere*. You may have to sacrifice space on the first floor or at loft level to squeeze in the staircase. It is most definitely worth employing an architect to get this absolutely right. My office often carries out detailed surveys for lofts, and we sometimes have to work out the exact design on CAD to get it right. Even then we still have to mark the staircase out on site to be 100 percent sure.

Converting your loft space into an additional bedroom or home office space is a very simple and affordable way to add space, as well as value, to your home and it will be a lot cheaper than moving.

below The position of the loft staircase can have a huge impact on the space you have in your loft as well as on the floor below.

above A typical loft conversion showing new floor joists and rafters in steel and wood, Velux roof lights and thick insulation panels on roof and walls.

Structural design

It is highly likely that you will have to put structural steelwork in the floor of your new loft room, to comply with the current building regulations. Have your structural engineer or architect keep the design as simple as possible – and the depth of the structural beams to an absolute minimum to maintain a maximum floor-to-ceiling height. Using more beams that are lighter and smaller also makes it easier for you to get the beams in place, as well as making your loft space feel bigger.

DUMMY WALLS

To create the simplest structural design it is best to build low-level dummy walls; these are the vertical walls used to form a practical loft space. The dummy walls should be built directly off the structural steel beams, around the edge of the room. The dummy walls provide an intermediate structural support to the sloping rafters, which are the main timbers that form your sloping roof structure.

STRUCTURE AND STORAGE

Make sure that you put access panels within these dummy walls, to allow access to storage within the triangular eaves area at the low point of your sloping roof. Otherwise, this is valuable storage space wasted.

There is a chance that your roof timbers may be quite thin, probably because your roof was not originally built to be converted. This may mean that you have to add increased depth to the sloping rafters – or you have to add extra rafters in between the existing ones. Alternatively, you can use structural plywood – which is a strong bracing material – and fix it to the underside of all of the rafters to provide a strong structural roof.

INSULATION

All of this has to be balanced with the need of your sloping roof to be newly insulated. In order to comply with current building regulations, there is a chance that the insulation required may need to be thicker than your existing rafters. This means that you might have to undertake a combination of the things I've mentioned:
• increase the depth of the rafters;
• add additional rafters; or
• go that extra mile and use structural plywood on the inside face. This plywood would then be covered in fire-grade plasterboard, skimmed and painted.

Positioning your furniture

Because there are areas of restricted head height in a loft, it is incredibly important to redesign your loft space both in 'plan' and in 'section'. The plan of a loft can often look incredibly large on paper; however, the trick is to work out the 1.8-metre (6-foot) height on the cross-section, so that you can clearly mark on the plan the approximate point that you would bang your head on the sloping ceiling!

GETTING IT RIGHT

The bed can obviously be positioned against one of the low-level dummy walls, but it's important to get the height of this dummy wall right so that you can sit up in bed without banging your head on the ceiling above. If possible, I always like to position a desk within the dormer window; it's a nice place to work, with plenty of natural light and a lovely view out over the rooftops.

Wardrobe storage is always more difficult because of the height restrictions. In general, this is better positioned against one of the end gable walls, so that you get a maximum height for storage. You are always juggling the need for maximum storage with the risk that too much of it can make a room feel smaller – particularly if it is full height. Storage needs to be beautifully integrated, without compromising the way the room feels.

Even if you don't plan to use your loft space as a bedroom, it's worth considering installing an en-suite. If you do ever sell your home at any stage, it makes the space that much more versatile. Try to position your loo opposite the loft staircase zone, to free up more usable space in the main room. Keeping your staircase alongside rooms that need services is always an efficient way of planning a space.

Good loft

Bad loft

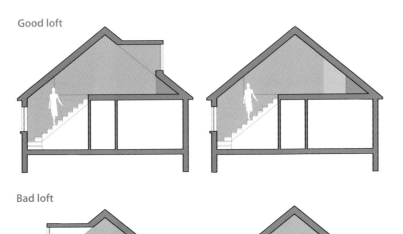

left Marking the 'clear' head-room zone onto the plan of the room will make you think very differently about the planning of the space.

Natural lighting

The best way to get natural light into a loft – while at the same time creating an increased area of loft space with a high ceiling level – is to install a dormer window to the back of the property. Dormer windows to the front of homes are rarely approved by planning authorities, particularly if you live within a conservation area. Planners don't particularly like the front profiles of roofs being extensively modified, but there are very rare exceptions to the rule.

SKYLIGHTS

A large dormer window to the rear is great as it often provides fantastic views over the back garden of your home. As well as the addition of a main dormer, there is also the possibility of installing Velux skylights. Carefully positioned over the loft staircase, a Velux skylight provides a dramatic way of flooding the stairwell with natural light – right down to the first floor. After consultation with the planners, it may be possible to install a Velux skylight on the front slope of the roof, although skylights on the rear slopes of the roof are far more common. Velux skylights are one of the most affordable and effective ways of getting natural light into your loft conversion, but a large dormer gives you more useable headroom and space.

Artificial light

Because of the sloping faces of the loft ceiling, the type of artificial lighting that you can install is likely to be restricted. Simple, hanging pendant lights can obviously be fitted to the high part of the ceiling; however, because they hang quite low, they can make the headroom within the loft space feel constrained. I prefer to go for a row of recessed downlights at high level, and then a series of 5-amp lamp switches in each corner of the space. This allows you to provide low-level lighting where you need it.

The use of your room

The way you choose to use your room really depends on your own personal needs; however, to add greatest value it's always a good idea to define the space as an additional bedroom. And, if you have enough space, consider installing a small en-suite shower room with a toilet and sink. Estate agents love this type of layout, because a self-contained bedroom and en-suite will add considerable value to your property. The en-suite shower room has to be carefully positioned to achieve maximum ceiling height, particularly in the area where the shower is being positioned.

opposite Lofts can often be made into the lightest rooms in the house with the best views out. Skylights allow the natural light to flood in.

Side extensions

above and opposite
Side extensions aren't particularly large in terms of volume or size, which means that they are often quite affordable. They can, however, create a dramatic transformation to a very important part of your home.

Side extensions have become an incredibly popular addition to British homes, particularly on terraced and semi-detached properties. They often form an important infill of the old external side-return yards. The kitchen and dining areas in most Victorian and Edwardian homes tend to be at the rear of the property, so a new side-return extension allows the creation of a much larger, combined kitchen-dining space.

It's important to consider the following when planning *any* side-return extension:

1 Consult your local planning department to get an idea of what size, style and scale will be appropriate – and acceptable.
2 Planning policies vary from council to council. Some departments may insist that the side extension is in keeping with the traditional style of your existing house, while others may insist that the style is distinctly modern and different from the existing style. Either way, you need to plan accordingly.
3 If your side extension does not exceed more than 50 cubic metres (or an additional 10 percent of the overall floor area of your house), you may be able to apply for your extension under 'permitted development rights' (see resources section). This is a faster, cheaper process!
4 In order to maximise the impact of a small side-return extension, it's important to ensure that the small space you've added is integrated with the existing building as much as possible. This will, no doubt, require a large structural opening to be made on the side wall of your existing house.
5 In order to create a large new structural opening, you must employ the services of a good structural engineer, who will calculate the size and loads on the new beam. A structural engineer will also decide if the existing walls at each end can support the beam, or if they will require underpinning.
6 It is critical that you spend as much time as possible at design stage – not only creating an extension that looks good on the side of the building, but has been carefully and efficiently planned to work well with the internal spaces.
7 If you live in a terraced property, your side-return extension will be built up to rest on the boundary wall between your property and your neighbour's. If this is the case, the extension cannot be built to a high level, as it will affect your neighbour's right to light. You have to be very sensitive about this element of the design.

8   If you're building right up to the boundary line of your property,
    you will be required to appoint a party-wall surveyor to form
    a party-wall agreement between you and your neighbour (see
    resources section). Your neighbour has the right to appoint
    their own surveyor to act on their behalf. Because this is your
    project, you will have to meet the costs for both surveyors. A
    party-wall surveyor is required where any structural works are
    carried out to any party, boundary or garden wall, unless you can
    reach agreement with your neighbour without the need for an
    independent surveyor.

Rear extensions

Adding to the back of your property can produce some fantastic extra space, particularly if you use it creatively. Depending upon your budget, and any light issues with your neighbours, you can go for a single-storey rear extension – or one that runs up the full height of your property.

Single-storey rear extensions

Single-storey rear extensions are a very simple and affordable way to add additional space to the ground floor of your property. Because they are just one storey, the scale of this type of extension rarely causes many problems with planners or your neighbours. However, even though these small, humble additions may seem unimportant – or unimpressive – within the bigger scale of home refurbishment, it is very important that any addition is carefully designed and integrated within the existing home.

Getting an architect on board

A single-storey rear extension offers the perfect opportunity for you to commission a good young architect – perhaps someone who has just started in practice. He or she will be bound to have some exciting design flair and will commit a lot of time to making your small extension something beautiful. Approaching a large architectural practice for work of this scale is a false economy. Their overheads and costs will be too large and they may not give you – or the project – the important time you deserve. A young architect will be hungrier and go the extra mile to create the perfect project for you.

opposite and above Rear extensions can add invaluable extra space to your home, and often, with minimal fuss and cost attached.

A recipe for success

For any single-storey rear extension, make sure you follow these rules:

1 Commission a good young architect who can service the project properly.

2 As the client, make sure you put in the time to produce a proper design brief. Ask yourself some testing questions, such as what you plan to use the extension for and how it needs to transform your spaces to reflect the unique needs of your family.

3 Pop into your local planning department with a set of your existing plans – or some photographs of your property – and discuss the potential for creating your extension. The planner will soon determine the restrictions and planning rules, and you'll have a clear idea of what is possible.

4 Flick through some good magazines and put together a scrapbook of all the single-storey extensions that you really like. This will be a great tool to brief your architect, and give the planners a good idea of what you would like to do.

5 Have a look over your garden walls to get a feel for what other people might have done in your local area. If a design precedent for something you like has already been set, this will go down well with the local planning department.

6 Remember that you may require the services of a party-wall surveyor if your new extension is being built up to the boundary line of your property.

Just because your rear extension might be small in scale doesn't mean that it can't be an architectural wonder. Investing in the addition of a small amount of space on the back of your home can make an enormous difference to the way it relates to your garden and the way the interior spaces are transformed. It doesn't take much to create a wow factor!

opposite A variety of rear extensions; it is important to consider all your options so you get what works for you.

Two-storey rear extensions

Although they are not *impossible* to get through planning, two-storey rear extensions are far more difficult. The main reason is that any two-storey addition to the back of your home is likely to be a substantial structure in terms of size. If you are lucky enough to have your home situated on a large piece of land – with your neighbours some distance away – then you are unlikely to come up against any significant problems.

However, in densely populated, urban areas – where your property is likely to be very close to your neighbour's – you will undoubtedly face a huge number of objections. It's not just the considerable visual change that poses the biggest problem – it's the fact that a two-storey extension can have an enormous effect on the rights of light that your neighbours' properties will have.

The success of any planning application for a large two-storey extension is always going to come down to the unique character of your home, the proximity of your neighbours and the policy of your local planning department. Frankly, however, there is no harm in trying!

A sensitive design

A well-designed, two-storey extension on the back of your home will make a huge difference – not just to the kitchen, dining and living spaces on the ground floor, but also to the house as a whole, giving you additional space to create bedrooms and bathrooms. The golden rule here is to create something incredibly sensitive in design. You not only have to respect the scale, style and proportion of the existing house, but the planners will be looking for something that actually improves on the quality of the architecture. Even this might not be enough to overcome some of the stringent planning policies, but there is no harm in popping in to your local planning department to test the water. It's worth noting that even if you're lucky enough to get the planners on board, it's going to be a much harder job to convince your neighbours.

Making your two-storey extension work

- The ideal two-storey extension involves transforming your living, kitchen or dining space on the ground floor, while adding an additional bedroom and en-suite on the first floor.
- A large first-floor bedroom to the rear of the property can make the most fantastic new master bedroom suite.
- Consider lifting the ceiling in this room up to the roof level, for an even greater architectural space.
- You could consider exposing the rafters of the roof to create a more dramatic space.
- If you aren't short of bedrooms, perhaps you could consider a double-height living or kitchen/dining space. This is incredibly dramatic. I would only suggest this on a larger property where additional floor area is not required, but an architectural 'wow factor' it certainly is.
- If you do want to add bedrooms to your home, consider using the space to include en-suites, or perhaps a fabulous new family bathroom.
- If you already have a single-storey extension, it may also be possible to add a second storey. A builder will be able to tell you whether or not the foundations are deep enough and if the walls can take the weight.
- Consider the appearance of your extension; do you want to make a statement, with something bright, new and bold, or would you prefer to extend in the same style as your existing property?
- Think about how much garden space you'll be giving up with your new design; if you are massively extending to the rear, you may create a property that is out of proportion. Losing prime garden space might not be a good idea and any four- or five-bedroom house should have a garden large enough for kids to play.

below Two-storey extensions are relatively rare, but if you can get the right planning permissions they can be really exciting architectural spaces to be in.

Garage conversions

Across the UK, there are countless homes with garages that are never used to store a car! I can't tell you how often I have visited properties to find the garage absolutely crammed with *stuff* – kids' bikes, fridges and freezers, lawn-mowers, pots of paint, tool benches, half-inflated paddling pools, and boxes that haven't been opened in years. And yet, there is no sign of a car!

Yes, yes – I know it's important that we have some storage space for essential things, but surely most of this stuff could be kept in a simple garden shed? Why use essential space that's directly connected to your home?

Your garage can easily be converted into much-needed living space. Before you get going, however, you'll need to check a few things:

1 If you live in an area where your car needs secure parking for insurance purposes, you might want to keep your garage.
2 If you live in a street where parking is unbelievably difficult – and off-street parking isn't so easy, either – then again you might want to avoid a garage conversion.
3 Speak to your local estate agent. If garages are an asset and maintain a high value for your property, then you need to do some calculations. Would the cost of converting a garage space into a habitable space actually increase the value of your property? If it doesn't, then you might not want to bother.
4 Always investigate other houses in your area, where similar conversions may have been undertaken. Find out how they used and reconfigured the interior space, and learn from their mistakes.

clockwise from top left
On *The Home Show* we transformed a garage in Bushey Heath into a fantastic living room. The wasted garage space; breaking through the garage during the build; and the garage converted into a great living space.

If there is no desperate need for protected parking within your garage – and you are in desperate need of more habitable space – then a garage conversion is a no-brainer.

What are the options?

A redundant garage that is cleverly integrated into the existing architecture of the home can have a dramatic effect upon the way the house works. However, the new use of the garage really depends on you, your family lifestyle and what your family needs. I have done so many garage conversions, and they have all had different functions. Some have provided an additional bedroom with en-suite on the ground floor – all very self-contained from the rest of the house. Others have been converted into a study for those who work from home. For larger properties that desperately needed more family services, we've converted the garage into a very functional ground-floor toilet and shower room, with an enormous utility room alongside. My favourite garage conversions involve creating much-needed kitchen, dining and living spaces.

Garage-conversion basics

The cost and complexity of a garage conversion will very much depend on the way the existing garage structure is built, as well as the standard of the fit-out for its new use. Whatever you decide to do with your space, it's really important that you are aware of the following things:

1 Many garages were never originally intended for habitable use; therefore, the walls are likely to be built from only a single leaf of brickwork. This construction is completely inadequate for today's building regulations. You will, in effect, have to build a new, blockwork internal leaf, with an insulated cavity wall construction. In other words, it's highly likely that you will have to create a new foundation on which to sit the new blockwork – unless the original concrete slab has been built to a high structural standard. Sadly, this is highly unlikely.

2 The original garage floor will probably be uninsulated; you will therefore have to build a new floor on top of the existing slab. This can be either insulation with a sand-and-cement screed on top, or you can build a suspended timber floor on top of the slab and place insulation in between.

3 You've also got to be super-careful of the existing services. Your garage might be home to existing boilers, tanks, electric meters, fuse boxes and your gas mains and meter. If they can be integrated into the design, then fine. If they can't, the cost of moving them all can be incredibly expensive. If I were you, I would design in a simple, safe and secure 'services cupboard' and leave everything where it is. If you've got a big budget, go for it!

Bushey Heath

When filming *The Home Show*, I visited the home of a couple in Bushey Heath. The husband had lived in this house for 30 years, and his wife had always felt in the shadow of her late mother-in-law's taste – and her possessions. I was absolutely astonished when they opened up the garage door to reveal boxes and boxes. It was a virtual mausoleum – a garage packed tightly with memories! The house was cramped and dated, and the massive garage space was totally wasted. It was a painful process, but the garage was cleared of possessions and we knocked through into this wonderful space and moved and expanded the kitchen into it, creating an open-plan kitchen-dining room, with a light, energised living space.

4   Your garage conversion will require planning permission, as you will be removing your garage door and replacing it with a new wall and windows. Please check with your local planning department before you spend any money on architectural services or building work, to make sure that your planning permission will be granted in principle.

5   Regard any garage conversion in the same way as any other house extension. The old interior spaces have to be perfectly integrated with the newly converted space. Even if you employ an architect for just a few hours' design consultation, it's worth the cost to avoid making any *very* costly design mistakes.

6   Although a garage conversion is not a highly specialised job, it's always worth using a contractor who has done this type of work before. There may be a great deal of structural work involved, as well as the prospect of moving your services, so your builder will really need to know what he's doing. Whatever you do, never attempt this type of work on the cheap or with a builder who hasn't got a proven track record.

below The transformation was so complete that the couple didn't even recognise their own home!

Before ...

and after ...

Converting existing cellars

If you are lucky enough to have a small cellar underneath your house – perhaps used for nothing more than some storage or a place to keep some wine cool – you may be able to change this into much-needed, usable space. One of the problems with existing cellars is that they have no natural light – and no natural ventilation. It is also common for cellars to have very restricted headroom.

Utility space

If you are working to a tight budget then your best option is to waterproof the existing space as it is, paint and decorate it, install some decent artificial light and some mechanically extracted ventilation, and then use the space as a decent family utility room. The great thing about putting washing machines and dryers in this sort of underground space is that the surrounding walls give a large amount of acoustic protection. It's great to move all of these noisy appliances from the ground floor down to the cellar.

If your budget can stretch a bit further, why not consider digging out the cellar's ground slab, and building in a new, insulated concrete floor at a lower level, to give you some increased headroom. If you have a few more spare pennies stashed away, you can always look at enlarging the cellar and extending it underground – either towards the front or back of the property. This may provide you with the opportunity to install some glazing at ground level – to allow natural light into the basement spaces and encourage some good, old-fashioned natural ventilation.

This makes your basement utility room a much nicer space in which to spend time – rather than being shut away in a dark and dingy dungeon. The truth is that any additional space for utility-room storage, which can be easily accessed by a cellar staircase, is always going to be a great asset and a selling point for any good family home. Even with the tightest budget, any conversion of an existing cellar is going to be a good use of space.

opposite Like garages, converting cellars is a fantastic way of making the most of the space you already have.

Creating new basements

If you are anything like me, and you've increased your sense of space by decluttering, knocking down walls, reconfiguring spaces to make open-plan areas work, done your loft conversion and your side-return extension – or even a rear extension – and had a go at converting your garage or cellar into a utility room or a little extra space, then you probably think you've reached the maximum that can be done to refurbish your existing home.

Well, there is one more thing you can do, and it may actually be easier than you think. I know because I've not only helped design these types of spaces, but I also created one in my own home. You can construct a full new basement underneath your house. Your first thought to this suggestion may be: *How the hell am I going to do that!* However, although the prospect sounds daunting, the reality of the project is definitely far less so!

New basement technology has moved on so much over the last 15–20 years and some pretty amazing things are now possible. When I started in practice it was common to see new basements being formed on sites where no existing buildings stood, but it is now possible for you to create a full new basement right underneath your old existing house. It's unbelievable!

above A clever way to maximize light in a new basement conversion.

Constructing your new space

The construction processes vary depending on the type of property that you live in, but the general principles of creating a new basement under an existing building go something like this:

1 The basement company constructs a hoarding at the front of your house, which allows them to start digging through your front garden.
2 Once they have dug down to the basement level, they then start to make their way underneath your house, by forming a one-meter-wide tunnel right down the middle of your home. They go down the middle because all of your structural foundations run along the edge of the house. For the time being, they have to stay away from them.
3 They then have a skip located on the road outside your house and a conveyor belt that goes from the underground space up through your front garden – over the top of the street footpath and into

the skip on the road. As the guys dig out the mud, they throw it on to the conveyor belt and it goes from the subterranean space and into the skip. The skip is unloaded regularly by a lorry with a grabber.

4 They then tunnel off to the corners of the house and begin to underpin the house with huge, deep, new concrete foundations. They gradually and very slowly do this in sections to provide the much-needed structural support to your foundations before they can remove the surrounding soil.

5 They underpin, remove a bit of soil, then put up some Acrow props to provide some temporary support for your flooring above.

6 Once all of the perimeter walls and foundations are completely underpinned, the remainder of all the soil under your house is removed.

7 Steel beams and steel columns then span beneath your existing ground floor to keep it in place.

8 Light wells are formed at the front and the back of the property, to allow in as much natural light and ventilation as possible. These can either be sunken external courtyards or glass skylights inserted at ground level.

9 Next, the waterproof tanking system is put up against all of the concrete walls.

10 Insulated concrete slabs, under-floor heating pipes and screeds are installed.

11 All the drainage and plumbing is installed.

12 The walls are timber-batoned, dry-lined and plaster-boarded before being given their final finish.

I am completely astounded by the simplicity of this process. Not only is all of this work done quickly and efficiently, but you don't have to move out for a single day! All of the work happens underground, while you remain living in the rest of your house. Being able to create this newly formed space from something that didn't even *exist* before completely blows me away. In fact, I was so blown away by the possibilities, that I decided to get in touch with the London Basement Company, to do one for me.

Basement worries

The main thing that concerns people about new basements is that they may damage neighbouring properties or affect the ground water table. Neither of these is true. What's more, with a good, reputable company running the project, any structural movement will be absolutely minimised.

Unless you live near an underground stream, the water table won't be affected, either. The biggest thing that you and your neighbours have to worry about is the disruption and the noise. But even that hasn't been as bad as I thought it would be!

below This is how they do it! A conveyor belt takes the newly extracted soil to a skip waiting on the road outside.

My new basement

When I'd refurbished my house from top to bottom, and added as much space as I possibly could, I decided to begin the design drawings for a full new basement under my house. I had to ask myself some very serious questions before moving forward, because I had to make sure that it made financial sense. From a family and lifestyle point of view, a basement made perfect sense. I didn't want to move house and even though we were comfortable in the space we had, having additional room was great for when parents and other family members came to stay. I also knew my kids weren't getting any smaller and that they would, in the long run, love some more space. But did it stack up financially? Some serious number-crunching was in order, and I asked myself the following questions:

- How much would a basement, with a footprint that was the same size as my house actually cost?
- Once the basement was completed to a high specification, what sort of increased value would it add to my home?
- Was there a danger that adding so much space and increasing the value of my home substantially would break through the ceiling of house prices that people would be willing to pay in my local area?
- How long would the build realistically take and what level of disruption would it actually cause for my family?
- Overall, was it actually worth it? With the extra capital I would need to spend, combined with the level of disruption, would I be better off just moving and buying a bigger house elsewhere?

With a little research, all of these questions could be quickly answered. The London Basement Company gave me a ballpark price based on some quick sketches. Yes, the price was only an estimate at this stage, but these guys have bags of experience so it was a pretty good guess. I was already aware of the property prices in my area, but I still put a call in to an estate-agent friend to find out if I was over-investing in the property. Even with all of my financial cards on the table, he said that there was no chance of my property going through the financial ceiling for our area. So doing the work as a financial investment made sense.

I then had to look at whether it would be easier and more cost-effective to move. Looking at bigger properties in my local area and some larger houses beyond, I realised I would have to commit a substantial amount of capital money in order to climb the property ladder while staying in the same area. Add to that the cost of selling my house, agents' fees and VAT, as well as stamp duty, legal fees, removal costs and potential refurbishment of a new home, and creating a basement looked like the best proposition by far!

In a matter of two days, the decision was made. It was new basement time!

At the time that this book goes to print the basement won't be fully completed. We were granted planning permission in the early winter of 2009 – relatively straightforward considering I live in a conservation area with very tight restrictions.

At the time of writing, most of the house has been underpinned and the majority of the underground space has been formed. The next stage is for all the waterproofing to be done, the slabs to go in, and the space to be made wind- and watertight. We can then begin fitting the internal walls and dealing with the finishes. I can honestly say that every time I go down the ladder to those newly formed underground spaces, I am absolutely amazed.

Due to new legislation that's been brought in to protect green garden spaces, this underground garden structure has to be built at an even lower level than the main basement, so that there can be a 1 metre clear zone on which the garden's top soil and grass can be re-established above the office's basement box.

The total floor area for this new basement is 1100 square feet! To put that into perspective, the area of the original two-storey house was only about 1600 square feet! You couldn't maximise a very ordinary, two-storey, Edwardian semi-detached house any more than this. I've used every single square inch of available space and more – and have managed to do all of this with a huge number of planning constraints that are the result of living in a conservation area.

What originally started as a simple, Edwardian two-storey house has become a four-storey home flooded with light from top to bottom.

I knew that if I overdeveloped my property to push it through the price barrier for my area, there would be a danger that someone would choose a better home in a better area, for less money than mine would be worth.

1. There is a light well to the front of the property where a new basement bay window has been built underneath the existing one. This provides natural light to a new double bedroom and en-suite.
2. This is a guest room for friends and family when they come to stay.
3. Towards the centre, and the darkest part of the plan, we have created a new utility room. All of our washing machine, dryer and butler-sink facilities can be relocated down in the basement. This frees up additional storage space, which is a huge bonus on the ground floor.
4. Alongside the en-suite and the utility area, there is a staircase that leads you from the ground floor to the basement.
5. Walking past the utility door, you go through to an area where there is a storage area on the right, and a new toilet, sink and boiler on the left.

My house ...
and the new basement

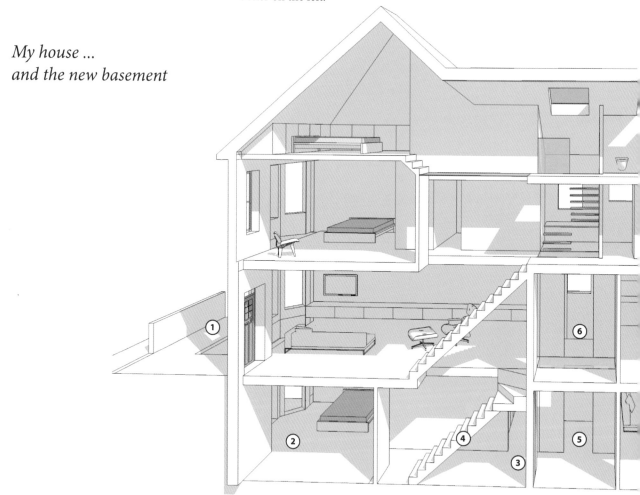

6. If you look up, you will see a clear, glass ceiling above you. Because I've got a clear glass ceiling in the corridor at ground level, you can stand in the basement and look straight up to the loft landing into the second floor and through to the glass skylight at the top of the house.

7. Walking under the glass ceiling, you'll reach a big TV area and snug. In effect, this is a sixth bedroom, as far as any estate agent would be concerned.

8. I've put in a glass ceiling to the back of this area to let natural light from the outside into the TV room.

9. There is also a new external staircase going up to the garden, so you can get direct access from the basement to garden level.

10. Probably the most dramatic move of all is that the basement continues *underneath* the garden, as far as I could possible go. This fantastic subterranean space underneath my back garden creates a new underground office, where I can work from home.

11. To get natural sunlight into this office space I've created an additional glass skylight at garden level.

As an architect who is absolutely obsessed with space, discovering that there is a way to create an entirely new space that presently exists as nothing more than mud and clay is nothing short of phenomenal.

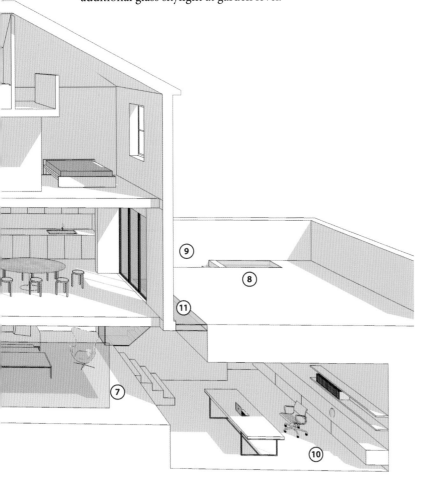

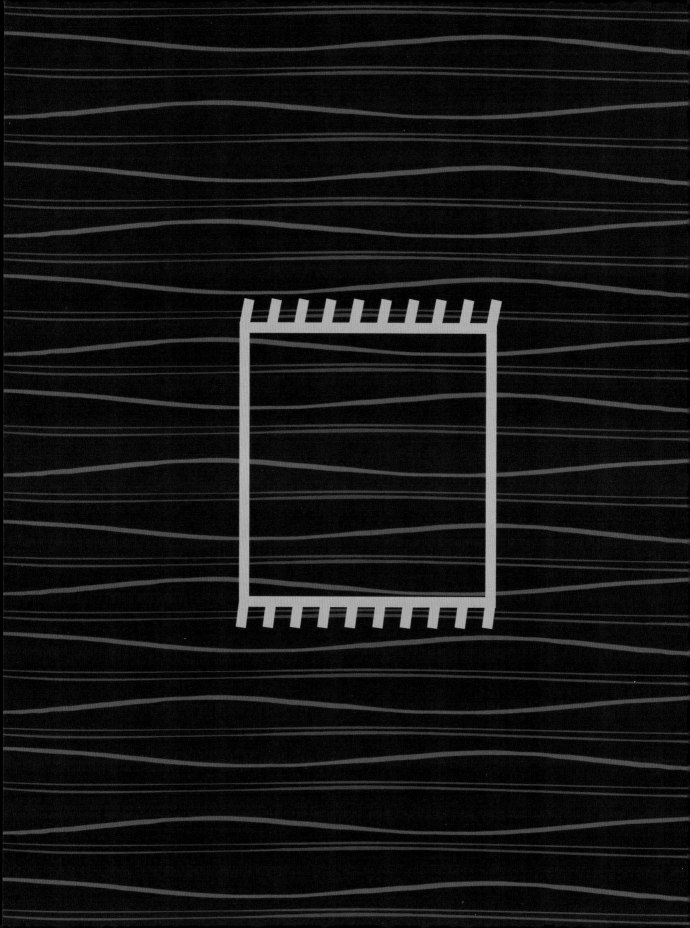

Section 5

Room by room

*'We shape our dwellings, and afterwards
our dwellings shape us.'*

Winston Churchill

Every single decision you make – from the smallest design detail to the selection of finishes and furniture, and the overall arrangement or layout of a room – has an impact on the way that your entire home feels. Together, these decisions can have a profound effect on the way you live your life, and the dynamic you create within it.

One question that I am regularly asked is: *Which rooms should I start refurbishing in my home, if I have a limited budget?* There are some pretty clear answers to this but they will, of course, depend upon the way that you use your home.

Take my home for example. After refurbishing every one of my previous homes bit by bit and room by room, over a long period of time, I was relieved – not to mention lucky enough – to be able to do the entire building from top to bottom at the same time. Well, not the basement, but I'm calling that phase two! This is undoubtedly the most cost-efficient way of doing a project, as you'll have all of the materials and labour on site at the same time, and they can get on with it in a faster, more efficient way. But this approach takes money, and that isn't always an option. You'll also have to factor in the cost of living in rental property while the building work is being undertaken – unless you don't mind living without electricity and loo facilities for a few months!

Kitchen and dining areas

'My kitchen is a mystical place, a kind of temple for me. It is a place where the surfaces seem to have significance, where the sounds and odours carry meaning that transfers from the past and bridges to the future.' Pearl Bailey

If one thing's for sure, kitchens are the absolute heart of the home. They aren't just places for cooking, but a hub for socialising with family, friends and relatives. The 21st-century family kitchen is a virtual hive of activity and, for me, it is without a doubt the most important room in the house. Dining rooms are, however, something completely different. There really has been a change in our view of these spaces, particularly in smaller homes. Sure, if you have a grand house with loads of space, then a formal dining room is a fantastic space for those special occasions – huge dinner parties, or family gatherings. However, whenever I visit smaller homes, I can't help but think that a separate formal dining room is a massive waste of space. If you need more space in your house, and need it in rooms that might sit alongside your dining room, then I really believe that this is the first room that needs to go.

opposite The modern kitchen: a place to cook, eat, socialise and take in the view.

A modern family's needs

Another reason why we are seeing the death of the formal dining room boils down to the fact that younger families simply don't use formal dining spaces in the same way that previous generations did. The modern family is much more relaxed and far less stuffy. Times are changing and we don't seem to mind the idea of entertaining in what is effectively kitchen space. In fact, most of us feel much more at home in a combined kitchen and dining space. As a modern architect, husband and dad, I'd be more than happy to announce the end of the separate formal dining room, replacing it with a far more exciting, spacious and enjoyable combined kitchen-dining space.

When you analyse the way that you live and assess spaces that are being used, under-used or unused, I think you'll find that a separate dining room in a smaller property is a space luxury that you cannot afford.

Planning your kitchen layout

I cannot stress enough how important it is to get the layout of your kitchen absolutely right. Your kitchen has to be ruthlessly functional, highly durable, and intelligently planned to suit the *exact* needs of your family. If it's not, then you have not only wasted a large proportion of your refurbishment budget (even the most affordable kitchens still cost money), but it will drive you mad every time you use it. Cooking for you and your family should be a pleasurable and rewarding experience, and not a source of frustration.

In the early 1950s, researchers in the US developed the idea of the 'work triangle'. This is an ergonomic concept derived from research to improve industrial efficiency, which was then applied to the domestic kitchen. Whether you are planning your own kitchen, or enlisting the help of a professional, you can use the 'work triangle' method to check the efficiency of your design.

The three points of the triangle correspond to the three main kitchen activity zones. There is the wet zone (the sink), the cold zone (the fridge) and the hot zone (the cooker). Their position and relationship to each other is critical to achieving an efficient and comfortable kitchen design.

How to draw and assess the work triangle

1 Have a plan of your kitchen-dining room drawn to scale, either on graph paper, or using a scale ruler (see Section 3).
2 Sketch different layouts over the plan of your room. You'll have to carefully consider the qualities and proportions of the existing space, as well as any constraints such as windows, doors and radiator positions. You also have to know – and implement – your family's needs.
3 Test each layout by marking the points of the three zones (sink, fridge, cooker) and draw your triangle.

The recommended overall distance (the total length of the three sides) is 6 metres (20 feet), with no two points being less than 90 centimetres (35 inches) apart. Sound complicated? It's not really. Read on! If the total is *less* than 4 metres (12 feet), then your appliances will be too close for comfort. If it's *greater* than 8.5 metres (26 feet), then your appliances will be too far apart and you'll waste time and effort trekking between them. A good way to burn off the calories that you are about to put on, but not an efficient kitchen design!

Try to assess the traffic flow across the triangle, too. If you have a large kitchen, people walking through the space may not be a problem, but in small rooms it can reduce efficiency even further.

Basic kitchen layouts

By adopting the 'work triangle' there are five typical kitchen layouts that can be created.

left A well-planned kitchen-dining area based on the popular island layout.

ISLAND LAYOUT

The primary benefit of an island layout is that the cook is looking out from the kitchen to the rest of the room and can relate to family and guests. This is a very a sociable and inclusive design. The downside is that an island layout takes up a lot more space and only works well in large spaces.

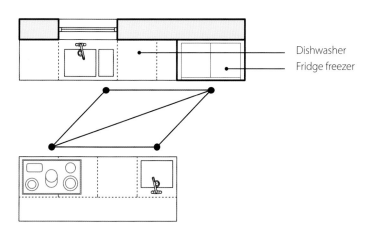

Dishwasher
Fridge freezer

L-SHAPED LAYOUT

Two adjacent walls at right angles allow the appliances to form a natural triangle. This is the perfect solution for a kitchen that opens onto an adjacent area.

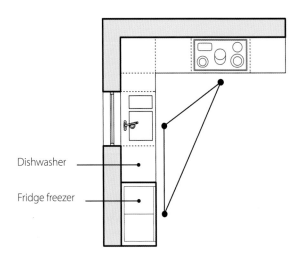

Dishwasher

Fridge freezer

U-SHAPED LAYOUT

A continuous countertop and storage system surrounds a cook on three sides, for maximum efficiency. There needs to be a minimum of 2 metres (6.5 feet) between the arms of the 'U' to make this work. The downside of this layout is that it can have an enclosed feel about it.

Dishwasher

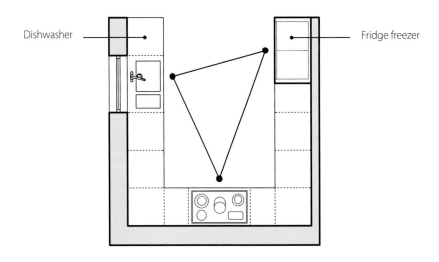

Fridge freezer

GALLEY LAYOUT

The galley kitchen offers one cook a very efficient space, with work centres on parallel walls; however, there is little extra workroom for more than one cook! The main disadvantage of this layout is that people will frequently pass through the space and disrupt the flow of the work area.

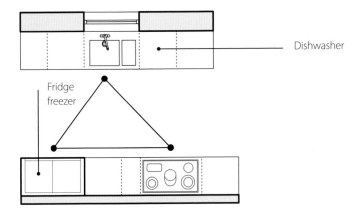

Dishwasher

Fridge freezer

ONE-WALL LAYOUT

As the name suggests, this is simply arranging all of your units and appliances along one wall – or in a single line. Unless you have a very small room in a flat or an apartment, this not the favoured option for many kitchen designers. Under the rules of the work triangle, this layout would be considered inefficient because you will be constantly walking along the line of the space to access the appliances. Having said that, I did bend the efficiency rules to suit my needs in my own kitchen! I went for the single-line option because even though it is less efficient in terms of the energy needed to work in the space, I definitely found it was the best use of my space. It freed up a usable area for the dining table and a relaxed seating zone.

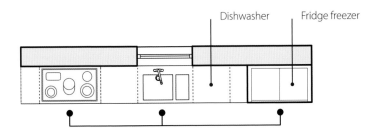

Dishwasher   Fridge freezer

following page It is vital to choose a kitchen layout that not only works for you, but makes the most of the space.

Dining tables

If your kitchen and dining area is the most important room in your house, then your dining table and chairs have to be up there with the most important pieces of furniture in your home. This is the one set of furniture used by everyone, and it will become the regular gathering place for the whole family. For this reason, it has to be ruthlessly functional as well as comfortable. Ideally, too, it has to be beautiful to look at. You'll be spending a lot of time sitting there.

The range of dining tables and chairs available today is absolutely enormous. Take the time to road-test as many as you can, to get the look and feel you want. Here are a few things you must consider to get your choice absolutely spot-on:

1 Consider how many people you actually need to seat around the table. If this is a combined kitchen-dining space, will you be hosting dinner parties? Do you regularly have guests?

2 What space do you have available? You'll need to be able to comfortably fit in the table and chairs, and have enough space to walk easily around them.

3 Take your tape measure wherever you go! You'll need to be sure that your table will actually fit in your space; it can be difficult to envision your measurements and your layout when you aren't at home.

4 What sort of look and style do you want to go for, and how will it relate to the rest of your kitchen-dining area design?

5 Consider what form of dining experience you want to achieve when you are around the table. For example, having high-back chairs creates a more formal dining experience, whereas low-level benches can be more relaxed and informal.

6 Consider the dining-table legs. Too many supports around the edge of the table can be a nuisance when it comes to organising chairs, and you may find that you are constantly banging your knees. Tables with a single central support work so much better.

7 If you don't have kids, or your family is small, you might want to purchase an extendable dining-table system for those occasions when friends and family gather.

8 The shape of a dining table has an enormous effect on the dining experience. A large rectangular table will automatically create clusters of smaller group conversations; it's hard for one person at the far end of the table to talk to someone at the other. Smaller circular tables are more intimate and make everyone feel part of the same conversation. Halfway between the two, there is the oval dining table, which can still make everyone feel part of the same group, while encouraging smaller group conversations at the same time.

top Your dining table is one of the most important pieces of furniture you will buy. Spend time getting the right one!

above Tables like this one from IKEA don't cost the earth and can add instant style to your kitchen.

My favourite tables

Personally, I've got two favourite styles of dining table. The first is a table that I designed myself, not long after finishing university. I wanted something that was large, rectangular and uniquely designed but, most importantly, simple. I also wanted the table to be strong, highly durable and able to stand the test of time. The specification of my table was something like this:

- The chrome base was made out of a series of simple, flat, metal bars.
- The metal flats were formed into two rectangular sections at each end, joined together by three horizontal chrome bars.
- In contrast to this slick metal base was the timber tabletop. This thick timber was made from 50mm 'fumed' oak. This allowed me to use a more affordable type of oak, which was not only strong and hard-wearing, but looked expensive! Fuming darkens the timber throughout its entire grain, and transforms it into something that looks more like American black walnut. It was an affordable way to get the darker look I wanted.
- Instead of going for formal high-back chairs, I chose low-back benches, which would create the atmosphere I wanted in my kitchen. To ensure that they were consistent with the style of the dining-table top, I formed the benches from the same fumed oak, at exactly the same thickness.
- The benches were designed to be able to fit perfectly under the dining table, sitting snugly within the chrome frame.
- The benches were designed to sit three people on each long bench, with two smaller, individual benches at each end. So, this was a table for eight.

this page This table was brilliantly made by a good friend of mine: Mark Darbyshire. He is an amazing craftsman and the table looks truly beautiful. Its style and quality mean that it looks as good today as it did 10 years ago. The downside of the design is that the older I get, the less I like the bench seats. When you start getting to the end of a big meal, you just want to sit back and relax – an impossibility with a low-back bench. So I've reluctantly removed my table from the dining area and put it to use somewhere else. In its place is one of my favourite design classics.

PURE DESIGN

One of my most favourite dining-table designs is the classically beautiful oval Saarinen dining table. Designed in 1956 by Eero Saarinen, it is manufactured and produced by Knoll. This table truly is one of the simplest and purest forms of dining-table design I've ever seen. To quote Saarinen directly: 'The underside of typical chairs and tables makes a confusing, unrestful world. I wanted to clear up the slum of legs.' What an *amazing* quote.

His table sits on a simple central pedestal, which has become known as the 'tulip'. The tables are produced in a whole series of different materials and finishes – veneer, laminate or marble tops, with a base in black, white or platinum. The white tulip base and the largest of the oval tops fitted perfectly with the design of the rest of my kitchen.

I could have gone with the classic Saarinen tulip dining chairs to match, but I thought this might be going a bit over the top on the tulip front – tulip fever! So, in the end, I decided to mix styles. I went for the Eames Eiffel plastic side chair (produced and sold by Vitra). This chair was designed by Charles and Ray Eames in 1950, and it became the first industrially manufactured plastic chair. The simple design has a bent and welded wire base with a sculpted plastic seat; it's comfortable and timeless, and it works beautifully with Saarinen's dining table. I now have a more sociable oval dining table, and chairs that are so much more comfortable than benches.

below One of my favourite dining tables. Beautiful, sociable and functional at the same time.

Kitchen lighting

If there is any room in the home where lighting has to be very specifically designed to be functional and flexible – but also create a wonderful atmosphere – it's in the kitchen-dining room.

Generally speaking, there are four types of light that can be used in a space.

1 General lighting. This is considered to be the all-purpose type of lighting that creates a comfortable and safe environment. General lighting needs to be balanced with other forms of lighting in a room.

2 Ambient lighting. This is lighting that illuminates each and every surface in a space evenly. This type of lighting is common in offices and schools.

3 Task lighting. You need this type of lighting to carry out daily activities, such as reading your recipe book, cooking and preparing food, and even finding the right piece of cutlery. Efficient task lighting enhances visual clarity and prevents your eyes from becoming tired.

4 Accent lighting. Lighting focused in a particular direction adds interest or highlights an object or unusual architectural feature in a room.

Who needs what?

A kitchen-dining room can use all forms of light, depending upon the way the room is designed – and your own personal tastes. For me, the most important part of any kitchen lighting design is to create flexibility – not to mention the ability to adjust the light source and the lighting level with the touch of a button. In my kitchen at home, I'm happy to be in quite low-level lighting. I'm just not a fan of bright lights at home – preferring a calmer, more serene atmosphere when cooking and eating. My wife likes the lighting to be slightly brighter than I do, and I know the kids like the lighting to be very bright indeed – so they can see what they are doing when they are reading, drawing or playing with toys on the dining table.

So, what do you do with one family, all using the same space, but with three very different lighting requirements? The answer is a multitude of different types of lighting, all of which can be adjusted to meet individual needs. Long gone are the days when a single pendant lightbulb and cheap lampshade were enough for a kitchen. Flexible lighting is everything to maintain the status quo in our house!

Technology is moving forward so dramatically with lighting controls that a single, hand-held device can adjust the lighting from the comfort of your dining table – or even remotely from your mobile telephone if you want to turn on your kitchen lighting for security purposes when you are away for the weekend. All this technology can take some getting used to, but your kids can teach you how to use it!

Kitchen lighting tips

In a well-designed kitchen-lighting scheme you need the following:

1 Strong task lighting over kitchen worktops, island units and preparation areas. It's important that this task lighting is glare-free, which is why lighting positioned under wall units works so well.

2 Integrated lighting inside your kitchen units, which is a massive help when you are looking for things.

3 A beautiful feature light centred over the dining table to provide task lighting when eating (yes, eating is a task).

4 Directional, recessed, downlights or spotlights can be used to pick out family pictures or artwork hanging on the walls of the room.

5 I like to have lamps in the corner of rooms, but I hate having to turn them all on and off with the lamp switch. Have the lamps connected to a 5-amp socket, which can be controlled from a light switch near the doorway to a space.

6 *All* zones of lighting in the kitchen-dining area should be controlled separately, so any zone can be dimmed or switched off to create a particular mood.

7 I'm a big fan of candles on dining tables. This creates a beautifully atmospheric light when all of the artificial lights are dimmed.

8 With all of these lights being independently controlled, there is a danger of having banks of light switches everywhere. To overcome these consider using a Lutron or i-light control panel.

below To be really effective, your kitchen-dining area will need a variety of lighting solutions which can all be controlled independently.

opposite Task lighting over your worktops is essential and, despite what the name suggests, it doesn't have to be boring!

Kitchen design features

Some of the integrated design features in kitchens these days are absolutely unbelievable. There is nearly as much technology in a kitchen as there is in a NASA space shuttle. The average price of a kitchen is usually around £15–20,000, but I recently saw one that was selling for nearly £180,000. For that price I think I would expect my kitchen to do the daily shopping and automatically prepare my food for the rest of my life! All joking aside, there is definitely something to be said for investing in a kitchen that is carefully designed and beautifully built, to withstand everyday use for many, many years to come. Those kitchens at the more affordable end of the market simply won't last the course. So, a good-quality kitchen is a must. Equally, however, there are some clever design features that will make your new kitchen stand out from the crowd.

Let's look at them now:

1   The Anima kitchen, by Binova Techno-Logical Kitchens, knocks down all the barriers of kitchen design. Their central island has a hidden section of storage in the centre, which, at the press of a button, displays a cabinet full of useful storage for utensils or cookery equipment. This truly is a brilliant piece of dynamic storage design.

2   Consider an integrated plasma TV screen within kitchen-unit design. Some plasmas can even be designed into splashbacks.

3   I am a big fan of breakfast bars within kitchens – connected to island or galley kitchens. They offer a great, relaxing way to chat with someone who is working in the kitchen.

4   On the other hand, I am *not* a fan of huge, ugly-looking cooker hoods! Thankfully, some innovative new designs have created a range of cooker hoods that are slimline, integrated, and packed with all sorts of technology, including integrated lighting and automatic sensors to adjust the levels of extraction needed when the kitchen is in use.

5   There is also a clever system called the 'up-and-down table' by Binova, which allows you to adjust the level of your table so it can be placed at the same height as the worktop when you need more preparation space, and electronically reduced in height if you require a lower dining table. So it can actually be three things: kitchen worktop, breakfast bar or low-level dining table.

6   Go for state-of-the-art drawer systems – particularly intelligent corner units. The corners of kitchens always used to be awkward; however, developments in clever design have overcome these problems.

above Pop-up plug sockets - a very simple but effective idea.

opposite top left Flexible taps like this look stylish but are also incredibly useful.

opposite top right Task lights under your cabinets are helpful when you are preparing food on your worktops.

opposite bottom New technology means that ugly cooker hoods can now be a thing of the past!

Intelligently designed storage compartments and recycling units are essential, and worth every single penny.

Kitchen storage

A kitchen really is a place where every *single* square inch of available space should be maximised for storage. The truth is that the kitchen is probably the most intensively-used room in the home – absolutely packed with everything from utensils to tablecloths, as well as different types of food requiring different levels of storage. You've got pots and pans, cutlery, small appliances and everything else, right down to the proverbial kitchen sink.

One very important decision to make is how much of this stuff you actually want to see. I personally prefer fully integrated storage with solid doors, so that all the clutter can be stored away out of sight. But you may have a preference for some open storage – with shelves, baskets and trays – so that all of your kitchen equipment is on full display. If you go down this route, you need to be ruthlessly disciplined and super tidy in your kitchen, otherwise it's going to look a real mess. With any kitchen storage, you should bear in mind the following:

1 Select a kitchen base unit where the available storage space goes all the way down to the bottom of the skirting plinth.
2 Try to design in very high-level storage that runs all the way up to the ceiling. This is ideal for those items that you don't need to access all that often.
3 Island units are a brilliant way to provide highly accessible storage on all sides of a unit.
4 Metal hanging rails alongside cooking areas are really handy for hanging pots and pans. These rails can be fastened to the ceiling, and are a great way to free up more space in your base or wall units.
5 My favourite fridge-freezers are the big double-door units that have very wide and deep storage. Small fridges, or those that are too subdivided, are incredibly impractical.
6 Make sure you go to town with your kitchen designer or supplier on very clever storage compartments and subdivisions within your cupboards and drawers. There are some amazing storage compartments out there to make sure your kitchen is organised like a well-oiled machine.

above This may seem a step too far, but you can work with a kitchen designer to get storage that perfectly suits your needs.

opposite top Island units are great for storage if you have the space.

opposite bottom Compartments within your kitchen units will keep things organised.

Whether you live in the smallest flat or the grandest house, cleverly designed and integrated storage is an absolute must. No space must be left unturned – or, more realistically, unfilled!

One thing that a decent family home should never go without is a good-quality dishwasher. When planning your kitchen, make sure you make space for a decent-sized dishwasher to cope with those big dinner parties. They're more environmentally friendly, too, as you won't need to run so many cycles.

Kitchen finishes and materials

The most important finish in any kitchen is the kitchen worktop. There are many types of products out there and your choice will be determined by the look and style you want to achieve – balanced by the level of durability you require. Bear in mind that the most durable materials may not necessarily be the most attractive! There is always going to be an element of compromise somewhere in the equation. The third element that necessarily comes into play is cost. In a nutshell, you get what you pay for, but inexpensive isn't necessarily unattractive or impractical.

The most common types of kitchen worktop material are as follows:
Timber There are all sorts of different types of timber, with varying levels of finish. Whatever type you do choose, make sure the timber is properly sealed and finished. If timber isn't properly treated it can become unhygienic and any fluids used on the surface can cause the timber to warp. The best timber worktops are protected with a coat of lacquer or linseed oil-based sealant. Over time, these lacquers will break down, so they should be reapplied every few years. For a matt finish on timber, you can use standard oil, which tends to improve with age.
Granite Granite is one of the most durable worktop surfaces around. A highly polished surface means it's protected from hot pans, stains, spills and marks. If you chop food on a granite surface there is more chance that you'll damage your knife than the surface itself. For all of these reasons, granite is one of the most popular worktop surfaces on the market. The only problem I have with granite is its speckled finish. As it's a natural material, there isn't much you can do about this; it just comes down to taste.
Tiles and mosaics Simple ceramic tiles or mosaics are an affordable way of forming kitchen worktops. They are a bit more labour-intensive, as they'll require lots of tiling, rather than simply fitting a single slab; however, tiles are very easy to clean and maintain. Tiled kitchen worktops tend to be used more in Europe than in Britain, but they are definitely becoming more popular. My main reservation about tiles is that although they can look great for years, the grouting tends to discolour over time.
Stainless steel Stainless-steel work surfaces tend to make domestic kitchens look incredibly industrial. Stainless steel can be matt, polished, patterned or sand-blasted. Although stainless steel is incredibly easy to wash down and keep scrupulously clean, it is very difficult to keep unmarked. Fingerprints, watermarks and scratches are very difficult to remove. One of the things I hate most is that if you leave any other carbon steel object (i.e., cutlery) standing on the surface for long periods, you will get rust marks on the stainless steel. For industrial kitchens they are brilliant but, for domestic use, I am not a fan.

above and opposite Make sure you strike the right balance between the cost, the look and the durability of a material when choosing your worktop.

Laminate Laminate worktops are incredibly popular and very affordable. Laminate comes in thousands of different colours and patterns, and the range just seems to get bigger and bigger. It's relatively maintenance-free, and can withstand a lot of heat and knocks. Laminate isn't great to use as a chopping surface, as it tends to scratch. However, if you have a very tight budget, then laminate is the way to go.

Concrete Concrete or cement-based worktops became trendy about a decade ago. Concrete is less susceptible to chipping than cement-based worktops, and both should be sealed properly to prevent stains from food and water. The downside of concrete is that it is *incredibly* heavy and needs to be designed and measured perfectly for it to work. Furthermore, unless the concrete is maintained properly, it can begin to look tired over time.

Stone Stone worktops can look astonishingly beautiful, but they are susceptible to two key problems. First of all, if the stone isn't sealed and maintained properly, it can stain badly – particularly if someone spills wine. In some cases, it can be impossible to remove stains without having to polish the entire surface again. Secondly, the edge of the stone at the front of the kitchen worktop will eventually become chipped. The majority of the limestone or sandstone used for kitchen worktops is relatively soft, and it's nearly impossible to put these chips or damaged areas right.

Corian Corian is a resin- or acrylic-based material and it is extremely practical. The nature of the material means Corian is non-porous and any scratches in the surface, or any damage caused by burns, can be easily sanded out. It's actually joined together with the liquid version of itself, so there are hardly any joints in sight. The thing I love about Corian is that it can be ordered in any colour; it is also super-easy to clean and maintain. Overall, it is, by far, my favourite worktop material.

Splashbacks, worktop surfaces, drainage grooves and even sinks can be formed from Corian, creating a seamless series of surfaces that are not just durable, but exquisitely beautiful.

Kitchen costs

previous page An affordable kitchen with lots of storage.
opposite The affordable kitchen that I designed for my last home - it looked top-spec!

The range of affordable kitchens on the market today is fantastic, which is great news if you have a tight and challenging budget. When I was struggling for money in my early years as an architect, I always had to go for the most affordable option when replacing an old, shabby kitchen with something new. Without a doubt, the very best place to buy an affordable kitchen was – and still is – IKEA.

I find it incredible that you can buy a very simple and minimalist kitchen with semi-gloss doors, a half-decent laminate worktop and all of the fixtures and fittings that you need – including your appliances – for a couple of grand. It's pretty obvious that a kitchen like this isn't going to last 20 years – and some might argue that it's not very sustainable to have a kitchen with such a short lifespan – but if this is all you can afford, it's absolutely brilliant.

There are now so many companies competing at the affordable end of the market – a situation that can only be good for all consumers. Even high-end and incredibly good-quality kitchen manufacturers such as Poggenpohl are constantly pushing the boundaries to make their products more affordable. You could never compare the standard of an IKEA kitchen with a Poggenpohl kitchen, but I suppose affordability becomes something relative as you gradually make your way up the property ladder.

One I made earlier

Here is the unique, affordable kitchen I installed in my previous house. It was a galley kitchen, running along two equal and parallel walls, measuring 4.5 metres (almost 15 feet) on each side. It was actually quite big!

1 Designed by me. Cost: £0.
2 All kitchen carcasses came from a local home-improvement store. Supply and install cost: £1200.
3 My joiners made up MDF doors, with a simple detail on the top edge to open them, as I didn't want any projecting handles. Material and labour cost: £600.
4 The doors went off to a spray-paint workshop, and I had them sprayed on all sides in a deep bluish-grey. Gorgeous! I chose 30 percent gloss to create a low reflective surface. Super-gloss finishes can often look 'plasticky' and cheap; however, low-gloss shines with quality. It's also easier to clean and hide your children's fingerprints! You can specify the level of gloss you want. Cost: £500.

Take a look at some of the top-of-the-range kitchens available and work out what you really love. Choose some detailing and get a joiner to help you make it a reality. If you use cheap carcasses, you'll have a bit more money in the budget to play with the finishing touches.

5   A stone supplier measured up and supplied thick limestone worktops along the length of both sides of the kitchen, allowing spaces for the sink, cooker and fridge to be installed. This was a bit of a luxury (considering my budget); it was, however, more than worth it. Supply and install cost: £2000.

6   I needed to leave a reasonable gap between the top of the sprayed doors and the underside of the stone worktop to get a finger in to open the doors. This would normally mean seeing a strip of white, from the carcasses behind. So I had my joiners cut out the top edge of each carcass and install a strip of walnut flooring that was leftover from the floor. Quality! Labour cost: £200.

7   I also needed a skirting plinth to match, so again we used a leftover length of walnut flooring. Labour cost: £150.

8   I bought high-spec (but not over-the-top) appliances: a double-door, American-style, stainless-steel fridge, a top-of-the-range cooker and a very, very top-spec dishwasher (we use it a lot). Cost: £4000.

Total kitchen cost: £8650!

Hand on heart, I can honestly say that it felt and looked like a £25,000 kitchen. Everyone who visited the house thought we had spent a fortune. A bit of creative thinking, combined with time doing research (not to mention running around sourcing the right products, suppliers and installers) is well worth it. You get a beautiful kitchen for a third of the price, and it's totally unique.

Costing your kitchen

- It's easy to forget the little things when costing out your new kitchen space. Door knobs or handles, light fittings (and even light bulbs), skirting boards, fill-in cabinetry, internal storage, plumbing, joinery and grouting will all cost cold, hard cash, so make sure you factor them in.

- It may sound crazy, but don't forget the VAT on your builders' bills. This can add up to an unexpected overspend if you don't factor it in.

- Similarly, remember that in a good kitchen, you'll need a variety of tradesmen, from plumbers to joiners. They all cost money.

- Don't hesitate to haggle. If you need a lot of flooring – or you can find a lighting company that has everything you need – talk to them about a discount. You may be surprised what you can get.

- eBay it! Although you may not get exactly what you expected, chances are you can find a bargain for some key elements of your kitchen, and wipe pounds off the overall cost.

- Do your homework. Home-improvement stores, specialist retailers and even good department stores often have sales or special offers, and you can pick up a bargain.

Tricks of the trade

'A budget tells us what we can't afford, but it doesn't keep us from buying it.' William Feather, American publisher and author

How to get a unique and great-looking kitchen on a tight budget

If you are working to a very tight budget, there are some fantastic affordable kitchens around. The standard and quality of kitchens from the home-improvement stores we all know and love are better than they have ever been, and, better still, they are available at very low prices. One of the problems with these kitchens is that they are – in some ways – victims of their own success. So many people have them, they become instantly recognisable as being 'that' particular product from 'that' particular store.

I have to say that I'm a big fan of these kitchens; however, if you are willing to add a little more to the budget and do a bit of legwork yourself, there are ways to have a truly unique kitchen that will look like it's worth at least three times what you actually paid for it. Unique and affordable, but looks top-spec? That's win, win, win!

above One of the most miserable kitchens from *The Home Show*. Poor worktops and cupboards, terrible flooring and depressing lighting. Time for change!

below The same kitchen once we'd finished with it!

The unique affordable kitchen

1   Design it yourself. Investing time in the research of products, and sketching your own design layouts, is great fun and hugely rewarding. In the past, after working out design options on paper, I've gone as far as cutting out sheets of card that are the actual size of the units and appliances. I then arranged them in the space to mock up the design and test that it worked before ordering anything.

2   Buy all of your kitchen carcasses from your local home-improvement store. The kitchen purists will say that they aren't top quality, but the truth is that they are cheap and the quality is really very good. Just how good does a wooden box that you hardly see have to be? It'll be holding a few pots and pans. It's fine.

3   The doors are an opportunity for you to make your mark. If you can't find a style of door that you like from the store, have your joiners make up timber doors to your own design. You'll be stamping your mark on the kitchen from the outset.

4   You can now choose the colour and finish of the doors you want. Don't be afraid to be bold and creative; it's a great opportunity to express yourself.

5   Go to a separate company that specialises in making the type of worktop you'd like. There are many standard options – timber, slate, stone, marble, stainless steel or Corian (see pages 204-205). Order your worktop directly and have your manufacturer fit it for you. You can, of course, be extremely inventive and make your own from reclaimed materials. A friend of mine once used the slate from a snooker table he bought on eBay!

6   Choose your own handles from any ironmonger's shop. Think practical, durable and beautiful – not to mention original!

7   Buy the very best appliances you can afford. These are the ones that have to work very hard in the kitchen. There is no point in buying the cheapest models and then having to replace them not too far down the line. Take the long-term view.

The result is that you get a kitchen that looks like no other, without breaking the bank.

Don't be afraid to be creative. Off-the-peg kitchens may look great in the showroom, but you don't want to see the same one in every house on the street. A few tweaks and individual touches can make your kitchen not only look unique but express your personal taste.

Kitchen ecology

Modern technology
Owes ecology
An apology. Alan M. Eddison, Environmentalist

Your kitchen is one of the most energy-intensive rooms in your home, and it's one place where you can take enormous steps to be environmentally friendly. We now live in an age where we expect instant hot and cold water, electricity and energy at the flick of a switch, gas at the turn of a knob, and food with the push of a button. We live a resource-intensive lifestyle and unless we start making some very simple ecological changes to the way we live our everyday lives, the environment is going to be in very big trouble.

below and opposite bottom Bringing in masses of natural light reduces your reliance on artificial light.

opposite top Recycling storage systems like this one from IKEA make recycling easy and clutter-free.

There are some very simple ecological steps you can take to help you do your bit to reduce your impact on the environment. The good news is that you'll also take a big step towards reducing your energy bills.

1   Invest in an energy-saving kettle. The kettle is the devil of household ecology. It uses more energy than nearly any other appliance in the home – and just so you can have a quick cup of tea. An energy-saving kettle makes sure that you only heat up the exact amount of water that you need, and allows you to adjust the temperature to which you want your water heated. If you can heat your water to less than 100 degrees, and still be happy with your brew, you'll be making a massive energy saving every single time you switch on the kettle.

2   Use energy-saving lightbulbs within your kitchen design. The standard and quality of the light that emanates from these bulbs is infinitely better than it was when they were first produced. There is absolutely no excuse for you not to use them.

3   Consider creating a kitchen worktop from recycled materials. This is a booming industry! What about this, for example: glass that is recycled from old wine bottles can be crushed up and mixed with resin to form a composite worktop. How cool is that?

4   Use energy-saving appliances, such as ecological dishwashers and fridges. They might cost you a little bit more initially, but they will save you a lot more money in the long run.

5   Use environmentally friendly detergents and cleaning materials, such as Ecover.

6   Make sure you have a fully integrated recycling storage system, and that it's big enough to clearly separate and recycle all of your paper, plastics and glass. It looks like the UK will soon be upping the ante on recycling, so add some extra bins for the other things that are likely to be recycled in future.

7   If you are good at turning your hands to a bit of DIY, you could take an ecological kitchen to the absolute extreme. Why don't you build your very own and unique kitchen, made completely from recycled or reused materials? There is nothing more ecological than being creative and inventive – and reusing old materials in a new and clever way.

It's amazingly easy to make changes to your kitchen that will support the environment and save your electricity bills. Look for energy-efficient appliances when you are in a position to buy, and integrate environmentally friendly features in your design. You won't regret it, I promise!

Ideal kitchen design

There is no single kitchen design that is perfect or ideal. The success of any good kitchen is really based upon how well it works for you and the way your family lives and uses the space in your home. Some people prefer traditional kitchens, some modern. Some people love island bars, while others don't. Individual taste and living arrangements are the reason why it is absolutely essential to fully understand your own personal needs when you analyse your existing space.

There are, however, some fundamentals that every good kitchen should have:

1. An efficient layout based, in one way or another, on the principles of the 'work triangle'.
2. As much preparation and layout space as possible.
3. Hard-wearing and durable work surfaces.
4. The best possible appliances that you can afford within your budget.
5. Maximum storage within drawers, cupboards and wall units.
6. An orientation that makes it sociable; ideally, the person cooking should feel part of the overall space, and able to socialise with others.
7. A view from your sink; looking out of your kitchen window is essential to prevent boredom!
8. A hard-wearing and easy-to-clean floor finish. This area of flooring in your home will undoubtedly be used more than anywhere else.
9. Underfloor heating is your best bet, if you can afford it. Not only is it comfortable underfoot when you pop down to make a cup of tea on those wintry mornings, but you'll free up valuable wall space by foregoing the need for radiators.

below A simple kitchen. Good storage, functional island unit, great space for the dining table and access to the outside. And what a fantastic view!

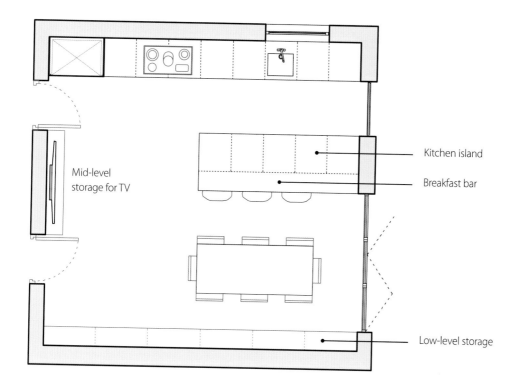

Kitchen island

Breakfast bar

Mid-level storage for TV

Low-level storage

10 Integrated recycling bins are an absolute must in any eco-friendly 21st-century home.

11 Well-designed and -considered lighting will define the whole kitchen environment. You not only need good task lighting to cook and prep food properly, but well-designed architectural lighting to make the space enjoyable at any time of day or night.

12 Hard-wearing, durable and easy-to-clean splashbacks; these can often take as much of a knock as the kitchen surfaces.

13 Super-strong drawer runners and door hinges. These elements of your cabinetry will be in constant use, and pushed to their limits – especially if you've got kids. There is nothing worse than finding your drawers don't open properly and the doors start falling off as soon as you put your new kitchen to work.

14 Soft closes are an absolute must in any family kitchen, to stop your kids banging drawers and doors all day. In fact, they represent one of the simplest and most beautiful elements of good kitchen design, and go a little way towards giving mum and dad a slightly quieter everyday life.

If you can get all of these elements in place – perfectly suited to the needs of you and your family – you are well on your way to creating the ideal kitchen.

Drawers maximise storage space making it easy to access the darkest corners of your kitchen. Go for extra-deep options, which are perfect for pots and pans, and all those baking and roasting trays. Shallow, extra-wide varieties are hugely useful for storing cutlery.

Utility rooms

'After enlightenment, the laundry!' Zen proverb

I absolutely love utility rooms! Yes, I know, very sad for a bloke to be confessing such a thing! But I'm serious here. Even the smallest family home should be redesigned and pushed as far as possible to integrate some form of self-contained utility space. A utility room is a brilliant way of hiding away noisy appliances such as your washing machine and tumble-dryer, as well as the piles of clothes, boxes of detergent, and all of your other cleaning paraphernalia. Most importantly, however, it allows you to free up important and useful space within your kitchen and dining areas.

In my view, a family kitchen should never have a washing machine or tumble-dryer within its space. In even the smallest apartments and flats I always try to get the washing machine and tumble-dryer into a separate cupboard, away from the kitchen. There is nothing worse than being invited over to someone's house for dinner, being seated in their lovely kitchen-dining area, and then staring at the washing machine in the corner. It ruins the atmosphere. It's noisy. It just looks messy.

Your new utility room should be ruthlessly planned and efficiently designed to maximise every single square inch of useable space, so that everything that you need to make your house function – such as irons, ironing boards, mops, buckets and cleaning equipment – can be hidden completely. Your utility room needs to work harder than any other room in your house.

opposite A place for everything. Hang towels, bags of laundry, baskets, shelves and wall-mount the ironing board.

above Narrow but tall storage will come in really handy in your utility room, as will space saving devices like wall-mounted ironholders like this one from IKEA.

Making the most of your utility room

1 An efficient ground-floor utility space can also contain your ground-floor toilet and handbasin. Putting these within the same room makes the planning and drainage incredibly efficient.

2 Consider choosing a large butler's sink for your handbasin. The butler's sink in my home has to be the most often used piece of sanitary wear in the entire house! Why? Well, we all use it to wash our hands after going to the loo, but it also doubles up as a brilliant utility sink for washing and rinsing clothes – particularly useful after my boys have been playing football or covering themselves with paint after an art session at the kitchen table! A butler's sink is super-functional and incredibly practical.

3 Your washing machine will obviously make its home here, so make sure it is in a position that is easy to access, for regular, everyday use. In our house the washing machine is used more than any other appliance, and it's great to know it's whirring away without disrupting our peace!

4 If you've got the space, it's worth installing a tumble-dryer. I always prefer to put the dryer directly above – stacked on – the washing machine. Not only is the access at a good height for retrieving clothes for folding, but you will maximise your usable space. Always try to provide direct ventilation for your dryer. Many now come with an extractor pipe that runs through an external wall. This high level of ventilation will mean that your tumble-dryer is less likely to overheat, thus extending its life significantly. In my house, the washing machine and dryer are stacked against the external wall, with full external ventilation. If I hadn't done this, the dryer would probably only have lasted a couple of years.

5 Create space to store mops, brooms, buckets and hoovers. For this, you'll generally need narrow but tall storage.

6 Provide a big compartment for a substantial dirty washing basket – preferably one that keeps it well out of sight!

7 You will also need a compartment to temporarily store your clean washing, after it has come out of the dryer.

8 It's also a great idea to provide as much additional storage as possible to store clean sheets and towels.

9 Provide a storage cupboard for all detergents, cleaning products, washing powder or liquid, tumble-dryer filters, stain removers and everything else you use to clean your home.

10 As your utility room is a highly intensive and often noisy area, it may well be the perfect location to design in your boiler system. Any boiler, hot-water storage tank or megaflow system should integrated within this room, if you have the space.

11 In areas where your mains water supply may be 'hard' rather than 'soft' water, it's well worth investing in a good mains water-softening system. There are some enormous benefits to these systems. For one thing, soft water prevents the build-up of limescale in your pipework, shower fittings and taps, and even shower screens and partitions that are often damaged by these deposits. Severely hard water can destroy *all* of these fixtures and fittings within a few short years. A water softener guarantees a longer life for some of the most expensive fittings and appliances in your home.

12 The utility room is a fairly sensible place for you to locate the mains water stopcock to your house; in any emergency, the stopcock can be accessed and your entire water supply isolated and cut off. The alternative place for this is under your kitchen sink, but my preference is to locate it in your utility room.

13 If possible, arrange direct access from your utility room to the outside of your property. This may not be possible, but it's worth considering. It will improve the functionality of your room – perfect for when the kids come back from a football match, or if you've all been out in the rain or walking in muddy boots. Coming straight into the utility room, where you can discard dirty clothes, grubby shoes and wet gear, allows you to get things straight into the washing machine, and keeps the rest of your house free of clutter. Having direct access to the outside also makes it easier to get clothes on and off the line.

14 Make sure you provide adequate heating for this space. Under-floor heating is always favourable, but you'll also want a good-sized radiator or towel rail to provide the perfect environment for drying.

15 If you've got the space, install an additional fridge or freezer. This is certainly not essential, but in most family homes it's useful to have a little extra storage for food, topping up the kitchen appliances as required.

16 Think about providing space for your iron and ironing board; the latter can be kept in your tall utility cupboard, or hung on the wall. There are some great wall-mounted iron holders available, too.

It's a good idea to keep cleaning products that you use frequently in a 'housekeeper's box' with a handle, so you can grab the whole lot when you feel the urge to clean.

Planning your utility room layout

My favourite utility room layout is the double-galley utility room. If you have the space, it's well worth going for this option. You may find it becomes one of the most-used rooms in the house!

It goes without saying that the layout of your utility room will be defined by the size and proportion of the space you have available, but you *really* don't need much room to plan an efficient utility space. The most important thing is that it is a separate, self-contained room, away from the other rooms of your house. In an ideal world, you will want to access your utility room from your kitchen – or have a short walk between them – but this isn't set in stone. Some people make fantastic use of walk-in cupboards upstairs, and find it convenient to have the washing machine and dryer close to the bedrooms, where their clothes are kept.

As a very general rule of thumb, utility rooms tend to work much better when they are long, thin spaces. The reason for this is that you can have a long run of utility units and appliances down the length of the space, accessed from a long circulation route running alongside. Rooms that are too wide – or substantially square in plan – are generally less efficient, as there tends to be too much circulation space. The golden rule for a utility room is to maximise the available storage and minimise the amount of circulation. At the same time, you'll need to provide a reasonable level of access to all of your storage units. The things you keep in your utility room will be used a *lot*!

right A clean, simple, efficient and affordable utility space. Every family home would benefit from one.

Basic utility room layouts

Let's look at some of the different layouts, which demonstrate very efficient utility-room spaces.

THE UTILITY CUPBOARD

The utility cupboard is very useful in small apartments or flats. The principle here is that you have a double sliding door, which is very space efficient; you don't have to allow a zone to for an 'in' or 'out' door swing. Sliding doors give access to a very small but efficiently planned cupboard. To one side you have the washing machine at low level, a tumble dryer stacked on top at high level; to the left, you have low-level storage, a small, integrated sink, and a wall-mounted unit above the sink to store cleaning products.

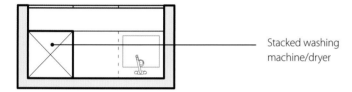

Stacked washing machine/dryer

THE SINGLE-GALLEY UTILITY ROOM

This is an efficient, long run of utility cupboards down one side of the space. Low-level base units running the entire length provide maximum storage, and there is a sink for handwashing clothes and rinsing. High-level wall storage can also be provided along the entire length, with a washing machine at low level and a tumble-dryer stacked above against the external wall to provide ventilation. Circulation runs the full length of the space alongside the units, and there is an option to provide direct access to the outside. You'll only need about 1.5 metres (about 5 feet) for the width of this layout, which means you can squeeze an awful lot into a very small space. Very generally, the split of circulation to storage space within the single-galley utility room is about 50:50.

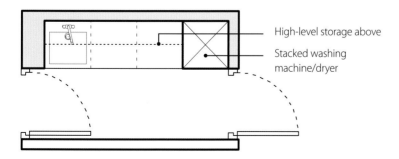

High-level storage above

Stacked washing machine/dryer

THE DOUBLE-GALLEY UTILITY ROOM

This layout requires a wider space than the single-galley option, but it is incredibly efficient. You have a long run of efficient storage down either side of the space, with a central circulation route providing access to both sides, along the entire length. In general, a double-galley utility room needs to be a minimum of 2.1 metres (a little under 7 feet) wide. That allows for 60 centimetres (about 23 inches) of utility storage down one side, the same down the other side, and a central circulation route of approximately 90 centimetres (35 inches). With this option, there is a far higher percentage of storage space to circulation space. Again, if possible, try to provide direct access to the outside.

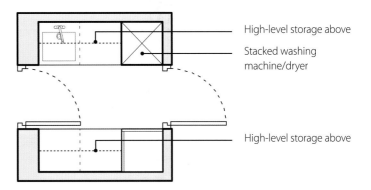

High-level storage above

Stacked washing machine/dryer

High-level storage above

opposite Butler sinks are perfect for utility rooms .

THE L-SHAPED UTILITY ROOM

L-shaped utility rooms are normally created in spaces that have more of a square than a long linear plan. This layout is the least efficient of them all, as there tends to be more circulation space than you actually need. This may not be a problem for larger square plans, as the additional circulation space could be used to erect your ironing board for the daily ironing – or even leave it up, if you wish. If you are able to create a much larger and grander utility room, all the better! You can maximise the storage area, while providing a large area of circulation space that can double up and be used for other utility-room tasks.

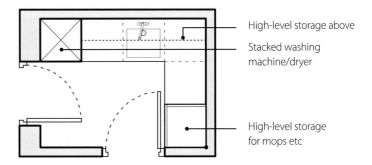

High-level storage above

Stacked washing machine/dryer

High-level storage for mops etc

Lighting your utility room

Ambient or atmospheric lighting in a utility room isn't really a priority. A utility room needs to be lit sufficiently, with as much task lighting as possible, so that you are able to work within the space. Ideally, you need to be able to clearly see stains or marks on clothes, and keep all areas of the room as clean and as hygienic as possible. It goes without saying that you'll need plenty of bright light for this!

Cold white light

Fluorescent lights aren't particularly popular in other rooms of the house, as they give off a very strong, white and often cold quality of light; however, this is just the type of light you need for a successful utility room. Because they are strong and clear, they make excellent task lighting in utility rooms; but, they *only* work well when they are installed under the pelmet of your wall units. Having fluorescent lighting overhead in an attempt to illuminate the entire room produces the most awful and depressing quality of light.

Functional fluorescent lighting should only be used as task lighting, very close to the source of the activity you are trying to carry out. It's miserable when used to illuminate an entire room.

When lighting your utility room, consider the following:

1 Fluorescent lighting, which is used as task lighting and hidden behind wall-unit pelmets, providing light to worktop areas.
2 A number of recessed downlights in the ceilings, which can be used to light the whole room. Make sure you have a sufficient number to give an even spread of light across the room, to avoid shadows.
3 It's always useful to have small lights installed within storage cupboards, which come on automatically when you open the door. This makes it much easier to find items quickly and easily within units that can often be cluttered with stuff.
4 For utility rooms of a decent size – in which you may spend time carrying out tasks such as ironing – it's always preferable to have a reasonable level of natural light. If possible, design your utility room against an external wall so that you can get a view out of the window or a glass-panelled external door. Any view can go some way to reducing boredom, and will make the space feel a lot less institutional!

Utility room finishes and materials

Most utility rooms never see anyone but family members, and then only when they are working. This is a space that will be heavily used, and needs to have finishes and materials that will live up to the job.

Such an intensive space is susceptible to a large amount of wear and tear; most utility rooms become a dumping ground for dirty clothes, cleaning equipment and products, and often wellies and sports equipment, too! Some people I know keep their tool boxes in the utility room as well as the drawers full of household essentials such as lightbulbs and batteries. So we're talking multi-purpose space here.

There is usually a large amount of water being splashed around, and a large amount of heat being emitted by appliances such as tumble-dryers.

These top tips will help to ensure that you choose the most appropriate finishes and materials for your utility room.

1　Install a hard-wearing and easy-to-clean floor surface. Tiles are ideal, but make sure that they are properly sealed and the tiles and grout are easy to clean. One of my favourite floor surfaces is rubber. Use a sheet and the rubber can be turned up the side of the wall which makes the floor and the lower levels of the wall very easy to clean.

2　Install the most durable kitchen carcass base and wall units. They are very rarely seen, as they are always full of stuff, so don't worry about looks – just make sure they are robust.

3　Worktops should be the toughest around. If you have a reasonable budget, install granite. You may feel that this is a bit over-the-top, but it will last forever and take a pretty heavy beating. More affordable options are laminate worktops or Corian.

4　Utility rooms can be messy spaces, with a lot of water being splashed around, particularly around sinks. Make sure you install tiled or glass splashbacks and simple tiles with easy-clean grout.

5　Install the largest and most durable sink available. Wherever possible I try to specify a large butler's sink, which is ideal for handwashing and rinsing clothes. Avoid Corian sinks, as they stain over time. If you are working to a budget, a large stainless-steel sink is probably the best choice.

6　Avoid too many white materials; white tiles with white grout are difficult to keep clean and may discolour over time. Go instead for some vibrant colours to make an ordinary utility space into a dynamic and exciting room.

7　Make sure your paint finishes are washable, too; and choose a colour that won't show the dirt, the splashes and the inevitable mucky handprints.

There is absolutely no reason why your utility room can't be attractive, but if there is a choice to be made between functionality and style, then functionality should always come out on top.

Utility room costs

Posh utility rooms are a huge extravagance! Don't get me wrong: I absolutely love them because there are ways of integrating all sorts of modern technology, from additional fridge freezers to fancy wine coolers. If you can afford a high standard of finish to combine the functional and stylish look, then go for it! But (and this is a big but), it should never be at the expense of compromising on the finish on other rooms in the house. I would much prefer you went for the cheapest functional look, if it means saving the money to apply to a better look elsewhere.

When I'm designing utility rooms on a challenging budget, I force myself to think about other spaces outside of the domestic home that need to be built affordably, with relatively little maintenance, and at the same time easy to clean and as hygienic and sterile as possible. If you think about the cleaning and washing spaces that are in our hospitals, or perhaps the kitchen of an industrial chef, you'll come up with the type of finishes and materials that are appropriate; they'll also be affordable and stand the test of time.

1 Stainless-steel worktops and sinks.
2 Very cheap but robust taps and fittings.
3 Single-sheet or tiled flooring.
4 Ceramic tiles and splashbacks.
5 Colourful laminate worktops combined with laminate splashbacks.
6 Strip fluorescent lighting or affordable recessed downlights located close to counter tops, to provide the best task lighting.
7 Base-range white goods. Buy the most affordable toilets, sinks and towel rails.

The most affordable products are usually highly durable, but they don't always look great. The golden rule is to choose colours carefully and keep things as simple as possible. Plastic, laminate, rubber, ceramic, metal and any other high-gloss finishes generally look the best. Any natural products – such as timber worktops and timber doors – really can't stand up to the intense use and tend to look pretty shoddy after just a couple of years.

When it comes to washing machines and tumble-dryers, it's not always the best idea to go for the cheapest. They don't have a particularly long lifespan, and they may be a source of frustration if they aren't up to the job. Even if you are on a low budget, try to invest as much as possible in your appliances and make further compromises on your finishes.

Utility room ecology

The utility room houses most of the home's utility controls. It is also the space where you can find the most energy-intensive appliances, such as your washing machine, tumble-dryer, and perhaps even your hot-water storage tank and boiler. Add to this the fact that you'll constantly be using a large amount of water, and it's pretty clear that this room can have some serious ecological implications!

Consider the following, to make your utility room as environmentally friendly as possible:

1 Install an energy-efficient boiler. If your boiler is over 10 years old, it is likely to be horribly inefficient and potentially dangerous. Energy-efficient boilers may be slightly more expensive, but they can be more than 40 percent more efficient when compared to an old, standard model. This will provide a huge reduction in your annual energy bills, and play an environmental role, too.

2 Any hot-water storage tank, such as a megaflow tank, will be a highly insulated unit, and have modern thermostatic controls to efficiently maintain levels of heat in your tank for as long as possible.

3 The tumble-dryer is usually the second-largest consumer of electricity in a typical household, coming a close second to the fridge-freezer. Choose an energy-saving dryer, and minimise its use as much as possible by drying clothes outside or on a radiator. Only turn it on when the dryer has a full load. But don't overload it either. Clothes dry more efficiently when they can be tossed around in the warm air. If you jam them in, your drying cycle can take hours.

4 Most households do nearly 400 loads of laundry annually. At around 40 gallons (180 litres) per load, that is a lot of water! The latest washing-machine models can cut energy consumption by as much as 70 percent, and can clean your clothes just as well – if not better. They can also work at a much lower temperature than older models, which is another environmental benefit. Go one step further and use environmentally friendly detergents.

5 Always install a mains water-softener within your utility room. Soft water is a brilliant way of reducing limescale build-up in hard-water areas, allowing your taps, boilers and appliances to last longer and work more efficiently. There is nothing worse than having a shower where the showerhead is working at a reduced level of efficiency because it is clogged with limescale. A water softener will also prevent streaking and limescale build-up on shower screens and doors.

Ideal utility room design

You need to consider the design of your utility room in a similar way to a functional lab. The design shouldn't really be about style and taste – instead, think about creating a space that is durable, functional, easy to clean and relatively maintenance free. There are, however, some amazing design features and products out there that will make the everyday use of your utility space so much easier.

To make your utility room incredibly functional, try to include the following:

1 The very largest butler's sink you can fit into the space. You'll be amazed by how much you use it!
2 Intelligent storage solutions to create as much high- and low-level storage as possible.
3 Storage compartments within cupboards and drawers, which are a brilliant new trend! People are obsessed with having their utility rooms really well organised. The range of cleverly designed storage compartments on the market is increasing every day, so make as much use of them as you can. One really cool thing that you might like to consider is creating a laundry chute from your first floor, directly down to the ground-floor utility room, so that the washing can automatically go down to the basket without the need for transportation! I didn't manage to create one in my house but – believe me – I wish I had.
4 A pull-down ironing-board system for larger utility rooms. Rather than having to drag the ironing board out of the cupboard, fold out its legs and try to get it into position, you simply pull down the ironing board, which is integrated within the design of a storage wall. This is super-easy, inexpensive and simple.
5 Lots of little storage. This one might sound like I have OCD (I think I might have!), but I like to have individual storage containers to store washing tablets, detergents, powders and bleaches. Having randomly branded bottles and tubs all over a utility room just looks a mess.
6 Cupboards with doors. Make sure you design in a combination of storage cupboards with doors to hide away the messy stuff, combined with open shelving for easy access to folded sheets and towels.
7 Utility-room shelving, which doesn't always have to be shelves! Wicker baskets or storage containers make perfectly good decorative accessories within your space, and are amazingly functional.

above Design in as much storage as you can, I guarantee you will use it.

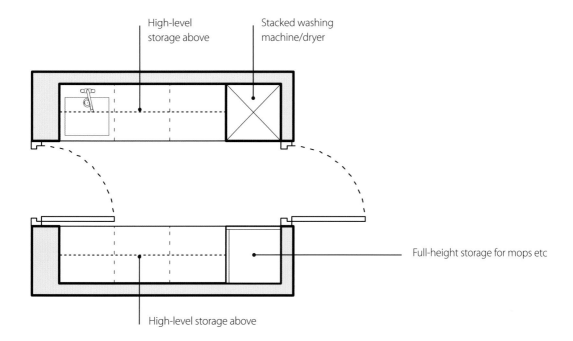

High-level
storage above

Stacked washing
machine/dryer

Full-height storage for mops etc

High-level storage above

8 Recycling compartments; these are often associated with kitchens, but there is a huge amount of packaging and waste generated within a utility room, too. If you have the space, try to design in a recycling hub here.

9 An integrated water-softener, to provide soft water throughout the house. And don't forget to allow for a compartment to store the block salt, which is regularly used to top up the softener.

10 As much natural and mechanical ventilation to the space as possible. Your tumble-dryer will belt out a lot of heat in this highly intensive area, and clothes drying on rails or rads can generate a fair bit of moisture. You want this space to be a comfortable environment when using it.

11 A pull-down drying rack, if you like to dry your clothes naturally. There are some great models that can be suspended from the ceiling. You draw it down to hang your clothes, and pull it back up again for the clothes to dry, well out of the circulation area. In a warm, well-ventilated room, clothes should dry quickly.

I always think that recycling becomes an easier habit to acquire if you have a series of recycling hubs around your home, rather than having one single point in your kitchen. One in the utility room makes complete sense.

Living rooms

'A man travels the world over in search of what he needs, and returns home to find it.' George Moore

I am fascinated by the way that living rooms have changed so much over the last few generations. In the good old days, your living room might have been known as a sitting room, a drawing room, a front room or a parlour. The living room was often the space in which you could grandly declare your style, status and taste, because it was here that visitors would be invited when they came to your home. In many families, the living room was a child-free zone, kept for 'best' to impress!

Times have undoubtedly changed, and not that many houses have space for such luxury – spreading out to fill every room in the house instead! In fact, as far as I am concerned, the separate 'formal' drawing room often feels like a fairly boring and redundant space – rarely used and usually not very comfortable.

Family space

Thankfully, I was brought up in a more relaxed household, where the living room was somewhere that we would all come together as a family, chill out, have a chat and watch some telly. We had a completely separate kitchen area – which was quite small – so it wasn't really the heart of the home for us. Instead, we shared the living-room space and I have incredibly fond memories of the many hours spent there.

Here in the 21st century, we are much more adventurous with our use of space, and it's increasingly common to combine the kitchen-dining area, making the kitchen very much the central hub of the home. Many kitchen-diners have their own TV screens, and most homes have a number of TVs scattered throughout. For this reason, the 'new' living room isn't necessarily a place for sitting down to watch TV. In fact, in my home we watch more TV in the kitchen than in any other room. So maybe it's time that we rethink the way we use our living spaces. Sure, get a TV in there for times when you really want to flop and chill out; however, it makes sense to think about giving your living room a new role.

If the kitchen-dining area is now the busy hub of the house – with noise, activity, socialising, eating, drinking and watching TV – maybe the living room should be the place for a peaceful retreat.

There are so many affordable places to shop for furnishings these days. IKEA is a good place to start.

By the fire

Today's living rooms can provide space for reading, listening to music, having a relaxed chat and gathering around the fire. Where kitchens can often feel like 'harder' spaces, with functional flooring and finishes, the living room wants to be a place where you can curl up and get cosy.

It's important that any living room feels relaxing and comfortable. It's undoubtedly a space where you can hang out with your kids, but there is also an opportunity here to make this a space that is a little more grown-up. The TV will always be the inevitable focus of any living space (or, indeed, any room in which it is situated), but by planning a room properly there are ways to give equal priority to a beautiful, real fire. Real fires have such a powerful psychological appeal, and represent one of the very best ways to truly relax. In my home, when I'm sitting in my lounge chair looking into the fire in the evenings, it takes me a while to realise that my thoughts have often been lost for hours, as I sit there and gaze.

below Fires add real character and atmosphere to a room.

Planning your living room layout

If I'm being completely honest, I think the living room is one of the most difficult rooms to plan within a home. They really can be quite complicated spaces. For one thing, you want there to be enough room for the whole family to come together. This means being practical, and fitting in the right number of chairs and sofas. You also want people to be sociable – and able to communicate together within the space – as well as organising the furniture in such a way that everyone can properly see the TV.

On the other hand, however, you don't want the arrangement to be completely *dominated* by the TV. It's important to be able to display personal possessions and belongings, such as artwork and family photos. And you'll also need a reasonable level of storage to be able to display books and hide away magazines and DVDs. Most importantly, however, I always want a living space to have a beautiful, real fire, which can also be the focus of the space.

Getting the focus right

With so much modern technology and the ever-present, dominant, wide-screen TV in the average 21st-century family home, it can be difficult to get the focus right within the room. What takes priority for you and your family? Is it being able to see the TV? Or would you like your fire to become the absolute focus, and dominate the TV instead?

Are you a family where relaxed conversation and interaction are more important than TV viewing or gazing into the fire? It's *so* important to be able to test out all of these complex space issues at the earliest possible stage of the project. You need to make your available space work hard for you, to create a living room that does exactly what you need it to do.

Planning it out

Make sure that you have a scale plan of the existing room and rigorously test out how the space will work. Make some little cut-outs of every single piece of your furniture (also to scale), and move them around until they work. The key is to be absolutely clear about how you would like your family to come together and interact within the room.

If you have a larger living space, consider designing it as a number of separate zones. You may have an area with a large sofa and chairs where the entire focus is towards the TV. Then, alongside the TV area, create an even softer, cosier space where the focus of this zone may be the real fire. This can be an area where you can relax in front of the fire with a glass of wine and a good book.

opposite top left and right In one of our *Home Show* projects, the existing living room was badly furnished with little consideration to the layout of the space. The selection of finishes and materials was inconsistent and the lighting was poor.

opposite bottom In the new space, we reorganised the furniture layout and chose a contemporary style to suit the client's taste. For this owner the TV was the focus of the room.

LIVING-ROOM GOLDEN RULES

1 Decide upon the focus of the room. Is it the TV? Or is it your new fire? If you're not a fan of fires, then the decision is easy. I would, however, encourage every single homeowner in Britain to have one; they create the most beautiful atmosphere within your living room, and they also go a long way to keeping you warm in the cold months.

2 Don't let your plasma dominate. One of the biggest mistakes people make in living-room planning is putting their flat-screen plasma TVs *above* the mantelpiece; in other words, *over* the fire! This never, ever works. First of all, you don't really know what you are looking at and you'll get a headache flicking your eyes up and down. Secondly, because of the height of a fireplace, the TV is normally mounted too high, leading to a bad neck. Ideally, you need to look *across* to a screen, not up.

3 Make sure you have selected furniture that is an appropriate shape and size to suit the size and shape of the room – and the level of comfort you are looking for.

4 I love having huge sofas. It's a brilliant way to have the whole family snuggle up together to chat or watch TV.

5 Select a size of TV that is appropriate to the size of the room. I am not a fan of TVs that dominate too much.

6 Carefully designing a series of separate and distinct zones within one space is a brilliant way of resolving the various demands we expect of a living room. The position of the sofa and chairs is everything. This is where you are going to sit when you are in your living space, and it is important to ensure that you've got their positions absolutely right. The positioning will dictate how you relate to all of the people and objects within the space, and also how you relate to windows and openings – to get the best view out.

7 Avoid having too much circulation space in your living room. The living room should never be a space that you have to walk through to get to another room. If your living room becomes a grand corridor, the distraction will drive you mad.

8 Make sure the door to your living room is very carefully positioned. Once you have arranged your furniture in the space to suit your way of living, you may find that the door is in the wrong place. If it needs to be moved, then move it.

9 Consider installing underfloor heating in your living room. Unless there is an obvious and dedicated space for radiators (and they have absolutely no impact on your ability to space-plan your room properly; for example, your radiators are situated under the sill of your bay windows), then you might find they get in the way of the room working properly. The last thing you want to do is push your sofa up against the radiator. All that is going to do is heat up your sofa. Underfloor heating solves all these problems.

Before ...

... and after

Lighting your living room

You could go to the absolute non-functional extreme and select lighting as artwork. I've seen all sorts of weird and wonderful lighting installations commissioned by clients as a feature of their homes – from light sculptures to words and personal messages created from bold neon lights.

Lighting is responsible for generating the mood and atmosphere in a space more than any other architectural element. It is *incredibly* important to get living-room lighting right – not only to ensure that the space can be functional, but also to create a life-enhancing environment within it.

As it is with so many other forms of lighting, flexibility really is the key to the success of the scheme. The living-room lighting levels in my home are changed on a regular basis – without a doubt, more than any other room in the house. When the room needs to be cleaned, all the lights are turned up to 100 percent, so that we can see every speck of dust. At the other extreme, when my kids want to sit down at night to watch a movie, it's nice for the lights to drop down to a lower level with a single flick of the switch.

Getting the light right

Here are a few steps to help you get the lighting right within your living room.

1 Pendant light fittings give you an opportunity to provide a lighting focus to the room. Investing in a beautiful lightshade for your pendant light gives you the opportunity to really celebrate the style, taste and character you want to achieve. The position of any pendant light should always be aligned to the centre of the space. It goes without saying, too, that your choice of light fitting should be to the correct scale and the right proportion for the room.

2 Side lamps are such an important feature in any living space. They can be an important design feature, and also provide a quality of light that is softer and at a lower level, to illuminate specific zones within the room. Ideally, these lamps should be connected to a 5-amp plug socket, so that they can be controlled by a main switch as you walk into the space. You also have the option of controlling the light by the switch on the lamp itself.

3 If you are displaying any pieces of artwork or family photographs, you may choose to design in architectural light fittings to illuminate and celebrate your personal belongings. You can choose from fixed wall lights, shining directly onto a specific area of wall, or directional recessed downlights, which are inserted into the ceiling and have adjustable bulbs that can be redirected into any position.

4 If you just want to have a bit of fun with the space, you can really go to town on decorative lights. These don't really serve any specific lighting function, other than being very beautiful and decorative things. There are so many to choose from, such as fairy lights, star lights, fibre-optic lights or even sculptured lights.

opposite Architectural lights at their best.

below Decorative lights can give more personality to a room.

Living room design features

There are certain design features that every living room must have, no matter what your budget or your space constraints.

Sofas

The most important design feature of any living room is a super-comfortable sofa. A huge sofa, big enough for the whole family to snuggle up on together, is brilliant in *any* living room. It's somewhere to have cuddles, read a book, stretch out, watch TV or fall asleep. Huge, is, however, relative! If your room is tiny, you don't want to have to squeeze round it, or forego any other furniture because there simply isn't space. On a very practical side, make sure your sofas are the right colour to suit your room and, if you've got kids, the covers must be removable and washable.

Your TV

I love to chill out and watch TV with my kids, but it's important that you get the right size, shape and make of TV to suit your room and your budget. Now I might sound like a technical snob, but I don't think there is any point in buying a new TV these days unless it's HD. Don't go overboard on the size, though. If it's the first and only thing you notice when you enter your cosy living room, then it's too big! And if you've got gorgeous, traditional furniture, don't go for a techy finish that will look odd in your space.

In my home, we installed a beautiful wood-burning stove that belts out so much heat during the winter months that we hardly ever have to put the heating system on. It not only functions incredibly well, but it also looks so beautiful as a design feature. I have to admit that it has transformed the way that I use the living room. I prefer to sit by the fire with a good book any day of the week.

right Decide what you want to be the focus of your living room, the TV or the fire.

Fireplaces and stoves

Real fires are such beautiful things in any living room. A fire can completely transform the atmosphere and feeling within a space, while at the same time generating heat to provide comfort. I always go for a real-flame fire, but your choice will depend upon your lifestyle and the availability of different fuels. A gas fire is obviously clean, easy to use and hassle-free, whereas a coal or wood-burning fire can sometimes get a bit messy. I do think this mess is sometimes a price worth paying to get the real thing.

The type of fire, and its setting or surround, is an incredibly important design choice and will say so much about your own style and personal taste. This will be a powerful focus to the room, so be sure to get your decision absolutely right. You'll also need to consult with a fire specialist to be sure that you have the right sort of fire, flue, hearth and design to suit your home. Be aware that if your chimney and flue have to be aligned to work, it can often cost more than the fire itself.

Please make sure that your fire is installed by someone who is fully qualified and approved to do it. This is vital to guarantee the safety of everyone in your home.

Lounge chairs

My favourite feature of all in a living room is a beautiful, relaxing lounge chair and ottoman footstool. I went for the Charles and Ray Eames classic (see page 58), but the range of lounge chairs out there on the market is so huge, you will easily be able to find something to suit your home and budget.

Tables

No living room will ever be complete without a selection of different tables. What good is it settling down with a glass of wine, if you haven't got a place to rest your glass? If your space is small, it's a great idea to go for tables with plenty of storage. I also like to choose tables at different levels – elegant, higher tables to hold feature lights that will illuminate a corner of the room, display some family treasures and allow you to rest a cup of tea on their surface, without having to bend over double, and lower, more practical coffee-style tables that can hold a big jigsaw or board game, allow the kids to get out their drawings, and even serve as an impromptu dining table for those meal-on-laps evenings. Once again, however, although big is great, it has to be in keeping with the scale of the room. Constantly edging around the coffee table, or banging your shins, is no fun at all.

above Find a chair that you can really relax in and will look forward to sitting in at the end of the day.

following page The living room should be a place to relax.

Living room storage

The living room is no exception to the idea that the modern family home needs as much integrated storage as possible. Even with all the developments of modern technology – with digital music systems, movie libraries and e-books – we are still not at a stage where our living areas are empty.

Furthermore, families do tend to collect and create a lot of clutter. Having space to tuck it away at the end of the day will make your living room a much more relaxing place to be.

TV storage

Personally, I'm a big fan of the award-winning, modern, wood-burning stove and integrated storage system designed by Peter Maly. The system is a seamless piece of design, which fully integrates the fire along with storage compartments for logs. There are optional extras for bench seating, drawers for DVD storage, and even a TV stand. This design is one of the most integrated and slick storage and TV units I have ever specified. It may not represent the traditional look that you want to go for, but there is no denying that it's a beautiful system.

When you choose your TV storage, look for something functional and purpose-built. It might seem like a grand idea to place your TV in an old antique cupboard, but if it's the wrong height or the doors interrupt your viewing, it's never going to be hugely successful. There's a lot on the market, so take a look around. If you don't see what you want, ask your joiner to build something to your own specifications. It can end up being far less expensive than you'd think.

below The storage unit we have for our TV and DVD player in the living room.

If you are mounting your TV on the wall, avoid placing it over the fire, and make sure it is at the right height for viewing while you are seated. Gazing upwards for hours will not make for a relaxing evening.

Book storage

I love living rooms with lots of books. Books are so incredibly personal and say so much about both you *and* your home. I might be a fan of modern technology, but I really do hope that the modern e-book complements rather than replaces the good old traditional paper book. Books should be proudly displayed, and with the range of shelving options – from the affordable end of the scale all the way through to the most expensive – now so incredible, you can really showcase them in style.

Built-in shelving certainly gives a more integrated appearance, but there is no reason why you can't take standard shelving from most suppliers and integrate it into your design. The most important lesson here is to keep all of your clutter down to an absolute minimum and celebrate the best books that you have. In other words, keep the tatty paperbacks to a minimum, and get your classics and your favourites up there on show.

Accessible storage

Storage needs to be as accessible as possible, otherwise you will tend not to use it and clutter will start to spread elsewhere in the room. If you have to move the TV every time you want to reach the cupboard where you store your DVDs, chances are they will end up everywhere but! There are so many clever design solutions around, including movable systems that allow you to rotate shelves, and slide-along modular shelving units to allow you to retrieve items simply and return them to their rightful place with minimum effort. It's worth investigating all the options, particularly if you've got a small space where storage is going to have to work hard.

Coffee tables

Coffee tables are another way of providing some storage. CDs, DVDs and magazines can be slotted into some ingenious coffee-table designs, so everything you need is within easy reach of your sofa. This also gives you another chance to make a clear design statement. Side tables can be equally functional, with slide-out baskets or drawers for the things you need for your usual living-room activities.

Books come in a range of shapes and sizes, so I would always recommend a flexible system of shelving that can be adjusted to suit your personal needs.

below If you don't want the TV to dominate the room, storing it within the bookshelf can make it less of a feature.

bottom This coffee table holds everything you might need when you're relaxing on the sofa.

Living room finishes and materials

Choosing your floor finishes is one of the most important decisions that you have to make for any living room. If you've got kids, remember that the majority of their very early years will be spent actually playing on the floor, and chances are that you'll be down there too. The whole family will be acutely aware of the comfort element of your flooring, so take time to get it right.

Hard surfaces are obviously more practical and easy to clean, which is an incredibly important factor when you've got kids around. On the other hand, however, hard surfaces can also create poor acoustics – all the noise generated by your kids, your TV and any socialising will be literally bouncing off your floor surfaces.

Carpets and rugs

Carpets can provide a very high level of comfort, as well as softening the acoustics; however, they are difficult to keep clean (particularly when you've got kids running in and out of the room all day), and can date quite quickly.

A happy medium is to lay timber flooring throughout your living areas, but also provide some zones that have a softer surface. You can achieve this by using rugs, or simply carpeting certain zones within a room. Obviously, the latter approach would only work if you have a large enough space to justify a complete change of material, or if there is a change of level within your living area.

Whatever you choose, remember that these soft areas within your living room are an essential part of your children's daily life. They will be drawn to the rug or carpeted surface whenever they choose to play on the floor. Buying a good-quality rug can represent a real investment and it's worth looking at the broad selection available before you choose. Many good rug companies will let you take a rug home so you can test how well it works before you buy it.

Timber flooring

There is a huge (and ever-increasing) range of natural types of wood to choose from when selecting your flooring. The most common type of flooring in the UK is oak, which is a strong, resilient hardwood. But the choice you make for your living room really depends upon your style and taste. If you prefer a lighter timber, you could select an ash, sycamore or Douglas fir; if you prefer darker floor finishes, you could go for an elm, walnut, American black

We've created zones in a number of our living room projects. For example, there might be a timber floor in an area where there is a lot of walking about (such as a TV entertainment space), and then the floor surface is changed to carpet where there is a raised area or a cosy snug. This is a great option if you want to give different parts of your space designations and it also keeps the noise down!

walnut, mahogany or sepilia (which is a durable, low-maintenance, semi-hardwood). The list is relatively endless.

WHICH BOARD?

Once you have decided on the type of wood for your flooring, you then need to select the width of the board and the quality of the grain. Some people prefer a more rustic look, full of knots and heavy grain; others prefer a fine-grain timber, with minimal grain and knots. Once you have made these decisions, you then have to decide upon your type of board.

The options are quite straightforward:
- solid-timber board
- engineered board (which is in effect a very thick timber laminate on top of man-made plywood)
- a very thin laminate board bonded onto a man-made board underneath (the most affordable end of the range)

LAYING THE BOARDS

A great floor-layer's tip is to lay timber floorboards in the direction that light comes into your room. It emphasises the grain, and the direction of the boards even more. So, if you put down boards in your living room, and you have a bay window at the front, you should run the boards from front to back in the room, rather than going from side to side.

From an architectural point of view, I love this look, as it reinforces the depth of your space. Use the same technique in halls and corridors too, running your boards the length of the space to make it feel more dynamic and, of course, much longer!

FINISHES

Finally, when you have selected all of these things, your last decision is how you want to finish it. All timber needs a protective sealant or it will stain. The treatment you go for can make a dramatic difference to the characteristics of the finished wood. The options open to you are to oil the timber, wax it, hard-wax oil it, varnish it or use an acrylic sealant.

Your best option is to visit a timber-flooring supplier and ask to see a series of samples to help you decide. For my own living room, I went for a wide engineered board with underfloor heating beneath. It has a thick oak, fine-grade laminate on top with a very natural oil sealant that has maintained the colour, quality and grain of the natural timber. And to provide lots of soft areas for my kids to play, I went on a shopping spree to buy lots of beautiful rugs.

Under-floor heating
If you want to go for an under-floor heating system with a timber floor on top, the best option is the engineered board. The heat from your under-floor heating could cause a solid-timber floor to move excessively and in some areas even warp. An engineered board can withstand (and transmit) the heat and you will get very little movement of the timber.

above There is a huge range of timber flooring options. Lay the boards in the direction that light comes into the room for best effect.

opposite A good example of a rug defining the room it is in.

The affordable living room

The best way to get more for your money is to choose furnishings that have function as well as beauty. Look for tables with drawers and shelves, an ottoman footstool with a top that lifts up to store your winter throw, or a window seat with baskets underneath to tidy away the magazines or toys.

above This is a living room that we created on *The Home Show*. It is full of character and perfectly fit for purpose.

Every single thing I've outlined in this section can be achieved on an affordable budget; in fact, there is absolutely no reason why you can't get a great look at a low cost, irrespective of your taste and the style you want to go for. Just follow these simple rules:

Get the design and layout of the room absolutely right.

1 Create a flexible lighting system with dimmer switches. Even if you can't afford a high-spec electrical installation, there is no reason why you can't have simple dimmer switches to control your pendant lights, downlights and side lamps. Changing the level of light can create a new atmosphere in an instant.
2 Get yourself a large, comfortable and affordable sofa.
3 Even at the low end of the market, there are some great, comfortable chairs out there. While you might be tempted to make a style statement, the truth is that the most important element of any living room is comfort. If you fill a great space with uncomfortable furniture, it will effectively be wasted.
4 A real fire needn't cost the earth, but will add quality, focus and comfort.
5 The price of flat-screen TVs is dropping by the day, and it's worth investing in one – not just because they look great and take up less space than box TVs, but because the quality of the viewing is improved, making your room that much more pleasurable and functional.
6 There are some fantastic, affordable storage systems from most home-improvement stores and DIY companies.
7 Timber flooring doesn't need to be expensive. It may cost more to lay than carpet, but it's not that difficult to have a go laying it yourself. Choosing a good laminate or timber board will buy you decades of decent flooring for your home.
8 There is also a range of affordable carpets on the market, which are not just inexpensive to purchase, but also reasonably cheap to lay. If you are zoning your room, you can probably get what you need from offcuts.
9 Rugs are a fantastic way to make a room more comfortable and jazz up your space on a budget. The range of rugs is incredible, and there is no reason why you can't pick up a bargain.

Living room ecology

Like all of the rooms in your house, your living room should be as environmentally friendly as possible. It really is important to take an ecological approach to the materials and products that you select. Bear in mind the following:

1 Always consider the environmental impact of any timber flooring that you choose. As a renewable resource, wood is potentially very environmentally friendly, but you need to choose carefully. Any endangered species of wood, such as mahogany, teak or ebony, should be avoided if possible. Please make sure that any timber you specify is obtained from a sustainable source. Check that your wood has an FSC (Forestry Stewardship Council) certification, which guarantees that the wood comes from an environmentally managed source.

2 Consider natural-fibre floor coverings, which are flatwoven (in other words, without a pile) in a range of designs. They tend to be made from a range of grasses and leaves, and are derived from natural, renewable resources. You can't do much better for good, environmentally friendly flooring. The most popular types include seagrass, coir, sisal and bamboo. There is also abaca fibre, which comes from a species of the banana family, or even paper flooring, which is a woven paper yarn that produces an attractive and durable floor covering.

3 Always check how carpets and rugs are made, and ensure that the materials are environmentally friendly. Wool carpets are very luxurious underfoot and remain a very popular choice for a soft and comfortable covering. Luxury wool carpet can be quite expensive, but there is such a broad choice of types and qualities available that there is nearly always something to match even the lowest budget. Wool is a sustainable resource.

4 A real fire is a beautiful design feature, but always consider its environmental impact, particularly if you are looking to burn fossil fuels.

5 Only turn on your TV and other appliances when you are actually using them. And the eco-rule that we always forget about is to turn your TV off completely rather than leaving it on standby.

The ideal living room

Planning your living room isn't as easy as it may seem. The size and proportion of the room, as well as the way that you access it, will define the qualities of the space, and your options for arranging furniture. It is vital that you coordinate your electrical, lighting and IT requirements as early as possible, to suit the layout you decide to go for. If you don't, you're going to end up with cables, wires, extension leads and banks of plug sockets everywhere, in order to make the space function. This is a messy route to take, so design co-ordination from the very beginning of your project is everything.

Achieving the ideal living-room layout

For wall-mounted TVs, make sure you fix a length of vertical trunking (plastic tubing) into the wall, to allow you to feed cables from your AV equipment at low level, up to your TV at high level. There is no point in simply plastering your cables into the wall. AV technology and cabling is changing so fast that you need to be able to feed new cables through the trunking, without having to hack out plasterwork and then redecorate.

1 If you choose to have a TV or a fireplace, their position will define the layout of the room.
2 Place the TV alongside your fireplace and have the TV as close to eye-level as possible, when you are in a seated position. Don't be tempted to place it above the fireplace or you risk having a cricked neck for life.
3 Create as much storage as possible beneath and around your TV, for DVDs and equipment storage.
4 Provide as many low-level plug sockets as possible beneath the TV, as TVs, DVDs and the growing list of other equipment, such as satellite boxes and recorders, need loads. Try to integrate them within a low-level storage unit so they cannot be seen.
5 If possible, integrate the installation of your speakers in a square or rectangular formation in front of and behind your sofa, to get the most out of surround-sound technology.
6 Your sofa needs to be as large, deep and comfortable as possible for TV viewing and chilling out. But, make sure the sofa suits the proportion of the room.
7 If you've got kids, think about providing a few cosy beanbags that they can fall into while watching TV. My kids love them and have to have one each!
8 Use lamps to provide lighting to the corners of the room. These should be connected to 5-amp light sockets, so they can be controlled by the main light switches as well as with the lighting controls built into the lamp itself.
9 Make sure you install a double power socket alongside the 5-amp socket in each corner of the room, too. You really can't have too many electrical points in your living room.
10 Depending on your sound requirements, your electrician should install cables in the right location for your speaker sockets, to get the perfect level of surround sound.

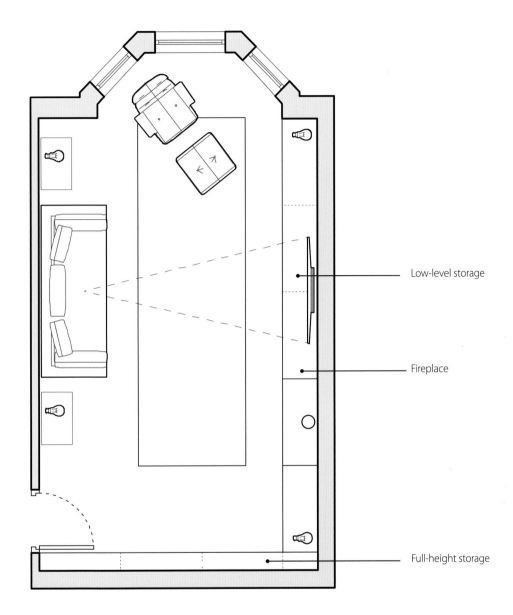

Low-level storage

Fireplace

Full-height storage

11 If you can, install underfloor heating. Arranging furniture and storage to avoid a large radiator position is just a pain. Under-floor heating gets rid of the problem straightaway.

12 Provide integrated areas for book storage. Your books are a personal expression of you and your family, and help to personalise a living space.

13 You may consider moving the existing door into your living room, to make the circulation in the space work properly, while at the same time allowing you to integrate more storage.

Extensions

'No money is better spent than what is laid out for domestic satisfaction.' Samuel Johnson

Building a conservatory or an extension on your home can add massive value. Not only can it transform the quality of the architecture in your ground-floor spaces, but the additional space will also increase the overall floor area of your house, which will automatically increase its value when the estate agent whips round with his tape measure. Best of all, if your new spaces are well designed, you'll certainly add that 'wow' factor.

In fact, extensions are a magical way to flood your house with light, create space where you didn't even know you had it, and open up the rooms in your home to make them work the way you want them to.

opposite A classic rear extension.

below Doors onto the garden will bring masses of light into the room and create a stronger connection with the outside world.

Adding an extension to your existing home can often be a cheaper and more effective way of gaining space than moving house. Why move and pay all the associated costs for stamp duty, estate-agent and legal fees, and removals, when you can stay at home and add value to the property that you've got?

below and opposite An example of a successful modern extension to a period property.

What do you need most?

The first question that you have to ask yourself is what kind of extension you want and why? Before even considering your options, you need to analyse your existing house plans very carefully to fully understand the impact your extension will have on the design of your existing house. You also have to be sure that whatever you build completely fits your needs. The most common form of extension on a property is a ground-floor rear extension; the most popular form of *extension* is a rear, ground-floor *addition*. Both of these can have a substantial and dramatic effect on the way that the ground-floor spaces work.

In many cases, these types of extensions are used to expand the kitchen-dining area, which has pretty much become the heart of the typical British family home. Creating additional space where the average family needs, wants and uses it most means that you'll not just be making your home more productive in terms of space, but you'll be in a fantastic position if and when you do come to sell.

Conservatories

Standard conservatories bought directly from a manufacturer can be even more affordable, but it's worth being wary of this approach. If selected in the wrong style, a standard, off-the-shelf design can conflict with the architecture of the existing house. This doesn't have anything to do with whether the extension is modern or traditional – far from it. Personally, I don't have a preference for either style, as long as the design of the extension is good – and appropriate for your house. Often, however, I find that the standardised conservatories in mock Georgian, Tudor or Victorian styles don't really work well when added to the back of a house from a different period.

A well-designed and well-built extension will always be my preference over a low-budget PVC conservatory that won't necessarily enhance the standard of your home.

The truth is that I sometimes wonder why people *do* go for fully glazed conservatories with glass roofs, which they then cover completely with blinds because they are worried about their privacy! This high level of glazing is not necessarily very comfortable, either! In the winter months you can end up with a freezing-cold extension and, in the summer, the equivalent of an indoor greenhouse.

A more considered design, which overcomes the issues of privacy, heat loss and solar gain, is by far the best way forward. Planned correctly, you'll still be able to achieve fantastic views and access to your back garden.

Planning your extension layout

The design and layout of your new conservatory or extension will in many ways be influenced by the views and policies of your local planning department. Make sure that you consult with the planners at the earliest possible stage, or risk having your ideas dashed before you've even got started.

Planning policies vary from council to council and they can be far more stringent if you live in a conservation area or a listed building (see Section 6). Some planning departments like any new extension to be traditional in style – and in keeping with the architecture of the existing house. Other departments may have policies that promote the design of more contemporary glass extensions onto older properties, so that the new addition looks distinctly modern, compared to the old house. I told you it was confusing!

So, before committing too much of your hard-earned money on consultants' and planning fees, and getting lots of finalised plans drawn up, pay for some preliminary work to be done by an architect with experience in exploring the planning options available to you. This initial consultation work will prove to be invaluable and will inform the rest of the design process.

Here are a few top tips to keep in mind when planning your new extension:

1 Consult your planning department as early as possible, and outline what you have in mind.
2 Appoint a local architect to help you produce some initial sketches and design information; you'll then have some options to provide to the planning department. I can't tell you how important it is to have a few different ideas. If you show that you are prepared to be flexible – and don't set your heart on one particular layout or design – chances are you'll get your plans through more quickly, and be able to get something closer to what you want.
3 Look through magazines and any other architectural books to get some ideas about style of extension you want to go for. You'll cut your bills if you have some ideas of your own, and you'll also find it easier to envision your new space and the role it will play in the overall scheme and dynamic of your home if you have some visual images to play with.
4 As much as possible, try to integrate the design and layout of your extension with the internal spaces to which it will be connected.
5 I sometimes feel that standard conservatories plonked on the end of a building feel like a completely separate space. If you want a self-contained room – for an office or a study, for example – then that's fine. If, however, the idea is that your extension will expand

below Extensions don't have to be dramatic to make a significant impact on the space you have.

your way of living, then you need to carefully integrate the design of the extension space with your existing home.

6   If you are considering a rear extension, try to make a positive and clear connection between the new building and the garden beyond. I'm a big fan of bi-fold doors that can concertina back to one side to allow the internal spaces to flow directly out to the garden. In my home, this has completely transformed the way that we experience our kitchen-dining room on a daily basis.

7   If your extension faces north, make sure you don't include too much glazing, particularly within the roof. The space may feel cold in the winter months.

8   If your extension is south-facing, it's also important to avoid having too much glazing. The space within your extension could dramatically overheat during the summer months because of the direct solar gain from the sun. This might seem like a bonus during the winter, but if you have to draw down all the blinds and suffocate in the summer, your space will only ever be useful for part of the year.

9   Make sure you are aware of permitted development laws within your area. Permitted development rights allow you to build an extension on to your home of a certain scale and size without having to make a full planning application. You will have to inform your local council of what you intend to do and apply to use your permitted development rights; however, if the design of your scheme is within the permitted development laws then this is a fast-track planning process, allowing you to proceed despite objections from your neighbours or planning officer.

10 Make sure you spend as much time as possible integrating your existing internal layout with your new extension. This is essential for the success of any structural addition or alteration to your home.

There is no doubt that the British planning system can be over bureaucratic and confusing, so it's well worth taking professional advice from your architect and making a pre-planning enquiry to your local council to find out exactly what you are and are not able to do with any extension.

following page A fantastic rear extension.

One I did earlier

One of the most amazing extensions that I've ever created featured on *The Home Show*. Jo and Grant live in Worcester Park with their two young daughters, in the tiniest house I've ever seen. When I first arrived I felt like I'd entered a doll's house. Jo was forced to keep her pots and pans, and her tumble-dryer, in a shed in the garden. The kitchen was so small that there was barely room to open the oven door, let alone allow more than one person in there at any time. The living space on the ground floor was cramped and awkward, and the storage was phenomenally poor. This was a family in need of usable space that was actually conducive to family living.

Planning constraints were ridiculously tight, but we were able to turn the ordinary into the extraordinary with a small extension, a whole load of glass to bring in the light and open up the house to the garden, and a total replan of the ground floor to create a gorgeous kitchen-dining room, a smart, functional living room and even a downstairs loo and utility room.

Here's what I did:

1 Jo and Grant had already acquired planning permission for a conservatory on the back of the house, to match the white-plastic one that their neighbours had installed next door. I hate this type of conservatory, because they overheat in summer and are far too cold in the winter. I think people also become confused about what they should be used for! Are they an extension of the home? If so, then they should be clearly integrated with the ground-floor spaces. Unfortunately, they rarely are, and tend to feel like separate rooms. They also become something of a 'garden room', feeling more like part of the garden space. A room with this type of designation doesn't lend itself to net curtains! So you are in trouble on the privacy front from the word go. I hate net curtains anyhow; they are a complete waste of time! The view out to your garden becomes something akin to a bride looking through her wedding veil!

2 So, my design had to work within the scale and shape of the already-approved conservatory. But instead of a glass horror, I designed a brick building with bi-fold doors to the back, to open out onto the garden. I topped it with a solid-slate roof, so it didn't overheat in summer or feel cold in the winter. But I did glaze part of the roof in the central ch, keeping the panels beautifully aligned with the bi-folds beneath, to allow in a controlled amount of natural light. It absolutely flooded the space. This made what would have been a very ordinary extension in shape and form into something completely different – simple, but architecturally quite interesting. The family loved it!

Old layout

New layout

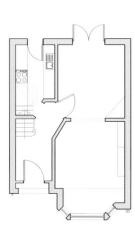

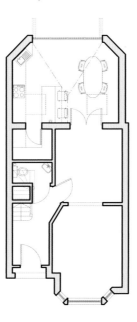

left The existing plan shows a kitchen that is far too small for a family home. A lot of their pots and pans were stored in a unit in the garden! The family had little room to cook and then ate their food on their knee in front of the tv....not ideal! There was also no ground floor toilet so the family were up and down the stairs all day.

The proposed plan shows the new kitchen extension. The old kitchen was divided into two to provide a new ground floor toilet accessed from the hallway and a small utility room accessed from the kitchen. The new extension created a fantastic new kitchen and dining space that transformed the way the family lived.

3   Inside the new space, I used the old kitchen area to create an ultra-modern utility room, complete with appliances (and an extra freezer), worktop and storage, and behind it, facing the front hall, a downstairs loo, which has since proved absolutely invaluable.

4   The new kitchen was spacious and well organised, with lots of circulation space, storage and countertop areas, as well as a breakfast bar and a substantial seating area.

5   The living room was designed to feel like a major part of the house as a whole, but it was tucked neatly into the new L-shaped downstairs layout, to offer a little respite from the more vibrant activities in the kitchen-dining area.

6   Although the extension was small, the ground-floor space felt dramatically different, and for the first time the family were able to spend time together cooking and preparing food, chatting while Jo or Grant were busy in the kitchen, and making use of the fantastic storage to keep clutter out of sight. What's more, by connecting the garden to the extension, the girls had a safe haven in which to play. There is no doubt that it changed the way they lived and interacted as a family, and they were now living in a home for life.

The simple message here is that you don't need loads and loads of space to change your home; a small, affordable extension to the back or side of your home will allow you to reconfigure the space you have already, and produce something the works for you and your family.

Lighting your extension

When you add a new extension onto your property, you will need to have a full review of the electrical layout for the entire ground floor of your home. It's important to remember that you will be removing a number of existing walls to form the new openings to allow access to the new extension, and this will undoubtedly mean a major disruption to the existing services.

A number of electrical circuits will no longer work and, within the newly designed layout, light switches and sockets may be in the wrong positions. This opportunity to review the electrical design also offers a fantastic chance to upgrade your lighting system and wiring to suit your new needs.

When considering your new artificial-lighting scheme, bear in mind the following:

1 Replacing and upgrading all of your switch plates in a more contemporary style throughout the existing and new space can achieve an updated and unified appearance. There is a fantastic range of switch and socket plates to suit your personal style and space, and many of them are most definitely affordable. Think about the ground floor as a whole, rather than changing your scheme from room to room; this can create a sense of space as your theme flows from room to room.

2 Your new extension is an intervention between your existing internal space and your garden. Lighting is a way of bringing together your house, extension and garden space. So, when you consider your lighting needs, consider all three elements as a whole.

3 Consider designing some form of small canopy to the new extension, so you can open your extension doors to enjoy the outside, no matter what the weather. A canopy provides a simple form of protection, while also offering you a brilliant opportunity to install lights beneath it – illuminating the space between your inside and outside.

4 If there is a large amount of glass in an extension overlooking your garden, it is essential to provide lighting in your garden area to illuminate key features, such as existing trees, plants and external seating areas. There is nothing worse than looking out into a dark void when you are sitting in your extension at night. Exterior lighting brings this dark world to life.

5 As always, go for dimmer switches; this will allow you to gently increase the light indoors, as it fades outdoors.

6 Make good use of table lights and other 5-amp lighting, to illuminate corners where the sunlight may not quite reach.

above The most successful extension is seamlessly and fully integrated, and this applies to all of your electrical and servicing requirements, too. Take the opportunity to assess your needs, and light and service your entire ground floor in the very best way possible.

below Canopies like this really make it feel like you have another room, albeit an al fresco one!

Extension design features

The two most important design features of any new extension are skylights and doors – these are the two elements that make your extension connect to the outside world. For a highly contemporary and modern extension, the lightest and most minimal touch would involve creating your entire new addition out of structural glazing. The advances in glazing design have to be some of the most exciting developments in domestic architecture today. There are now so many options to create a flow of natural light in any space, using glass as walls, flooring and even roofing. While artificial lighting can work wonders in confined spaces, there is no substitute for natural light in your home.

Light from the sky

Skylights can take the form of simple sheets of glass that are fully fixed and bonded together, or you can specify more standard skylight units, such as those developed by brilliant companies such as Velux. I am a massive fan of standard Velux windows, largely because they are very simple, always well designed and, above all, affordable. What's more, they can have so many different domestic applications.

Top light is so much stronger than the light that comes through a normal vertical window so, even if you are designing an extension on the lowest budget, always try to install a skylight if possible. They will absolutely transform the quality of the space. If you have a few more pennies in your budget, then you can approach other glazing companies to be more intrepid with glass technology.

One of the most adventurous extensions that I've done recently was for a curved, double-glazed, structural glass extension that used heated-glass technology. The heated glass, similar to your car windscreen, has a metal oxide film across its surface. Given a little bit of electricity, this metal oxide heats up, making your double-glazed unit an amazing glass radiator, with incredibly high thermal qualities. This innovative and contemporary extension was placed onto an old Scottish icehouse. The contrast between old and new couldn't have been more extreme, but it was for this very reason – and because it was so well designed – that the extension worked beautifully.

The client nicknamed the extension the 'Fox's Glacier Mint', because it was so light, minimal and devoid of any structural support. What a fantastic addition to a beautiful old building!

Designing in as much glass as you can, particularly in the roof, will bring in heaps of natural light. Even on a dark day, your space will be illuminated and bright, which reduces your need for artificial lighting.

above Skylights like these are the most effective at bringing in light as they allow light to flood in from above.

Doors and windows

Over the last 10 years, developments in glass technology have been phenomenal; these days, glass can do so much more, providing structural support, a source of heat and even a form of insulation.

The doors and windows for your extension comprise a vital design feature, for the simple reason that the way you are able to move from inside to outside space is a key element of architecture.

By now you are probably well aware that I am a massive fan of bi-fold door systems, which can concertina to one side and give direct access to terraced or garden areas. In most cases, they are generally aluminium or timber-framed; however, there is an increasing wealth of options out there, and it's worth checking them out to see what works best with your space, style and taste. You can go for traditional French doors, large sliding doors, or those that concertina – and if you want to do something completely different, I have even seen some extensions that work in a similar way to garage-roller doors, or 'up and over' doors. There are so many fascinating products on the market, and this is one area of your extension where you can really have fun. Simply bear in mind that the more glass you use, and the greater the expanse, the lighter, brighter and airier your room will be, creating a space that will be truly dynamic and integrated to your property as a whole.

below These doors onto the garden make the room feel so much bigger and brighter.

Extension storage

The scale and size of most domestic extensions on standard types of housing mean that we are inevitably trying to add a small-scale addition to achieve maximum impact. When designing extensions, I always try to apply my favourite design philosophy – trying to get maximum effect from the smallest affordable change.

So, if your extension isn't particularly large, you'll need to work very hard to ensure that all of the spaces work, there is direct access to the garden, and everything is as integrated as it is possible to be.

The level of storage needed will obviously depend on the function of the room. If the extension is being created to house a large kitchen, then make sure you allow for as much wall area as you can, to permit wall units to be integrated into the architecture. Having said that, it's equally important to the get the balance right – achieving the maximum amount of usable wall space, while freeing up enough wall space on the garden facade to allow ample and easy access to your outdoor space.

The golden rule of extension storage is to ensure that it is of a scale, proportion and level that provides all the storage you need for the space to function, without undermining the quality, character and feel of the additional space you've created. It's all about balance.

Using the side walls

In any rear extension to a home, the two side walls should be used to create space for masses of storage, leaving the end wall as free as possible to produce good access to your garden. It's also worth remembering that external walls provide fantastic opportunities to bring light into the room, so try to ensure that you utilise them for windows, doors and glass walls rather than covering them from floor to ceiling with storage that can make your space feel confined.

If the extension is to use for dining, using the side walls for storing plates, cups, cutlery and servers is ideal. While some full-height storage is essential to maximise the use of space, there is a danger that it can make your extension feel quite narrow. For a dining area it may be more appropriate to set your storage at counter-top height, so that the top of the unit can double up as a serving area when you have large dinner parties or family celebrations. Otherwise, choose the corners facing the access wall to go full height on the storage front.

LIVING SPACE

If your extension will be an addition to your living area, then these side walls become an ideal place for book and magazine storage, as well as TV display areas and DVD storage.

If the extension will be your study or an office, then fully integrated storage and shelving is even more essential. The most important decision to make here is where to have your desk. To be able to work creatively, your desk should be in the most perfect position for you to get the best view. Great views can sometimes be a distraction, but they are, more often than not, a welcome break from hard work. What's more, a little natural light shining in on your project – and a glimpse of nature – can lift your spirits.

opposite If your budget is smaller than you would like, always opt for a smaller but higher quality extension.

below If your extension is wide enough, use the side walls to create extra storage.

Extension finishes and materials

Your selection of finishes and materials will depend on the architectural style of the existing house and the degree to which you would like your extension to contrast. If you decide to design a traditional extension on an old house, it's absolutely imperative that you choose materials that are respectful of the period in question. Reclaimed goods, such as bricks, fireplaces, lighting, flooring and any surfaces are ideal; however, if you do go for new materials, aim for something that produces a high-quality design. Cheap and cheerful will not work in an older property.

If you choose to design a modern extension on a traditional building, there is a huge amount of scope for the selection of new materials to contrast with the old in an extreme way. Once again, however, it's all about selecting products that are appropriate to your new build as well as being respectful of your existing building.

Respect the original

A badly designed extension with poor-quality finishes will not only be a waste of time, but you are in danger of reducing the value of your investment. A worse sin than that is building something ugly. An extreme case in point – and unfortunately something I've seen many times – is for an elegant home, with nice timber sliding-sash windows, to have an extension dropped on the back with thick white UPVC frames. There is no excuse for doing this and it's not acceptable! If you have a contemporary house full of existing UPVC windows and you choose to build a new UPVC extension, then that's your call. I suppose you could argue that it's in keeping.

But don't ruin the character of a more period-style home by adding an unsightly extension.

To avoid making mistakes that could ruin the overall look, feel and value of your extension, bear in mind the following:

1 Take time to really understand the architectural characteristics and materials of your existing home. Do your research, by looking through magazines and books to find extensions that are appropriate and respectful to the existing building, whether it's modern or traditional.
2 Visit other extensions that have been built in your area to learn from the bad ones, as well as the good ones.
3 Prioritise your budget. In order to get the best design, you may need to spend a little more on the doors and skylights, choosing to compromise on some of the internal features that can always be updated at a later stage.

4   If you are struggling to find the budget for a large extension that has finally been approved by the planners, don't be tempted to produce something large and ugly. It's a much better idea to buy something smaller, and put the money you've saved into a better design with fantastic finishes. Small and beautiful is better than big and ugly.

5   Frankly, too, if you can only afford finishes and materials that fall below the standard that you have in your existing house, then don't bother doing the extension. Upgrade the house you've got, and do the extension later.

6   Don't forget the importance of colour; if you are creating a vast open-plan space with your new extension, you can cleverly use colour to define zones; try to carry the same colour across the seams of the extension, so it doesn't look like an 'add-on' or an afterthought.

7   Similarly, bringing vast amounts of light into your new space will be undermined if you go dark in your colour scheme. While you don't want reflective surfaces that could be blinding, choosing colours that throw back the light a little can keep things bright and beautiful.

8   Consider your flooring carefully. If you plan to venture in and out of the garden regularly, there is no point in having carpeting that will be almost instantly ruined. Similarly, if it's your main access point to the garden, anything that will be stained or damaged by water should be avoided.

9   I always think that flooring closest to the garden should be as natural as possible, to make the transition from home to garden as effortless as possible. If you have a timber deck on the other side of your bi-fold doors, then consider matching your flooring to draw the eye outwards and make your new space look absolutely huge.

right Natural flooring in your extension will help maintain continuity between the inside and outside spaces, making your extension feel that bit bigger.

The affordable extension

Most of my clients consistently underestimate the cost of a build, whether you are creating something massive or very small. A house extension is *never* as simple as knocking up a few walls, sticking a roof on it, and installing some walls and doors. The truth is that if you want to do the job properly and create an extension that is going to be a substantial improvement to your home – not to mention a good investment – then you've got to get it right. There are, for example, a number of costs that you'll need to be aware of before you even begin the work.

Considering the costs

It's very important to factor in:

1 Your architect's fees. Your architect is going to need to survey the existing house to produce good, accurate drawings of the space you have now, plus the proposed new build. He'll need to be paid for drawings, design meetings and design time, as well as the supervision of your planning and building regulations application, and the build itself.

2 Your structural engineer's fees. You will need calculations to open up existing walls and form the new extension structure, and this will need to be undertaken by a professional – unless you don't mind your new home collapsing at some point in the future.

3 Party-wall surveyor's fees. If the structure of your extension is being built into or forming part of your party wall (see Section 6) you will have to appoint your surveyor and your neighbour has the right to appoint their own, too. You'll need to meet the costs of both.

4 Payment of your planning- and building-regulation application fees. Put aside a little extra in the event that you have to resubmit or appeal.

5 Schedules and specifications. These can normally be produced by your architect or, in some cases, a project manager, but they are necessary. Everything that will go into creating your build needs to be detailed and communicated to your builder. Only then can he accurately price the job.

Getting it right on site

After instructing, paying for and taking delivery of all of this work, you will then be in a position to be able to start on site. This is when your costs become even more important.

The simplest and most affordable extension should not – and doesn't *need* to look cheap. The golden rule is to carefully design the addition so that it is sensitively proportioned – avoiding awkward angles, and respecting the existing house.

There are two other things to bear in mind constantly: scale and proportion. These must be applied to every single element of your extension, from the overall scale and proportion of the building itself, to the type, size and colour of the bricks, your skylights, the glazing, glazing frames and glazing materials. Don't underestimate the importance of getting this right. These individual decisions need to come together in an elegant way to create one single, beautiful building.

As a starting point, consider these ideas for creating the simplest and most affordable single-storey rear extension. You can work upwards for larger projects, with the help of your architect – and imagination.

above Simple finishes help keep costs down.

1 Go for solid-brick or rendered side walls, making it easier to create integrated storage that can be set against them.

2 The scale of the extension should just be enough to do the job that it needs to do. Don't design a large extension if you're struggling to pay for it, and it is providing space that you don't absolutely need. Make the plan work as hard as possible at design stage, and make the scale of the extension small and efficient.

3 Buy some very simple, thin-framed, aluminium bi-fold doors so that the rear end of your building can open out onto your garden. Make them as large and wide as possible, without compromising the potential storage space on either side or the internal layout. If possible, choose bi-fold doors that open out into the garden, and not into the space. Doors that open in can create a real obstruction in a small extension.

4 If the planners will allow it, design your extension with a flat roof, which is the simplest, easiest and cheapest to build. Flat-roof technology has moved on so much that the problems that were once associated with them no longer exist.

5 Within the flat roof, place a number of Velux skylights that are appropriate to the design and your budget, to allow in lots of top light.

6 Keep your internal finishes very simple, with plastered walls and a hard-wearing, relatively maintenance-free floor. It will be put to the test with people moving in and out of the house to the garden.

7 To maximise the available storage space and to free up as much available wall space as possible, look at underfloor heating.

These very simple measures will create the most affordable extension.

Extension ecology

Even if you are designing a small-scale extension, you should always be aware that all of the decisions you make will have a big impact upon the environment. Money may be tight, but there are a few simple and inexpensive steps you can take to keep your environmental conscience clean.

1   Use as much insulation as you can possibly afford. If it were my project, I would go way beyond standard building-regulation requirements and put in as much as I can. Remember that good insulation keeps a space cool in summer and warm in winter.

2   If your extension has a flat roof, make sure you paint the surface of the roof either silver or white to reflect as much heat as possible.

3   Check that your external glass doors are at least double-, if not triple-glazed, with the highest level of thermal performance glass that your budget can stretch to.

4   Choose skylights that can be opened with a radio remote control; in the summer months this can be an invaluable source of natural ventilation.

5   The roof of your extension will be bombarded by the great British weather, which means your biggest challenge will be to get rid of large amounts of rainwater. Try to harvest as much of this water as you possibly can, by allowing your rainwater downpipes to drain into a large plastic container or water butt. This water can be used for watering your garden, or even filling the paddling pool.

6   If your budget can stretch to more modern technologies, consider investing in a small solar panel or solar-roofing slates. These photovoltaic collectors can generate energy in even the coolest, cloudiest locations, and knock some money off your electricity bills. But take specialist advice about this, to ensure that your panels are facing in the right direction and working to maximum efficiency. If you don't get it right, it can take a long time to recoup your money.

7   Recycle or reuse any materials and finishes that you've been able to salvage from other building sites or reclamation yards. You might then end up with a project that is quirky, but it will certainly be unique – and environmentally friendly!

following page Once you've finished your extension, it is worth spending a bit of time making your garden attractive.

The ideal extension

I am a big fan of really well-designed rear extensions that can transform kitchen-dining or living spaces. Replicating it in the existing architectural style of your house is absolutely fine, as long as the design and the planning are good. Personally, however, I really prefer a bold contrast between a traditional house and a slick modern extension. The plan and layout still need to be fully integrated, but the new design style can be something that is architecturally inspiring and positively changes the way that you experience the house.

Consider the following, to achieve your ideal home extension:

1 A seamless floor finish between the existing space and the new space, which can help to integrate the extension to the new house.
2 Try to bring in as much natural light as possible with the design of the glazing and the roof of your extension, while maintaining a comfortable environment during the winter and summer months.
3 Building your extension will obviously mean removing some of the external walls of your old house in order to link to the new extension. Make sure you carefully consider how much of the structure will need to be removed in order for the design between the old and the new to be balanced and proportioned.
4 Make sure you employ the services of a good structural engineer to help you with these alterations. His or her services will be invaluable, and will save you a lot of money later on.
5 If you have a lot of glass in your extension, make sure that you factor in screens or blinds. Both you and your neighbours will need to maintain a reasonable level of privacy. A cool option is shutters, which can be folded closed when you want a little privacy (or darkness), and folded open to reveal the garden and let in the light – in varying degrees. These are functional, inexpensive and seriously trendy, and because they are usually made of wood, they'll look great against the garden view.
6 Prefabrication is an increasingly popular option for home extensions. These are factory-built in a highly controlled environment, and can be lifted into place very quickly and easily on site. In many ways, you can get a better standard of build realised much more quickly on a more affordable budget. But – and this is a big *but* – you definitely need to make sure that the prefabricated design is appropriate as an addition on your existing home. Get it wrong, and the whole space can be unattractive and unwieldy.

'Houses are built to live in, and not to look on: therefore let use be preferred before uniformity.'

Francis Bacon

Window seat

Extension

Lounge

Kitchen

Extension

Dishwasher

Fridge freezer

Full-height storage

7   The best thing about creating an extension – with the additional space it offers – is that it can often free up *other* space in the house that can be put to good use. So make sure you consider the entire ground-floor plan of your property when proposing any extension. It isn't just an isolated project, but a magnificent opportunity to redesign the way you live.

8   Any successful extension should add value to your home. It's worth running your initial design by your local estate agent to make sure you will get a return on your investment.

9   Always build the right extension to suit your property *and* your needs. For a narrow house, a side-return extension may be the best option to make the internal spaces work by maximising the width of the property. Alternatively, if you have a substantial garden, a full-width extension – which runs from one side of the house to the other – may be the best way to go, even if it seems ambitious at the outset.

10 Your extension should have a strong and direct connection to your outdoor space. This doesn't just mean creating doorways or even windows overlooking the garden; you'll also need to consider how the flooring works with any deck or patio, how the light flows in and out, and how you can open up the indoor rooms to make access to the garden as natural as possible.

11 Remember the old architectural maxim about increasing light and space. You'll need to maximise as much controlled natural light as possible into your extension, creating a bright, airy atmosphere that will appear to achieve a greater sense of space.

Studies and offices

'I know what I should love to do – to build a study, to write, and to think of nothing else.' Lew Wallace, American author

This is a painting of St Jerome, painted in 1475 by Antonello da Messina, probably in Venice. It currently hangs in the National Gallery in London and it is, beyond doubt, the most beautiful, romantic painting. It's had an inexplicable effect upon me since I was a small boy.

My career in architecture is such an important part of my life. I love to work, and I have always dreamt of having a beautiful study like this one. Apart from needing an Apple laptop, an iPhone, a few other gadgets and perhaps a different set of clothes than old Jerome, I could work quite happily in this study.

The truth is that the architectural principles of study spaces have changed little over the centuries, and the same things remain important to us today. There is a comfortable chair, a beautiful desk and sufficient storage, and it's all contained within a magnificent space with what I can only imagine is a wonderful view from that large window. I would give anything to have a study or an office like this one. I think most people would.

Working from home

One of the biggest changes that has occurred within the family home over the past 10 to 15 years is the growing popularity of the home office. An increasing number of people now choose to work at home, either to create a better work-life balance, to avoid the misery of commuting, or simply to undertake the work they love in the comfort of their own homes.

Britain has become an entrepreneurial state, with many ambitious individuals and small groups keen to set up companies on the lowest possible budget. It's undoubtedly true that setting up at home cuts overheads significantly, and allows you to work long, productive hours without completely giving up family or home life.

Just over 10 years ago, I remember leaving a large practice to start my own business from my spare bedroom. It was an enormous downscale – believe me! However, even though I now have a much larger, fully staffed office, I still like to spend time at home in my own study, in quiet contemplation. It can be an amazing place, allowing me to avoid the distractions of the outside world and focus on delivering work that needs high levels of concentration.

above 'Saint Jerome in his study' by Anatello da Messina.

opposite My office at home. A beautifully simple space with few distractions...apart from the view over my garden.

Whether you choose to use a corner of your living space, or create a study or home office in a designated room, it's undoubtedly important to keep it tidy and make it ruthlessly efficient. But that doesn't mean it can't be beautiful. Seamless, integrated storage will keep chaos at bay, and you can focus on creating a comfortable, motivating place to work.

Finding the space

There is no reason why you can't have a 'study' or home office integrated into another space in your home. Some rooms obviously lend themselves to this sort of approach, including those with an L-shaped layout or a nook or enclave that you can adapt to your needs. If you need to fit a study into a rectangular room, you'll have to work a little harder, but it's possible to delineate your room into zones with colour, clever use of storage or screens, and functional furniture that allows you to hide away your work when the day is done.

Why not consider the following options:
- Use bookshelves or open shelving as a screen. This will neatly divide up your room, while providing privacy and storage options for your study space. Your storage effectively becomes your screen.
- Open shelving can prevent your room from looking too boxy and feeling too claustrophobic. If you get some deep shelves to screen off your study area, you can use one side for study storage and the other to display books or other items in your living or dining area.
- You'll have to be incredibly organised to keep your work from spilling over into the accompanying space, and if that just isn't you, consider a pull-down desk or screen that can mask it when you aren't at your desk.
- Check your under-stair space; there are some clever options now available to make use of this area of the house, which usually ends up being a repository for household implements. Opening it up and sliding in a desk with some functional storage and good task lighting can create a perfect little office. Consider installing bespoke bi-fold doors that concertina back and forth to hide away your work when you need to.
- Study-bedrooms are increasingly popular as these rooms are far enough away from the activity of the house to allow you to get some work done. Use a massive wardrobe to house a desk that can be pulled out, and integrate shelving around and under it. You can close the doors at the end of the day to get a good night's sleep.
- Good cabinetry in your living area can provide a dual purpose – allowing you to display books or personal belongings over and around the desk area. I love the Neville Johnson bespoke furniture solutions that allow you to blend the latest technology into a neatly fitted study area that works in the room as a whole. A good joiner can create a similar look.

Planning your study layout

Working from home can be an enjoyable experience, and because you aren't out there creating a bigger carbon footprint in your car or on the train in a daily commute, it's pretty environmentally friendly, too.

There are, however, downsides to working at home, even if you do so only occasionally. As human beings, we are torn between the relaxed pleasures of our homes and the demands of work, and we have to be seriously disciplined to get the work done and not be drawn into the comfort of being in our home environment, with all its distractions.

Moreover, we face a huge number of unique challenges if our home life is to remain enjoyable and our work life is to be productive. It's easy to be lured into a home office when we should be spending time with our families or relaxing, and it's possible to work crazy hours just because we are 'on site', so to speak.

It's important that you take all of these very delicate issues into account when you are trying to create a space for you to work. Let's look at the best ways to create a workable and productive office – one that isn't so comfortable that you drift off – or spend your entire life in there – or so streamlined that you can't relax and settle into the job.

The location of your study is everything. If it's too close to your other living spaces, it's easy to lose your concentration. The old saying 'out of sight, out of mind' applies pretty well here: if you can see the TV or you're distracted by other activities in the house, you're unlikely to get much work done. Similarly, if your kids can see you, they aren't going to let you get on with the job, either. Ideally, you need to be in a room that is as isolated as possible. One of the best places to achieve this is to find space in your loft, your basement or in a converted bedroom that is well away from the others. The golden rule is to stay as far away as possible from your kitchen, dining and living spaces.

1   There are certain views that can encourage concentration. For me, being able to gaze out of a window over a beautiful garden allows my brain to take a mini-break that is part of the process of shaping ideas in my mind. A view gives you a little much-needed respite from the pressures of work.
2   Natural light is essential. Working in a dark space that is illuminated only by artificial light for hours on end can be miserable and depressing. A reasonable level of natural light and natural ventilation makes for a comfortable working environment. It's worth noting too that natural light raises the level of 'feel-good' chemicals in your brain that will make you happier and more productive.

above Whenever possible, put your desk by a window.

3 Buy yourself an incredibly comfortable, beautiful office chair. It needs to be highly ergonomic and relate perfectly to your desk and the height of your computer screen. If you get this wrong, you're in danger of causing yourself long-term physical damage. What's more, you'll be up and down like a yo-yo, trying to get comfortable.

4 A fantastic ergonomic desk is the centrepiece of any office. As an architect and designer, I'm a bit of a fanatic, and a little obsessive when it comes to stunning furniture. As we speak, I'm sitting on a comfortable, padded Eames chair in front of a simply designed but elegant desk. A desk should be functional, but also handsome, to draw you to it when you enter the room, but also comfortably hold everything you need to get your work done properly.

5 Make sure your computer is mounted so that your eyes look directly at the screen. Being forced to look either up or down for long hours at a time will make you tense and uncomfortable, and you could end up with some nasty neck problems. Remember that you can only be truly productive when you feel at ease.

6 Sufficient storage is absolutely essential. Your office will become an unproductive mess unless there is enough storage space.

opposite Storage walls are a clever way of defining your study space.

this page Storage needs to be plentiful and easily accessible from your desk.

The layout of your study or office really depends upon the amount of room you have available, and the type of work you intend to carry out within it. Most of the offices that I visit within people's homes are generally the same. You need:

- A sturdy, comfortable place to sit
- A desk on which to place your computer
- Some additional layout space to spread out your work and consider it properly
- Space for files and storage
- Room for all those gadgets that we use, such as printers and scanners
- Shelving for books and other reference materials
- Something inspirational, such as a treasured print or photograph
- Plants, to bring the natural world inside.

When brought together, it is the layout – combined with your choice of finishes and materials – that will produce a particular mood and atmosphere. These are the elements that are fundamentally important to creating the right working environment for you.

opposite One of my favourite desk lamps, the Kelvin LED lamp.

below It is a good idea to have blinds over your windows for really bright sunny days.

Study lighting

The type and style of lighting for your office/study space is very much a personal choice. It all comes down to what will create the right atmosphere for you to be productive in your work. Having said that, ambient lighting or atmospheric lighting isn't really the priority here; task lighting is the most important form of lighting in any workspace. It goes without saying that you should be able to clearly see the work you need to do!

Being an architect, I am obviously keen on the typical architect's anglepoise; in fact, in the office space in which I'm seated right now, I can see four of them – all in different designs and styles. I have a very tall anglepoise on a wheeled stand; it's beautifully made out of cast aluminium, and I can freely move it around the space to position it just where I need it. I bought this from a friend who runs an old antique, and reclamation place.

The next light is a more straightforward and affordable anglepoise that you can actually screw-fix to the end of your desk. I think these lights are beautifully functional, and they can be picked up very cheaply from IKEA and other home-improvement stores.

Then there is the classic anglepoise by Habitat; these come in a broad range of colours and can, again, be fixed to the desk. This type of lamp is hugely practical because it doesn't have a base to clutter your desk and take up valuable space, and you can position it so that it shines directly on your work.

My favourite anglepoise of all is the Kelvin light. It isn't fixed to the desk, but rests upon it with a very simple adjustable mechanism. It's an elegant lamp and brings a splash of style to my workspace. You can buy this lamp in a wide range of colours.

I'd always go for an anglepoise or two in any good study; however, you can choose a slightly more traditional, straightforward desk lamp. There is a huge choice of designs and styles available to suit your taste. Just make sure that it throws enough bright light on the areas that need it, and that its base isn't going to overwhelm your working space.

I am not really a huge fan of studies being absolutely flooded with light –particularly from large pendant lights or too many recessed down-lighters in the ceiling. I much prefer a lower level of task lighting to illuminate the desks and work areas.

Study design features

The most important design features for any study are the products that allow space-saving storage. You need to be able to hide away your stuff, while at the same time making it accessible. Small study rooms – or areas in your house turned over to study space – are a real challenge, so every single square inch of space has to be maximised.

Here are some of the best solutions:

1 The corners of rooms are the most difficult to use efficiently; however, you can purchase clever corner-storage units, which allow you to pull out the entire corner unit into the space. These tend to be more common in kitchen designs, but why not be inventive and integrate standard kitchen units like these into your study room design?

2 Use storage walls – such as bookshelving that is open on both sides – as architectural screens, to create intimate study spaces in larger rooms. This is a good way to prevent being distracted, and gives you the sense of being in a much smaller, designated space – particularly if you are using space within another room in your house, such as the living room.

3 Think about storage as art! There are some fun products that make for interesting storage. For example, a 'tree' shelving system is great for a kids' study room. It really is quite witty – after all, paper comes from a tree, so why not store your books in the branches of one?

4 Integrated 'wall desks' or 'wall beds' are a brilliant way of creating a storage wall that includes virtually everything you need. Pull-down desks can be folded away into a storage wall to free up more everyday living space – and then folded out again when you need to work. I love systems like this, which work really well in small spaces.

5 Make use of high-level storage that can be accessed via a sliding ladder. The ladder is the key. Although you may have plenty of up-high storage, you probably won't use it efficiently if you can't access it! Make use of every bit of space that you can.

opposite I love these desk beds. There are all sorts of clever designs – even a bookshelf that can be pulled down into a bed. Genius!

In every study, you need to maximise the usable space you have at desk level, so the more storage you can integrate at high levels, the better.

Study storage

'Organising is what you do before you do something, so that when you do it, it is not all mixed up.' A.A. Milne

Finding a self-contained and private space to work within your home is difficult enough, but there is an even bigger challenge involved in incorporating all the storage you are going to need for your office to function efficiently and properly. Very few of us have the discipline to keep our office spaces immaculate and free from clutter, and I certainly think we are a long way off from a study space that will operate as a truly paperless office. It is, however, important to run a 'minimal' office, and to do this you need to develop a simple archiving system that stores items depending on the level of accessibility required.

In simple terms the bulk of your stuff can be organised into three categories:

Permanent archived storage these are all of the items that are incredibly important to you, but don't need to be accessed on a regular basis. They can often be stored in high-level storage spaces that are more difficult to reach, such as loft spaces or high cupboards or shelves.

Semi-permanent storage This is storage in a more accessible location. such as lever-arch files that don't need to be near your desk. Semi-permanent storage will often have doors, to allow you to hide most of your clutter out of sight. There's no reason why you can't use tubs, baskets or boxes to organise your things; however, you'll want to tuck them away out of sight. There tends to be a lot of semi-permanent storage in the average office.

Easy-to-access, everyday-use storage This is the stuff you are going to need near or around your desk. Things like materials, writing equipment, books, paper and reference materials often need to be accessed constantly, so they'll need to be very close at hand. These sorts of items are far better stored in open shelving or drawer units, such as the classic Bisley metal-drawer systems or – one of my personal favourites – the classically designed and brilliantly functional art-storage unit designed by Joe Colorubo. More affordable study storage can be purchased from Habitat and IKEA, as well as many other suppliers.

The range in standards from high-end contemporary products all the way through to elegant yet simple products is absolutely huge. Measure your space carefully before you begin; you'll want to make use of every single bit of available wall space.

above Always go for a desk chair on castors so you can move easily about the space.

opposite A variety of storage options is essential and a view outside is a bonus!

Study finishes and materials

When selecting materials and finishes for your new study space, the most important thing to consider is to keep things as simple as possible. Too many changes in your materials or finishes will make a space feel even more cluttered and complicated than it needs to be. In order to achieve a creative and calm atmosphere, a minimal palette is certainly the way forward. You can then enliven the space through your own creativity, and selecting interesting design features and personal belongings to surround you.

Getting the finishes and materials right in your study

1   Select a hard-wearing floor surface. This is important for your office chair, which is bound to have castors, to move freely across the floor. If you can't move around easily, your ability to work efficiently in your space is going to be severely affected. So, all flooring needs to be smooth and even. Similarly, choosing coarse, textured or riven tiles will make it difficult to keep desks and storage units upright – and this is a big consideration if you have bookshelves that will topple if they don't have a sturdy, flat base. Flush and simple timber floors or stone, tiled or concrete floors are the best options. If you want to create an atmosphere of increased comfort, you can always select a good-quality rug, but make sure your chair castors can be adjusted to accommodate this.

2   I like to keep walls incredibly white, which effectively creates a blank canvas and a completely neutral palate onto which you can then impose your personal belongings or artworks. I think it's better to enliven the space with things that will inspire you, rather than colours that can create the wrong mood from time to time. Choosing white paint will also ensure that your space is as light and as bright as possible, which is the ideal environment for most tasks – particularly if you are working with photographs, drawings or artwork

3   Make sure that you have personal photos, pictures or messages that give you inspiration. This can be anything from pictures of your family, an inspirational painting or one of your favourite photographs that captures a fond memory. In those moments when work becomes too much, you can sit back and be inspired by the things that surround you. In my office, I have pictures of my family and a small abstract sculpture of a thinking man, which I first bought when I went into practice. This has been with me in every study space I have ever had at home.

opposite No structural changes were made here to make the space feel bigger. The trick was to declutter, provide more storage space and use furniture appropriate for the space. Simple!

below If you've got a joiner on site doing other work for you, why don't you ask him to create a bespoke storage system for you, which will incorporate all three types of storage in a beautiful, easy-to-access format that uses your existing space efficiently.

4   Go for simple, smooth surfaces that can be easily dusted and
    cleaned regularly. Fancy scrolling on desks and bookshelves may
    be gorgeous to look at, but they will be a nightmare to keep clean
    and free of dust.
5   Blinds – that pull up or pull down – can be a great way to regulate
    the light, to avoid it shining in your eyes while you are peering
    at the computer screen, or allowing it to flood in when you are
    working at a specific task. Blinds are also easy to keep clean, and
    won't trap the dust. If you are anything like most people, your
    study probably isn't cleaned as often as the rest of the house, in
    an attempt to avoid disrupting your work or dislodging piles of
    'essential' papers and books. So go streamlined wherever you can.

The affordable study

Great study spaces can be achieved on the smallest budget. In fact, the only product in which you'll really need to invest some good money is your chair. You'll be spending a lot of time sitting at your desk, so your chair needs to be ergonomically designed and correctly positioned to avoid any long-term damage to your back or neck.

Chairs

So make sure your chair is comfortable, adjustable in height and position, and suited to the way you work. Castors are a must, to give you the flexibility to move around. A good chair isn't always cheap, and you pretty much get what you pay for. If you find something unbelievably affordable, with all of these features, you can be pretty sure that it will break within a year and offer little comfort or support. So, invest in a good chair that will last you a lifetime. Some of the best study chairs from the best manufacturers often come with very long guarantees.

Desks

When it comes to desks, I've always wanted to get something absolutely stunning – a precious design object that sits, in all its glory, in the middle of a great space. Unfortunately, I've never had enough room to achieve this – although I'm hoping that when my basement is finished I will!

As a result, for the last 10 years, I've always used the simplest and cheapest IKEA desks – with a simple, rectangular laminate top with screw-in cylindrical legs. These are sturdy, functional, perfect for small spaces, and ridiculously cheap! I have four of them strung together, making my office desk space a perfect L-shape. I can type in one area and draw in another.

Flooring

Make sure you have hard-wearing flooring in your study space. Not only is it easier to clean, but you'll be able to negotiate it much more easily with your chair. Good-quality, timber-laminate floors (not the horribly cheap, thin timber laminate that feels like fake, plastic timber – please, please don't buy this stuff) are becoming more affordable by the day. Timber-engineered board is the best, as this is a thicker laminate – often around 6mm thick. If you want to soften the space up a bit, then use rugs in key areas where you would like a bit of comfort.

Laptops can be the worst offenders for long-term neck injuries as the screen is often too low when you are seated at a desk. Make sure you buy a stand on which to place your laptop, so the screen is directly ahead of you and at eye level when you are staring straight ahead. I have one of these stands in my own study and use a separate wireless keyboard for typing. It's the business!

Storage

Affordable storage units cover every part of the home-furnishings market. On even the cheapest budget imaginable, it is possible to fully kit out your study with some original storage solutions. If money is tight, don't bother going anywhere else but IKEA. I get home delivery every time to save the hassle. And, even though I hate putting the stuff together, the low cost makes it all worthwhile in the end. Using the same company for your storage needs (and even some of your other furniture) means that you can mix and match to create a unified look on a budget.

If you've got an unusual space, look at low-end kitchen shelving and units, which tend to be more flexibly sized. You can adapt them to your use, and if you are fussy about the appearance, get your joiner to knock up some splendid doors. Organise your belongings on shelves and within units with inexpensive baskets or plastic tubs; unless you've got the budget, there is no need for fancy fittings.

Lighting

Anglepoise lamps are fantastic for studies, and can be redirected to shine light wherever required. These can be purchased inexpensively from all sorts of shops. Get them in a few different colours, to provide a functional splash of colour. It's worth remembering, too, that light-coloured or white furniture will provide a great reflective surface to bounce around whatever natural light comes into the room, and make your light fittings work that much harder, too.

left An IKEA office. Timber floors, a comfortable chair on castors, natural and task lighting, and plenty of storage – it is all you need.

The ideal study

For any office space to function well, all of the services need to be very carefully located. There is going to be a huge demand for plug sockets to cope with all the technology in the room – particularly if you want to avoid messy cables, wires and extension leads. It's better to have too many points than not enough! Design in the number of sockets you need, including any TV aerial points and wireless Internet systems.

Although I would love a study with a similar design, style and scale to that of St Jerome, I am more than happy to accept something far more simple and humble in my own home. We recently turned one of our smaller bedrooms into a home study and office. It's a reasonable size, and seems perfectly suited for two people who may want to work from home.

It's difficult to generalise the ideal study, as everyone has very specific needs depending upon the type of work they do. Let's look at my study, which will give you an ideal of how my space works for me. Bearing some of these features in mind, you can then create something special that suits your individual requirements.

My study

My study measures 3.5 metres by 3.5 metres square, and is accessed by a door in the corner.

- Alongside the door – and against the back wall of the room – there is full-height and full-width storage. This provides an enormous amount of integrated storage space for all of my stationery, cameras, box files, drawings – and all of the stuff I need to store for my work.
- Rather than having full-height storage for books, there is, to one side, a simple low-level unit that runs the whole width of the space, which opens up the room.
- We have a number of desks that are the same width and depth, linked together in an L-shaped formation, with my 'workstation' directly positioned in front of the window. The remainder of the desk space provides layout room for drawing, as well as printers and scanners.
- As the desk turns round to form the L, there is an additional second desk.
- My layout of this study room could not work any better. I've even raised the ceiling height; instead of having a flat ceiling above me, it now follows the slope of the roof, adding to the sense of space.
- To allow the study to double up as a guest bedroom, there is a mezzanine deck where a ladder can be taken from the side and used to climb up to a deck to sleep. Unfortunately, with so much work to do, I haven't had the chance to use it!

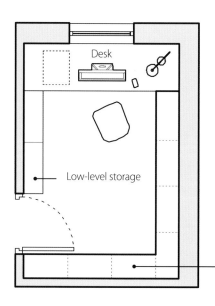

Desk

Low-level storage

Full-height book/file storage

Prefab offices

Thankfully I had a room to spare to create my own study room, but if you can't afford to lose any space in the house – and have room to spare in your garden – you can always consider having a prefabricated shed or studio built.

I would definitely *love* this type of space, but my London garden simply isn't big enough. An end-of-the-garden shed or studio is the perfect way to escape from the house and work with no distractions. In fact, it's a brilliant way of feeling disconnected enough from your home, while having a self-contained, private work space to which you can easily 'commute', with a gentle walk to the end of the garden!

This type of work space is become increasingly popular as more and more people set up work at home. These prefabricated studios can be ordered in all different shapes and sizes, as well as truly exciting designs. As there is such a powerful connection with your garden space – and just that small disconnection from your home – you have a little sense of 'travelling' to work, and may find it easier to close the door and get on with family life at the end of the day. You'll also be free of the distractions that can haunt or tempt you if you are inside your home.

If you are one of those lucky people out there who has one, I'm jealous!

above My office!

below If you can afford the space, a pre-fab office like this is ideal.

Playrooms

'Children's games are hardly games. Children are never more serious than when they play.' Michel de Montaigne

My kids are, without a doubt, the most important things in my entire life; and, if I'm honest, they bring the house to life. As much as I love to have a few hours of peace and tranquillity when they are not at home, the spaces just don't feel the same without them.

Kids do, however, present one key problem: an unbelievable amount of *stuff*! My kids are two, five and seven, and the amount of paraphernalia that they've acquired is absolutely staggering. And as they graduate up the years, it's getting worse! My two-year-old has an unfortunate obsession with anything plastic, which goes against the grain of everything that I hold dear! The five-year-old has made the step up from plastic to wooden toys and books, which makes me happier. These items do not, however, take up any less space! My seven-year-old? Well, he's progressed to gadgets and things like electronic drum kits. I'm bursting with pride, but the *mess*!

All this stuff needs a place to live. The kids all have decent-sized bedrooms, and we certainly *aim* to keep some of these things happily ensconced there, but there is a worrying creep effect going on, particularly at certain times of the day. And after the weekend, all this stuff is spread across the house at random. It's like living in a house with a trio of Tasmanian devils! We are now doing up our basement, and one of our main priorities is to create a separate playroom or den. There is something to be said for being able to close the door and forget that all that stuff is there.

If you can afford the space – either a separate room or even a separate zone within a larger room – creating a playroom will give you a fighting chance of keeping control of the chaos. It will also help your kids to realise that although you are happy to have a relaxed and playful atmosphere in your home, there are boundaries that need to be set! One of these is keeping toys and games in a designated space.

below On *The Home Show* we created this dedicated playroom – can you imagine anything better if you were a kid!

A space of their own

A playroom is very much your children's own space, just as your master bedroom or study is yours. I am not suggesting that we hark back to the Victorian days, where a separate nursery housed the kids, leaving the rest of the house feeling formal and stuffy. Equally, however, it does help to have dedicated zones where your children can have a sense of ownership, and let down their hair a little. Play is good for children, and there can be nothing worse than having constant interruptions because they are creating too much mess. It will also do wonders for your own spirit to have the clutter removed to one space.

All parents want to create an atmosphere that benefits everyone within the household, and if you can all get on with things without feeling as if you are on top of each other, you'll be that much closer to achieving that aim. Best of all, any playroom or den should be great fun, and designing it will give you the chance to create the space that you wish you'd had when you were a kid. It really is child's play!

Creating space

Kids don't actually need that much room to play. A quiet spot with a few square metres for them to sit comfortably on a rug is enough to keep them happy. One of the dangers of allocating too much space is that you end up collecting more and more stuff, which inevitably creates more and more mess. The size of the space you need will obviously depend upon the number of kids you have, but make sure you don't allocate too much space if you want to maintain an element of control.

Whenever people tell me that they want to move house to gain some more space, they commonly say that they need the room because their kids have so much stuff. I usually reply that it would be a lot cheaper to get rid of the stuff and stay where they are. The truth is that we do live in an age of materialism; never before have our kids been so fortunate, and had so many personal possessions. It's arguable that things have gone too far, and, with kids of my own, I just might agree. We can't blame our kids, because we are the ones purchasing the next best things; however, it is putting *enormous* pressure on the space in our homes.

When I am making *The Home Show*, I am often absolutely shocked by the amount of stuff that the British public hoards. So, before you complain that you haven't got enough storage space, undertake a mass clear-out of the hundreds of things you don't need.

Before planning the layout of your playroom

1   Be absolutely ruthless and declutter anything you don't use regularly. My house rule is that if my kids haven't seen it or played with it within the last six months, then out it goes – straight to the charity shop. The idea of a playroom is not to fill it to the rafters, but to provide a designated, inspiring place for your kids to play.

2   Put any very special objects that have sentimental value on display on shelving, or carefully pack them away into a more permanent storage area – preferably out of sight. You want your kids to use the space, not live in fear that they might damage a prized possession.

3   Provide a reasonable level of storage. High-level storage that is only really accessible to adults effectively becomes semi-permanent storage, which your whole household might need. It's also a good place to keep toys and games that may not be appropriate for all the kids, or which they may later grow into. Put doors on your units, to hide stuff away.

4   Low-level storage should be more open and easily accessible, and contain the books and toys that your kids use on a regular basis. If you have too much there, chances are that half of it won't get a play, or your child will feel too overwhelmed to settle into the fun. Some parents like to keep a rotating series of baskets or bins, so that every couple of weeks the toys 'change' and appear much more exciting again.

5   Consider designing in some desks for your kids. You may choose to locate these in the bedroom and away from the playroom, but I think that if your kids are disciplined enough to do their homework within the playroom, you can more easily make it part of their routine. There's no doubt that kids need to learn to concentrate in even a playful environment, but the other side of the coin is that they won't feel like they are being 'sent' to their rooms to do their homework as a penalty.

6   Kids love to play in light spaces. Try to get as much natural light as possible into the playroom, ideally locating any desks nearest to the window.

7   In most other rooms of the house, I always promote fully integrated storage. Here, however, I make an exception! Having bookshelves or units that can be easily moved around – and even having furniture on castors – allows you to constantly reconfigure the space to adapt to your kids' changing needs as they grow up. It's always great for your kids to be in a playroom that feels dynamic, exciting, playful and relaxed, rather than having everything stuck in its place and feeling quite stuffy.

Planning your playroom layout

The ideal playroom should be located in an area of a house where the kids are far enough away to feel free to make lots of noise and have fun, but close enough for parental supervision. As kids get older, moving them further away can suit everyone best!

If you have a large enough garden, one of the perfect ways to create a playroom is to actually build a separate playhouse. What could be more fun? These playhouses generally double up as summerhouses for the entire family, and come in a huge range of sizes. Take a peek at what's available on the market, and you'll come across all kinds of prefabricated playhouse structures – from the modernist cubes to the ornate, romantic and more traditional Hansel and Gretel-style house.

The style doesn't matter much, as that's going to be individual to you, but if you do decide to go for a separate structure, you need to remember that they may be underused. If it's cold or rainy the kids are unlikely to want to trek out there, and if you have to keep your doors and windows firmly sealed against the elements, you won't really be able to watch them either! For days like these, you are still going to need some form of play area within your home.

opposite A mezzanine floor is the perfect place for a playroom. This is a great space for kids to play - a range of colour, soft surfaces, natural light and, from the room below, the mess is out of sight!

Lighting your playroom

We adults can sometimes forget just what it is like to be a little kid. The growing-up process can erase some of that magic, and it can be hard to put ourselves back in that position again. But try you must! For your playroom to be a complete success, you need to get into the minds of your children, to work out what is important for them on a practical level.

It goes without saying that lighting is incredibly important to ensure that your kids can see what they are doing. They'll become frustrated and disinterested if they have to fiddle about with toys or artwork in dim light. Ideally, too, they'll want a reasonable amount of natural light during the day to make their playroom a fun rather than a depressing place. But, artificial lighting is something which you can really go to town over in a playroom!

As well as task lighting within the general ambient lighting scheme – to allow your kids to see their books and toys – the playroom is the most perfect place for decorative and sculptural lighting that doesn't really have any practical purpose other than adding to the fun and romance of the place.

Go kid-friendly

opposite Try to get as much natural light into the playroom as possible.

My kids are huge fans of sculptural lights that come in all shapes and sizes, but their favourites are undoubtedly the brightly coloured, randomly shaped objects that sit on the floor. Having lighting at a low level is great for kids – they are able to learn how to control it themselves because they have easy access to the switches. What's more, kids love being able to create their own ambience!

It goes without saying that safety is absolutely paramount with any easily accessible lighting. You need to steer clear of any lamps or fittings that can overheat and become hot to the touch. Always buy your lamps from reputable companies, whose products conform to all the rigorous tests and safety requirements for children's lighting.

The children's lighting departments within most home-improvement and furniture stores are absolutely incredible compared to what they were like when I was a kid. They are packed with starlights, LEDs, fibre-optic lights, fairy lights and lighting sculptures that can make your playroom beautiful, fun, atmospheric and totally original. There is absolutely no point in holding back – your kids will love it, and you'll be amazed by how inexpensive it can be.

Playroom design features

Any design feature for a kids' playroom has to be something that lifts their spirits, makes them smile and allows them to do things that they may not be allowed to do in the rest of the house. This is their space! Never forget that the enjoyable things that you produce for them in your home will stay with them for the rest of their lives. Magical environments create magical memories, and you can't put a price on that.

In my home, I have created unusual spaces with glass floors; when the kids lie on them, they think they are flying! This is powerful stuff! Design features like these will stay in their memories for the rest of their lives. So, really think about what unusual and interesting design features you can include in your kids' playroom. Here are just a few things that I love:

1   Built-in alcoves. Creating little alcoves built into the space can create small-scale and comfortable hideaways that your kids will love. Remember that when your kids are small, small is beautiful. Small recesses and alcoves can provide spaces where your kids can snuggle up, read a book, relax and feel like they are in a cosy, warm, protected space. They are also the perfect spot to create secret forts that only invited guests can visit.

2   Window seats. A large sill with a soft surface where kids can sit by the window to play with books or toys is a wonderfully romantic place to be. Obviously ensure that you have all the appropriate safety catches and locks on the windows. Use the space cleverly, too. A padded seat that can be lifted up to reveal a space with baskets of toys or books creates yet more all-essential storage.

3   Mezzanine levels or play decks. Changing the levels within a space makes an ordinary flat, boring room seem far more interesting in your children's world. Create raised areas of flooring to redefine different zones within the room. Some may be softer and cosier than others, and some can be harder and more practical. You can use rugs, carpeting or colour to define the zones if you don't have the option of creating different levels; however, it can be very simple to create a raised platform in even the smallest room, and it can become an impromptu stage for the inevitable dramatic productions that will take place over the years. Why not install a slide to allow quick exits from mezzanine spaces?

4   While making *The Home Show*, I've got myself into quite a lot of trouble by encouraging kids to draw on the walls. I'm actually quite proud of this! OK, I'm not saying kids should be able to draw on any wall in the house, but don't be so precious about playroom space. Provide whiteboards and blackboards on large areas of the playroom walls, so your kids can be set free to have

above Use colourful storage items to bring the room to life.

Your children have the most amazing ability to absorb the feeling and atmosphere of the environment around them, and the space you provide for them in the early years of their lives will completely structure their futures. Our ultimate aim as parents is to make our kids happy within a happy home.

fun and draw as much as they like. How often have you had to tell your kids not to draw on this or that, or be careful with their pens? The playroom is *their* space, so give them defined areas, chalk, washable pens and even paint, and let them loose!

5   Personal artwork. Animate your kids' rooms with all of their stuff. Most of our kids are creative from a young age, building, making and drawing things. Celebrate all of those creative things within their playroom; put up display shelves, pinboards for artwork and even suspend some creations from the ceiling.

6   Climbing walls. A wall that is a couple of metres high will seem like a mountain to a small kid. I know that my kids have got far too much energy and will find their own climbing surfaces all over the house to burn some of it off! Why not install a mini-climbing wall, surrounded by cushions, mats or beanbags? It will bring a smile to your children's faces – and their spaces – and hopefully not too many bruises.

7   Entertainment. This is a controversial area, because some parents will undoubtedly be keen to keep this as a creative zone, with books, toys and artwork to keep kids occupied. So, do you want a TV? Personally, I think this is not bad thing. I'm not a fan of TVs in kids' bedrooms, which should be more contemplative, quiet spaces, conducive to sleep. However, a playroom is intended to be a hive of activity, and can easily accommodate a TV. It can be a bonus as your kids get older and begin to want to watch their own programmes in peace, and can also be a bit of a godsend when they are tired and just want to flake out in front of a DVD. It's your call, obviously, based on how you view your kids' relationship with the TV in your home.

8   Arts and crafts centre. Kids love to get messy, and if you are careful to get in the right kind of flooring, it's great to allow them to exercise their creativity without worrying about the mess. Try to create a corner of the room where they can experiment with paint, glue, glitter and all the other bits and pieces that can completely ruin any other room in the house. Fix a roll of paper to the wall in a holder, which they can pull out and use as they need it, and build in some good storage for all their little pots of creative fun. A sturdy table is also ideal for this space, with a washable cover on top, and perhaps a mess mat underneath.

9   Durable, washable flooring. My favourite is rubber, which can be run up to the skirting boards to create an easy-to-clean, sturdy and almost indestructible space! It comes in a huge range of fun colours; it won't stain, and it provides a cushion for lively little ones.

Furnishing your playroom can be great fun, but bear in mind that kids grow quickly and the little tables and chairs can soon be too small. There are now some amazing products on the market to deal with this problem; for example, a three-in-one table from The Land of Nod, which adjusts to three different heights. They also have fantastic activity tables with built-in storage and rolls of paper to draw across the top; if you get one at the appropriate height, it will serve as a desk when your child needs to settle down to a little work; even teenagers will appreciate the opportunity to doodle!

Playroom storage

In any kids' playroom, the most important thing you'll need to do is to provide flexible storage solutions. Anything you purchase has to be durable and long-lasting, but also able to move with the times! As your kids grow, they are going to demand different levels of storage to accommodate their changing needs. Minimalism may have been popular within the family home over the past decade or so, but do bear in mind that kids are *not* naturally minimalist!

The best storage for kids

There are a number of different types of storage solutions that you must try to integrate into your playroom:

Hanging storage Low-level storage pegs or hangers are a great way of encouraging your kids to hang up their own gear. Within a playroom, you will always need hanging space for aprons, protective clothing for art, and bags (including school bags). Kids take a great deal of pride in having their peg personalised with their name, too! It is the kind of thing they become used to at school, so why not at home?

Display areas Your kids are busy little bees, constantly making and producing things. The tops of chests of drawers and open shelves are natural display areas for favourite toys and models. A simple pinboard is a great way to celebrate their creative artwork.

Bookcases Books are such a vital part of a kid's development and should be easily accessible within an open bookcase. Make sure the shelving is at their level; low, long bookcases are ideal. For little ones, baskets of board books will become a treasure trove of delights.

Built-in shelving If you do decide to build in any shelving or storage, make sure that works for kids, no matter what their age. There is no point in spending money building shelving for tots that becomes completely redundant when they become teenagers. Personally, I prefer more flexible storage solutions. Shelves at all heights will grow with your kids; when they are small, you can use the top shelves to allow a rotation system of toys, keeping some out of view and revealing them when they become tired of old favourites. As teenagers, they can use this space for their own things. This also works well if you have a range of ages within your family; teenagers will enjoy having their belongings out of reach of younger siblings!

Containers Over the last seven years or so, I have probably bought enough containers from home-improvement stores to last me a lifetime. They are, however, perfect for organising your kids' things. Stacking colourful plastic boxes or baskets within efficient storage units allow you to organise all of your kids' belongings. Containers

above Open shelves can be used for storage as well as for displaying things.

The market has finally realised that our kids are a fundamental part of a home and product designers and manufacturers have developed a whole range of different storage products to meet our individual needs.

above and left There are some brilliant products on the market which can make storage attractive and fun for kids.

on castors are also a great help as they can be wheeled in and out of storage units or from beneath raised decks. If your kids have a lot of sporting equipment that doesn't fit neatly anywhere else in the house, look for tall metal baskets that will hold a clutch of balls, and some bats and racquets, too.

Functional furniture Look for tables with shelves, drawers and cubbyholes, and desks that lift up to reveal space for stationery or books. If you do go for a TV, choose a stand that will hold the DVD collection, with a pocket to hold the remote. Shelving units with space to hold big baskets are also ideal.

As a parent you really need to be a creative storage designer so that you maximise every single square inch of space in the most efficient and easy-to-access way possible.

Playroom finishes and materials

When selecting the materials and finishes for your children's playroom, you have to balance the need for every surface to be practical, durable and easy to clean, with the equally clear need for comfort. This is one reason why creating different zones – or different levels – within the same space can work so well. It gives you the opportunity to vary the quality of the finishes to suit the particular mood of your child; does she want to snuggle up and read a book, or make a suitable mess with her papier mache project? She'll need room for both!

The best family homes are often those in which everyone feels relaxed and comfortable; within *any* playroom, you want to avoid the culture of 'don't touch this' or 'don't touch that'. In fact, a playroom should be designed so that you *never* have to use that phrase. You can't be uptight and worry about scratches, fingerprints and other signs of wear and tear, and you can't be precious about your kids exercising their creativity – with its accompanying mess!

below Storage bags like these are one of the cheapest and easiest ways of clearing away the clutter.

I always try to select materials and surfaces that wear well and actually look better over time. Wood and stone are perfect for this, and can provide the ideal floor finish. Highly durable carpets can be used for areas that you want to soften. The fantastic thing about carpet is that it comes in all sorts of finishes, designs and colours. But you must make sure you select a type of carpet that is maintenance-free and easy to clean. Rubber flooring is fantastic for kids' playrooms – it couldn't be easier to clean, it comes in a vast range of colours and textures, and it would take a herd of very messy elephants to make any impact on its surface.

The following tips will help you to choose finishes and surfaces that should make your life (and those of your kids) that much easier:

1 Choose floor finishes that age well, and look better with time. Scuffs, scratches and even splodges of paint will make them look suitably rustic. Stone and wood are good for this.

2 Avoid any finish that isn't durable and easy to clean.

3 Try to balance hard surfaces with soft surfaces, to provide your kids with some comfort. A thick rug or carpet in one part of the room, with some washable cushions in a variety of shapes and sizes, is ideal to create the cosy space.

4 Soft furnishings, such as carpets, rugs, cushions and beanbags will also provide some acoustic absorption, and keep down the noise!

5 Think about laying some floor tiles with games or numbers printed on them; I've seen some great hopscotch tiles, and even some that act as a road system for little trucks and cars. Educational suppliers are your best bet for these products. Use your imagination! When kids get older, a well-placed rug can hide the more juvenile elements, but you'd be amazed by how many teenagers find ways to use their old favourites.

6 I'm a huge fan of decorative wallpaper within kids' playrooms. Choosing an inspirational and colourful design that can allow your kids to dream of other worlds and storytelling can be life-changing. I can still vividly remember the character that I had on my wallpaper when I was a kid. Although their needs will change as they grow, wallpaper is relatively inexpensive and easy to change from time to time. You can also paint over the lot when your teenager demands a cooler space.

7 Blackboard paint. For just a few quid, you can buy a pot of blackboard paint and paint a wall surface within the playroom. All of us love writing messages and drawing on blackboards; creations can be easily be brushed away and redesigned again and again. This is a beautifully dynamic wall that will constantly change the way any playroom feels. Kids and grown-ups: please get drawing.

Whether your finishes are soft or hard, they should always be fun, colourful, vibrant and full of life. Durable, safe and easy to clean is also important!

Playroom costs

Apart from the thousands of toys that your kids will deem necessary, there are two primary things that will need to be paid for in order to create an exciting playroom space that is both practical and fun.

The first is to invest the right amount of money in the fixed finishes that will need to be part of the space for many years to come. These are items such as flooring, wall finishes, electricity-point positions and fixed lighting. You really should not compromise on these elements. If, for example, your flooring is timber or stone, then invest in a product that gives the highest level of durability, with the lowest level of maintenance. The fixed lighting positions need to have a long lifespan, so, again, make sure that you select the right product. Ideally, you'll want something that can be adjusted to change the height of the beams. As your kids get taller, they'll be working and playing at a higher level!

The second category of things that you'll need to pay for are those that will probably change in the short to medium term, in order to reinvent your playroom to adapt to your children's growth and development. So when it comes to flexible storage solutions, paint colours, rugs, decorative and sculptured lighting, and all free-standing furniture, go for affordable.

When visiting home-improvement stores and furniture shops, I'm always astonished by just how affordable these items can be. Unless you can find something that will grow with your kids, there is no point in investing heavily in things that are bound to change in a few years' time. The golden rule here is to invest your money wisely in fixtures and finishes that need to be more permanent, and go affordable for the things you plan to change.

Your carpets, flooring, light fittings and even your wall finishes need to last, so push your budget as hard as possible to invest in the best possible fixed elements you can afford.

Ecology

It is so important that you create an environment in your home where your kids are reminded of the importance of protecting the environment. They are obviously made aware of these issues at school; however, in order to take steps as a family towards an ecological and more sustainable way of living, we need to introduce our kids to the things they can do to make a difference at home. Your kids will become a part of the next, sustainable generation, and can adopt environmentally sound practices from a very early age.

Here's what to do:

1. When your kids get bored of toys, allow them to be part of the recycling process. If toys are damaged or unusable, then take them (and your kids) to the local recycling centre, and show them how they can be made into something new and exciting. Take toys they've simply outgrown to charity shops or car-boot sales. As long as they don't hit the bin, you've established good working practice.
2. Install a mini-recycling hub in the playroom. All you need is a few simple, colour-coded containers that your kids can use to throw away any paper, plastics, tins or juice boxes. This will make recycling a part of their everyday lives.
3. Use environmentally friendly paints whenever possible. The range is huge.
4. Make sure that all soft finishes, such as carpets, rugs and fabrics are from sustainable sources, and can be cleaned successfully at a low temperature in the washing machine.
5. Use energy-saving lightbulbs throughout the playroom.
6. Installing an ecological underfloor heating system within the playroom provides a fantastic level of warmth and comfort, particularly when they spend a lot of time at floor level. Running this heating system at a lower temperature can save on your energy bills, while avoiding the use of radiators that can often pose a risk of burning to your kids.

One thing that is worth spending a little money on is your paint. Eco-friendly is the name of the game when it comes to kids, so choose low-VOC options that won't release harmful chemicals into their environment.

The ideal playroom

All kids are different, and your playroom will have to be designed with your children's individual interests in mind. The most important thing to remember is that the space has to match their needs and moods. Every playroom needs a quiet space, and a place where they can get seriously messy. The whole point of a playroom is that it offers your kids the opportunity to do their own thing in their own environment; for this reason, they'll need to be able to operate it themselves! They should be able to reach their toys and games, turn on the lights or the TV, get out their arts, crafts or dressing-up gear and, most importantly, put it all away again!

The ideal playroom should include:

Enough space for your kids to play – but not too much Too much space means more mess.

Different levels within the same room This may not always be possible, but it's worth a try if you have the space. For example, if you are able to open up a flat ceiling to the slope of the roof you can create play or storage areas on mezzanine levels for first-floor playrooms. The kids will have a place to play beneath, and enjoy the light, airy space. If you do have roof space available above a room, then why not bring it into the usable space.

Direct access to the garden If your playroom is on the ground floor, try to arrange things so that your kids can access the garden directly. They'll be more likely to go in and out, and both spaces will feel more dynamic and fun.

Well-considered acoustic insulation Most of your playroom will be better suited to hard surfaces, which are easier to maintain and clean; however, the downside of this is that hard surfaces have poor acoustic qualities. There are clever ways of overcoming this. Locate storage walls against the walls that run between the playroom and any adjacent room. The storage itself becomes a buffer against the noise. If your playroom is on the first floor, and you have chosen a hardwearing floor finish, consider placing acoustic matting beneath the floor, as well as mineral-wall acoustic insulation between the floor joists. If this is too costly for you, make sure you place lots of rugs on the floor or even consider carpeting the whole area.

Flexible fixtures and furnishings Any dedicated playroom will be constantly changed. There is no point in having any fitted pieces of furniture as the room has to grow and develop as fast as your kids do. It won't be long before it is transformed from the plastic-toy workshop to the TV room, snug or multimedia suite.

below Playrooms don't have to be huge, particularly if you build in lots of efficient storage.

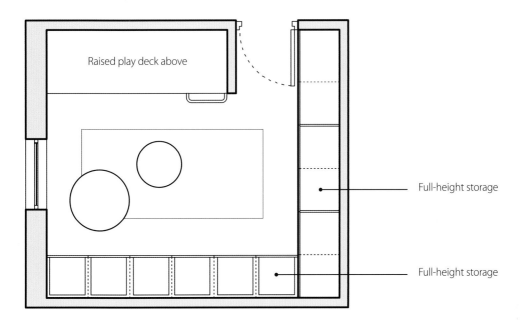

Raised play deck above

Full-height storage

Full-height storage

Colour and light You'll need natural and cleverly designed artificial lighting to illuminate those all-important tasks, and make the playroom cheery. Similarly, a playroom should be vibrant and fun in some areas, and soothing and restful in others. A great deal can be achieved with a few tins of paint. Why not go for restful greens and blues in one corner, and a riot of rainbow colours for the truck, Barbie and craft parts of the room?

Durable, easy-to-clean flooring Factor in comfort, too. Your kids will spend a lot of time on the floor in their early years, and probably as teenagers, too! A washable floor surface that improves with age is ideal; you can update the look and create comfort with some well-positioned rugs.

Storage, storage, storage – at all heights You can't really ever have enough, and kids love to be able to access baskets, bins and boxes themselves as they choose their own activities.

There are a few things to consider when creating your children's playroom. Your number-one priority is safety, so be sure that everything in the plan is kid-friendly and non-toxic. Secondly, focus on function. The furnishings and the space need to be used comfortably by your kids, and they should be able to access the things they need easily. They should also be able to put them away! Finally, create a space that can grow and develop as your children do.

Bedrooms

'The bed has become a place of luxury to me! I would not exchange it for all the thrones in the world.' Napoleon Bonaparte

Bedrooms must be beautifully calm and comfortable spaces, for adults and children alike. The ideal bedroom should be cosy and serene, allowing your mind to be cleared of the pressures of the day when you retire to bed. When you consider the fact that we do, on average, spend nearly a third of our lives sleeping, the quality of our beds and the rooms they sit in become that much more important. The space should be beautiful; the bed should be a haven.

It makes no difference if you are a traditionalist, enjoying an over-the-top bedroom and indulging in Louise XIV-style splendour, or an avid minimalist, with a room stripped bare of any ornament, decoration or distraction. In both cases, comfort and cosiness should be the order of the day, and a fundamental part of your design brief. This means that the selection of your finishes and furnishings is actually the most important choice you will have to make in your bedroom. However, to create a fully successful bedroom, all of the principles of good design need to work together.

And so to bed

Bedrooms need to serve a dual purpose – lulling you to sleep and allowing you to languish in bed for those all-too-infrequent lie-ins, but also stimulating you adequately to give you the get-up-and-go you need to get out of bed in the morning.

It's also an extremely personal room, where we undress, dream, mull over the day that has passed and plan the day ahead, and also spend intimate time with our loved ones. We take to our beds when we are ill, and retreat to our bedrooms when we want a thorough rest. It's not surprising, therefore, that creating the perfect bedroom is a challenge on a major scale.

WHAT DO YOU NEED FROM YOUR BEDROOM?

Before you begin to make changes to the décor, the layout or the space of your bedroom, you need to ask yourself how your current bedroom is working, and what more you might need.

For example:
- Do you long for your bedroom at the end of the day?
- Do you sleep well and find your bed comfortable?
- Do you feel refreshed and inspired to rise in the morning?
- Does the colour work to soothe *and* rejuvenate you?
- Do you have adequate storage to keep distracting clutter out of the way?
- Do you have space to display your most personal possessions?
- Are you able to organise your clothes and other belongings efficiently?
- Does the lighting create the right ambience and atmosphere?
- Is it easy to manage, maintain, keep clean and tidy up?
- Is the layout convenient, allowing you to switch off lights, file away your reading book and blow out the candle without leaving your bed?
- Do you have windows that provide a view and flood the room with light when you want it, but adequate coverage when you need dark?
- Is there somewhere to curl up and relax other than the bed?
- Is there space to move around?
- And, most important, is it comfortable and cosy?

Think carefully about your needs before working on the design brief for your new bedroom. A bedroom should be a sanctuary, but a functional one at that. Take your time to work out exactly what will work to create the optimum environment.

opposite top and bottom Before you redesign your bedroom, take some time to consider what your perfect bedroom would look like.

Planning your bedroom layout

When we look at the design and layout of the bedrooms in our existing homes, you can pretty well guarantee that there will always be at least one aspect that does not work. The main reason for this is that bedroom design has changed dramatically over the years, and bedrooms in existing homes really only satisfy the needs of a bygone age.

It's easy to suggest that a bedroom is only for sleep, but we all know that this is not entirely true. The 21st-century bedroom requires a very different layout to what might have been acceptable in the past. We now expect – and quite rightly so – our bedroom layouts to meet our modern-day demands. If you look at the way a simple Victorian or Edwardian bedroom would have been laid out, you'll see that there is room for the bed, a small level of storage for clothes, and usually a real fire inset within a large chimney breast in order to provide heat.

How things have changed!

Clever architecture

But the Victorians and the Edwardians were very sensitive to the way certain things should be done. Take the simple bedroom door swing, for example. In older properties, most bedroom doors always seem to be hanging in the wrong direction. The doors were hung in a certain way, to prevent you from seeing the bedroom when you opened the doors. In other words, if the bedroom space was predominantly to the right of the door, the door would be hung with its *hinges* on the right. And, alternatively, if the majority of the bedroom space was off to the left, the door would be hung with its hinges on the left.

This was a very clever and simple architectural device intended to act as a screen to the room; if someone tried to walk into a bedroom, where its owner might be in a compromising position, that owner would have a few seconds to redress the situation before the visitor could fully open the door and enter. If the door was hung on the other side, then as soon as you turned the handle and pushed the door open – by as little as an inch – you would be able to see everything in the room.

These are the subtle things that modern house-builders just don't understand; very clever, yet understated architectural devices built and laid out in a particular way can have a very powerful impact on the way a space works and feels. This is the level of very fine thinking that we need to get back into our homes today.

When redesigning your bedroom layout, make sure you consider the following points:

1   What do you consider to be the perfect position for your bed? If your ideal position means making substantial changes to the layout, then you should do it; the bed position is everything.

2   Unless you want a real fire in your bedroom (which would certainly be a beautiful thing), then there is no need for the redundant chimney breast. A redundant chimney breast within a bedroom is simply a waste of space. Take it out.

3   Your bedroom-door position is also important. If it's right in the corner of the room, it can actually be quite inefficient. If you need to open your door against the side wall of your room, a large area of that wall will be unsuitable for storage. I always try to move the bedroom door at least 60 centimetres away from the face of the wall, so that you can allow a clear run of wardrobe storage down the length of the wall. There's nothing worse than opening your bedroom door and looking at the blank side of a wardrobe unit.

4   The relationship between the door and the bed is very important. I hate it when you open a bedroom door and the bed is smack bang in front of you; it's not great for privacy and it's not the nicest way to enter the room. Ideally you would open the door, have wardrobe space to one side, and the bed positioned as far away from the door as possible – and perhaps even screened in some way to give you some privacy.

5   You need to make sure there is not too much circulation space wasted within the room; however, you *do* need to provide a reasonable amount of access to be able to get to the wardrobe, walk around three sides of the bed, and, of course, get dressed. In master bedrooms, you may also need to provide easy access to an en-suite shower room or bathroom.

6   If an existing radiator position needs to be moved in order to make the space work, then do it. Ideally, your radiator should be positioned beneath the bedroom window, which is always space that is difficult to use for storage. However, the perfect solution would be to install an underfloor heating system.

Bedroom lighting

The most important aspect of bedroom lighting is designing it to celebrate the architectural character of the space.

The most important lights in any bedroom tend to be the lamps sitting on either side of your bed. These lamps are used more than any others – to provide task lighting if you enjoy reading before falling asleep, or, indeed, illuminating any task you might undertake in or on your bed. You may, of course, opt for a central pendant light as well, as this can provide a key focal point within the room. It also allows you to select a light fitting that proudly declares your sense of style.

I have to say that I am not really a fan of recessed downlighters within bedrooms – unless they are used as directional lights to illuminate pictures or artwork on bedroom walls. Downlights tend to give a very harsh level of light, and if they are wrongly directed, they can end up shining straight into your eyes and producing a high level of glare. If you do use them in your bedroom, avoid placing them over the bed. It simply isn't in keeping with the creation of a peaceful, calm atmosphere.

Creating the right atmosphere

Low-level lights, recessed just above the skirting boards, can provide a soft glow of light across your floor, and this can be quite atmospheric. And, if you are really into your lighting and feeling quite brave, you could look into installing coloured lights to create a particular mood. I would avoid choosing the colour red, as this may raise a few eyebrows in your neighbourhood! Red is also a stimulating colour that may not be conducive to restful sleep.

The golden rule for any lighting in your bedroom is to ensure that every lamp or fitting is fixed to a circuit with a dimmer switch – to give you complete flexibility to achieve the mood and feel you want. This means that you will have to carefully select the number of fittings and the method used to be able to control them. If your budget is plump, and you like your gadgets, it might be worth going for a remote-controlled system to operate a small computer panel that can give you all the levels, variations and flexibility that you need.

If you have high ceilings in the room, it may be worth installing a number of wall lights that shine upwards (up-lighters) to enhance the sense of space above you.

Lighting ideas

1 When lighting dressing tables or vanities, make sure that you light them horizontally from both sides, to avoid casting shadows across your face. Equally, avoid any harsh fluorescent or white light near vanities; no one needs a reminder that the years are creeping on!

2 Candles can be a fantastic way to create an atmospheric, romantic glow. Place them in alcoves, if you can, and well away from any soft furnishings or the bed.

3 Fit lighting inside wardrobes and other units, which will come on automatically when the doors are opened.

4 Choose lampshades with a white interior and warm colours on the exterior, and fit them with a clear bulb to provide a warm, soothing light.

5 In children's rooms, you'll need to avoid having flexes and cords anywhere near the bed, or where little fingers can reach them. Best to avoid table-top lamps and fit something on the wall instead.

6 Choose your colours carefully when purchasing children's lamps – a hot pink glow might be fun in the daytime, but it can prevent your child from falling asleep!

7 Dimmers are particularly good for kids, as you can slowly tone down the light to prepare them for sleep.

8 Children's bedrooms often have desks, so ensure that there is good task lighting available – ideally lighting that can be directed according to needs.

above Soft lighting is best for dressing tables.

below Kids' rooms should have a variety of lighting. Go for bright colours when choosing the central and decorative lights and something a little more subdued for bedside lamps.

Bedroom design features

The most important design feature in your bedroom is, quite simply, your bed. Your bed is a key indicator of your design style; the choices you have available to you are limitless!

While you need to choose something that is durable and unmistakably functional, your bed is also a statement and the centrepiece of the bedroom. Practical, yes; fun, romantic, trendy or classic? Yes, yes, too!

1 For your kids' bedrooms, there is the classic bunk-bed – a brilliant, cost-effective and space-saving device.
2 If your kids need somewhere to work, the raised-platform bed with desk space beneath is an ideal solution. Teenagers may enjoy designs with a sofa or futon fitted underneath rather than the desk!
3 In your master bedroom, your bed will dictate the character of your space, so choose carefully. Do you want elegant four-poster, minimal timber, ornate antique or a bed with a substantial metal frame for a more industrial look?

What are you sleeping on?

While the selection of your bed frame most definitely defines your style, your selection of mattress (which says absolutely nothing about your style!) will certainly be a declaration of just how important comfort is to you. A bed frame can often be the most affordable part of a bed, whereas the mattress can set you back – a lot.

Mattresses are designed with varying levels of firmness, as a lighter person will obviously need light or medium support, and someone heavier will need something firm. You can actually purchase mattresses that provide light support on one half, and firm on the other, to suit the individual needs of a couple.

When you start to explore the mattress options, and the support they can offer, you'll realise that the bed frame was one of the easiest decisions you've had to make.

below One of the most important pieces of furniture you will buy.

Consider the following when choosing your mattress:

1 Would you prefer a sprung or unsprung mattress? A sprung mattress is basically made of open springs of coiled wire. An unsprung mattress is a foam mattress made of latex or slow-recovery foam.

2 What sort of base do you want the mattress to sit on? A divan can give a super-luxurious feel to your mattress, and can include storage drawers beneath, which is a bonus for storage. A slatted base on which your mattress will sit won't provide the level of comfort of a divan, but you will have space under the bed to organise some storage solutions.

3 You've then got to select the degree of firmness. Do you prefer something softer or do you like it hard?

4 How much do you want to spend? Some of the more luxurious mattresses can cost thousands of pounds; however, some of the bigger department stores now produce a range of economy mattresses that are good value and very comfortable.

5 If you are going unsprung, what would you like your mattress to be made of? Do you want natural or man-made fibres?

6 If you are adventurous, you could take the plunge and go for a water bed. This is a water-filled vinyl mattress that can support your body evenly, and eliminate any pressure points. Be careful with sharp objects!

Bedroom gimmicks

If you really are into designer fun, then you may consider buying a bed frame that incorporates a range of technology. There are beds on the market today that have fully integrated plasma screens within the base of the bed frame, which rise up as and when you need them.

Some beds have integrated systems where the mattress and base can change profile to suit any required position – and all at the touch of a button. At a recent home show, I climbed into a four-poster bed that could be instantly surrounded by screens! It was absolutely packed with technology – providing TV systems and surround-sound music systems to meet your every need.

The choices you make will, of course, depend on your individual style and taste, your level of gadget obsession and, of course, how important comfort is to you. Factor in your budget, and you'll be in a fantastic position to make the right decision.

following page A beautifully calm and comfortable bedroom.

Central Park, New York · Classic Photographs by Ralf Uicker

Bedroom storage

'Space and light and order. Those are the things that men need just as much as they need bread or a place to sleep.' Le Corbusier

The world-famous architect Le Corbusier famously said that storing clothes within the bedroom is 'unhygienic'. Corb lived a fairly minimal and monastic life, so he probably didn't even have enough clothes to fill a decent-sized wardrobe. This is most certainly not the case today! Our bedrooms have not only become places to sleep and wash, but they also play the role of storing and displaying our most private and personal belongings. For this reason, it is important to assess your bedroom-storage needs well before you reconfigure your bedroom space.

Before you begin, consider the following:

1. How much storage space do you actually need? The usual answer is 'as much as possible', but in order to decide if your design is going to work, you must have a rough idea how many linear metres of storage you'll need to store *all* of your clothing – and your partner's, too.
2. How much dedicated space do you need for the storage of shoes?
3. What bedside-storage requirements do you have? Do you like to read in bed at night? If so, you'll need a light fitting, lamp and places to store your books and magazines. If you use an alarm clock, you'll need a place to display that as well.
4. Do you want to have a TV in your bedroom? If so, then you may need to consider some sort of box storage for DVDs or CDs.

below Built-in wardrobe space will be the most efficient use of space, particularly in loft rooms like this.

5   What about highly protected storage, such as a small domestic safe? These are becoming more common in many domestic homes. Gone are the days when keeping your valuables under your bed was an option.

6   Do you need a dedicated dressing area within your master-bedroom suite? This will only be possible if you have plenty of space because you'll need to build in some floor-to-ceiling storage – and mirrors.

7   What balance would you like to strike between fully built-in storage, and wall space to hang personal pictures and artworks?

8   What combination of open and closed storage do you require?

Striking a balance

The golden rule here is to get the balance right, by providing the right *amount* and *type* of storage you need. This way, your wardrobes and cupboards won't be full to bursting, nor will your bedroom feel like a substantial storage facility!

No matter what your storage requirements, you will want your bedroom to remain a beautiful space. There is a broad range of products now available, but you'll need to consider carefully before making a purchase. I guarantee you that more mistakes are made in the bedroom than anywhere else in the house! Your choice is, of course, personal, but you'll also really need to think through the way you live. So, there are *more* questions for you:

1   How much open, accessible storage do you need to display books?

2   Which areas of your space would be better suited to low-level storage – to maintain the character and proportions of the room.

3   Similarly, which areas require full-height storage – or storage that will need to be fully closed and private?

4   Which wardrobes and storage units will require artificial lighting – and do you like the idea of lighting being installed inside the unit, and activated when the doors are opened?

5   What type of style and design are you looking for in your storage units? Have you got a feel for how you'd like to decorate and furnish the room as a whole?

6   Should your storage furniture be fully fitted into the space or be free-standing? This is an important design decision! Built-in furniture generally blends in with the walls of the room, whereas free-standing items tend to be individually selected pieces that may have greater design value for you. This type of storage effectively becomes an object within the space, but you'll have to allow some circulation area around items like this. There is nothing worse than ramming together unique, highly individual pieces of furniture!

Planning your storage

It's so important to provide the right kind of storage in the right way. You'll have to sort out all of the necessary compartments required for all of your clothing and belongings to be stored properly and carefully. This will ensure that your bedroom space is very well organised, and your personal belongings aren't damaged. There is nothing more depressing than opening a wardrobe door to see everything crammed inside.

The following, very simple tips will help you to store away your stuff in style:

1 Arrange clothes of a similar type, length and colour together.
2 Allow a depth of at least 60 centimetres for all of your wardrobe storage; this is a standard wardrobe size.
3 Make sure you are very clear about what compartments you need – such as double-hanging or half-length spaces for suits, skirts and long jackets.
4 Use wooden rather than wire hangers to protect delicate items.
5 Try to incorporate drawer dividers as often as you can, to separate small items.
6 Make sure you design in racks or compartments for all of your shoes.
7 Always provide an adequate number of shelves to store jumpers, sweaters and knitwear.
8 Purchase plastic or box containers for any other important small items you may want to access easily.

For an elegant bedroom look that is both practical and beautiful, make sure you think about every single aspect of your bedroom-storage requirements at the very beginning of the design stage.

above Consider what your storage requirements are so you can get appropriate hanging rails, drawers, shelves and dividers built in. This hanging device is from IKEA.

Saving space

One of the most extreme space-saving beds I've seen (and which I absolutely love) can work really well in apartments or study-bedrooms. It's a bed that can be pulled down from the wall, when required.

We're not talking about something you would find in a nasty bedsit or something from *Rising Damp* – there are now some truly fantastic systems on the market that are integrated into storage walls. For example, shelves of books can surround a central section, which can be easily pulled down to reveal the most comfortable bed stored inside. If you live in a small house or an apartment and you need space to be adaptable and flexible, this is a brilliant way to stow away a bed when you don't need it. It is clever, elegant and simple.

There are also some fabulous pull-down desk-beds (try Cabrio beds and the Wall Bed Workshop, for example), which incorporate your bed behind your desk space. The desk is raised, and the bed folded down for use.

You'll be amazed by the space-saving beds now available on the market, in all shapes and sizes – and tucked into the most extraordinary places!

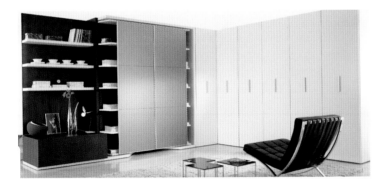

left The space-saving wall bed!

Bedroom finishes and materials

'Sleep is the golden chain that ties health and our bodies together.'
Thomas Dekker

opposite Our bedroom – perfect for us.

The finishes and materials that you choose for your bedroom are not only dependent upon your personal style and taste, but on the budget you have available. Obviously you want your bedroom finishes to be as special – and as long-lasting – as possible, so it really is very important that you allocate the right amount of money towards finishes that are going to have to withstand some wear and tear!

In my last house – where I had the tiniest budget to refurbish the master bedroom – I had little option but to sand down and whitewash the soft-wood floorboards and (in my usual style), paint the walls white. This was all I could afford, after redoing the heating, electrics and the window. The room was actually beautifully proportioned, so the whitewashing was simple and effective in creating a good bedroom.

In my current home I certainly learned from my mistakes and made sure I had enough in the budget to do the job properly. I also realised that I wanted more comfort, rather than a completely minimalist style.

My own perfect bedroom

To create the bedroom I really wanted, I did the following:

1. Laid carpeting. While timber flooring was placed in the rest of the house, it was an absolute must for me to lay carpet in the bedroom. Carpeting provides the ultimate level of comfort, making the room feel warm and cosy, as well as being quieter, as it absorbs noise rather than bouncing it around a room.
2. Installed underfloor heating. Combined with the carpet, this provided the perfect level of comfort underfoot. It's worth bearing in mind that you'll need to check that the 'tog' factor of your carpet isn't too high, or the heat won't make it through.
3. Installed dimmer switches so we can adjust the level of both the central pendant light and the bedside lamps.
4. Chose a leather, slatted-base bed with a half-decent, comfortable mattress. It's certainly not the best bed on the market, but it was good enough to suit my budget. For a few extra pounds, I bought a topper to provide an additional level of comfort.
5. Painted the room soft white. This lets as much light as possible bounce around the room. You can, however, choose to go for richer, deeper colours and possibly even wallpaper a feature wall.

While carpet is ideal for the master bedroom, you may want to think twice about your children's rooms. In my home, we had timber flooring laid, which can be easily cleaned in the event of spillages. We scattered rugs to soften certain parts of the room and add a dash of colour.

The affordable bedroom

It's easy to achieve a stunning, comfortable and functional bedroom on a budget, largely thanks to the massive number of home-improvement stores that are competing for your business. The most important thing to get right is the level of comfort and accessible storage, and, of course, spending money on the thing that matters most – your bed. With a few cool decorative touches and a clever use of lighting, you can create a sanctuary that will look like you paid a whole lot more.

When you are planning and designing your space, consider the following:

1 The most important item to invest in is your mattress. This was not only provides you with the comfort you need to get a good night's sleep, but represents a significant investment. The most beautiful bedroom is meaningless if you wake up with a bad back every morning. On even the tightest budget, your mattress should be a priority.

2 If you go for a divan, you'll need to purchase a headboard. These can, however, be knocked up quite easily using fabric or even a wall hanging behind the bed. But check out salvage yards or antique shops; I've seen some amazing wrought-iron headboards that just need a polish to do the job well. Similarly, once you've spent your money on the mattress, you can go for a budget bedstead. Simple is best, if you are on the cheap.

3 I'm a big fan of carpets in a bedroom – mainly to ensure that you experience comfort and not cold toes when you put your feet on the floor first thing in the morning. The great thing about carpet is that there are so many designs and levels of quality that you can always find something to suit even the smallest budget. And, in comparison to timber flooring, it is faster and much cheaper to lay.

4 Bedside units and lighting are very important, too, and the affordable home-improvement stores – such as IKEA – have a brilliant range of bedside storage units and bedside lamps. Make sure the lighting is adjustable and set on dimmer switches, to get the right atmosphere.

5 Cheap lampshades work well if you choose one with a warm-coloured exterior and a white interior; with a clear-glass bulb, you'll gently soften the edges of your room, and produce a relaxing, atmospheric glow.

6 Choose cheap carcasses and integrated storage from the budget range at your local home-improvement store, and ask your joiner to produce some original doors and drawer fronts. You'll save a

below The existing bedroom was a cramped and awkward space with very little width, no integrated storage and ugly downstand beams in the ceiling. On *The Home Show*, we relocated an old shower room alongside the bedroom we removed the dividing walls to make the bedroom much wider. We also redesigned the ceiling structure to remove the downstand beams creating a more elegant space.

fortune, and your wardrobes and other storage will look smart and unique.

7   Creative storage, which will allow you to declutter your bedroom space, is amazingly affordable; choose under-bed baskets and containers that keep things out of the way, and some inexpensive tubs to organise your belongings in your cupboard and wardrobe space.

8   When you purchase your bedding, buy several extra flat sheets, which can be used to create cushion covers, vanity skirts, basket inserts and even curtains on the cheap. The quality of bedding you go for will be individual to you – some people can't sleep between sheets that have a thread count of less than 200, but good sheets are still likely to be cheaper than furnishing fabrics, and they'll give your room a clean overall look.

9   Add colour and your own individual style by dotting small vases of flowers and pretty scented candles around the room, or add loads of inexpensive cushions to create a luxurious feel.

Feature walls behind the bed provide prominence to a wall, and draw your eye. This is a simple and cost-effective way to style a room using wallpaper. It can be expensive to paper an entire room, but one wall may well be within your budget. Wallpapering is an easy technique to acquire, too, so you can probably do it yourself. If you aren't into wallpaper, a splash of beautifully coloured paint will do.

The ideal bedroom

The ideal bedroom should be a perfect, personal refuge, where materials, colours, fabrics, lighting and products are very carefully selected in order to create the atmosphere you want to achieve.

Go for the best quality that you can afford, and try to keep the colour scheme in rich or pale shades; although you can most certainly have fun decorating your own personal space, some colours are more conducive to sleep than others. Staring at a vivid red wall all night long might do your head in. Get the finishes, storage, lighting and materials right and you could have the bedroom of your dreams.

Bear in mind the following when planning your new bedroom:

1 Select a bed that is the right size and style for you and your partner.
2 Buy the best-quality mattress your budget can stretch to; your choice of mattress cannot be overestimated! You need comfort and support to sleep well, so get this right. There's no point in having a smashing new bedroom that is actually unfit for its main purpose!
3 Decide whether you want a divan. A well-sprung divan can substantially alter the feel of the mattress, making it softer and more luxurious. However, it may not give the look that you want; divans are large-scale bed bases that usually run down to floor level. If you like minimalist – or a real sense of air flow around the room – they may not be right for you.
4 Make sure your bed is positioned so that it has the best aspect of the room – and a level of privacy in relation to the bedroom door.
5 Consider ways of moving the position of the door to make the room work more efficiently – and allow a greater area of wardrobe space.
6 Try to position the bed so that it has some form of view out of the bedroom window; ideally this view should be achieved from both sides of the bed.
7 Personally, I am a huge fan of carpets in bedrooms. There is nothing better than climbing out of bed in the morning and finding warm, soft carpet underfoot. Obviously, the same can be achieved with rugs, but the effect is lost when you step off the rug onto the harder surface alongside. Carpets may not have been particularly trendy over the last 10 years, but when it comes to bedroom spaces, they're certainly back.
8 If possible, install underfloor heating in your bedroom, to improve the level of comfort underfoot.
9 Make sure you install 5-amp light switches on either side of the bed, to control bedside lamps. The best case scenario is to have lamps that can be turned off manually from the bed, and via a switch by the door.

I'm not bothered about installing pendant lights in bedrooms unless you have high ceilings or a favourite light shade you really want to show off. I prefer to have bedside lamps that can be adjusted by a dimmer to create a more romantic atmosphere.

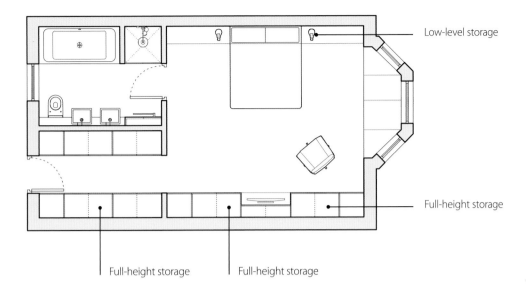

Low-level storage

Full-height storage

Full-height storage

Full-height storage

10 Try to create some sort of en-suite shower room, with direct
    access to your bedroom. Even the smallest en-suite will make a
    big difference to the way your master bedroom works.

11 Carefully consider all options when it comes to curtains or blinds
    in your bedroom. These can really define the style of your room,
    and provide colour and texture to the space. It is very important to
    consider the level of privacy you want, without compromising the
    amount of natural light coming into the space. You'll also want to
    think about the views. A flexible blind system, which can be adjusted
    to give you a combination of complete privacy and natural light, is
    ideal; good ones are retractable, to provide you with a view as well!

12 Maximise the amount of wall space available to produce as much
    storage and wardrobe space as possible. Inefficient, inadequate and
    even too much storage can begin to impinge on your bedroom's
    essential role as a refuge. Careful planning is the order of the day.

13 If you are able to have a real fire installed in your room, in the
    right position to make it work efficiently, then go for it. There
    is nothing like a fantastic, real-flame fire to create a beautiful,
    romantic ambience in your bedroom

14 If your budget can't stretch to a real fire, then the more affordable
    option is to invest in some scented candles. They are a great way
    of creating that calm and serene atmosphere, not to mention
    romance! Design in a few alcoves to hold them.

15 Consider factoring in space for an easy chair; bedrooms can be
    a wonderful place to curl up and relax, away from the hubbub of
    your family. And it's lovely to sit down to chat comfortably in the
    evenings, when you want a little privacy. You'll need some task
    lighting here, too, such as a floor-standing lamp.

Bathrooms

'There must be quite a few things that a hot bath won't cure, but I don't know many of them.'
Sylvia Plath

If I was refurbishing my home and had a very limited budget, there is no doubt that my first priority would be to build a new combined kitchen-dining room – creating a central hub or heart of the home. But second on my list would be to refurbish all of the bathrooms and shower rooms.

A smartly refurbished bathroom will certainly add value to your home and make it more appealing to potential buyers. But, more importantly, your bathroom should be a luxurious space where you can soak in the tub and relax, letting all of the stresses of the day disappear.

Getting everyone involved

With any bathroom or shower-room redesign, there are so many decisions that have to be made to get it *just* right. Bathrooms are hugely labour-intensive areas, where many different trades within the building industry will need to get involved.

- You'll need a joiner to form the space – putting up walls, moving the position of your doors, forming counter tops or vanity units, and probably integrating some storage.
- Then the plumber gets involved, to do his 'first fix' (see Section 6), after which your electrician will come on board to do his, too.
- You might need a plasterer to come in to do your ceilings and make good certain walls.
- And then comes your tiler, who will lay all of the tiles you need on your walls, floor and possibly your counter tops.
- Unless you are a dab hand with a paintbrush, you'll need a decorator to paint the walls and ceilings in the colour of your choice.
- Then *you'll* need to get out there to choose the right tiles, sanitary fittings and other fixtures, such as mirrors and towel rails.

Are you starting to get a feel for why your bathroom or shower-room redesign takes a lot of organisation and coordination? It's an *enormous* amount of hard work, but if you can get all of the decisions right along the way, it is so worth your while.

opposite You have an opportunity to be bold in your bathroom design. Be creative!

Refurbishing your existing bathroom is a great way of improving your home without having to spend a lot of money. Visit your local kitchen and bathroom companies and speak to their in-house designers. They will be happy to produce simple design plans for you free of charge if you are interested in buying their products. Shopping around in January and February also means you have the added benefit of getting good discounts on most of their kitchens, sinks, taps and baths because of the post-Christmas sales!

Planning your bathroom

If you are making substantial changes to the layout of your home, involving repositioning many rooms, it is important to consider the best place for a new bathroom or family shower room. This may be your one and only opportunity to get the bathroom you want, in the right location, as you'll have the builders already on site and probably the help of an architect to plan as well.

Waste pipes

Before you can move a bathroom or shower room, you'll need to do a bit of investigation work to find out the location of your manhole cover and the soil-vent pipe. The soil-vent pipe is the 100mm diameter, large plastic pipe located on the outside wall of your house, through which all of the waste and drainage runs to connect to the main sewage system. If you locate your bathrooms some distance away from the soil-vent pipe, you are going to experience some problems getting the toilet waste to reach it, in accordance with the building regulations for waste pipe falls.

Getting the waste from sinks or showers is easy because this flows through a much smaller pipe and can therefore travel longer distances to connect to the soil-vent pipe. But the large, 100mm-wide toilet waste is always the problem. It needs to be as close to the soil-vent pipe as practically possible, which really defines the location of the bathrooms within your house.

The best layout

The layout of the individual room itself will obviously depend upon the amount of space you have available and the details of what you require to suit the way that you live. With smaller apartments, you may be very limited with the amount of space available, which makes it even more important to plan the space efficiently. With family homes, where you have more space at your disposal, it's still important to be efficient. Getting your bathroom well placed and laid out can potentially free up additional space around it, for other use.

When I'm sketching over a bathroom plan, there are often six or seven perfectly good layouts that will work within the space. It's really important that you test all of these ideas and get the most efficient layout that suits you.

opposite You don't need to spend a fortune to create a stylish bathroom like this. Simple, white sanitaryware is often at the budget end of the range but can look really effective.

Family bathrooms

'Childhood is that wonderful time of life when all you need to do to lose weight is have a bath.' Richard Zera

What level of mains water pressure do you have coming into the house? If your mains pressure is low or if you have an old 15mm lead pipe providing the mains water to the house (rather than the modern 25mm plastic pipe), then it's highly likely you will have incredibly low water pressure. This simply may not be sufficient for certain taps or showerheads. There is no point spending lots of money on fancy fittings and fixtures if you only get a dribble of water coming out of your shower.

If you have an existing family space, you should ask yourself these questions at the very beginning of the process, in order to make your brief as accurate and useful as possible:

1   Every family bathroom should have a bath. Even if you're the sort of person who relies on showers, having no bath in the house will reduce its value. But what type, size and style of bath do you want to go for?
2   Do you want one sink or two in the bathroom? Two sinks can certainly stop arguments and battles in the morning in the rush to get everyone ready for school and work.
3   Does the bathroom need a shower? And, if so, is it a walk-in shower separate from the bath? Or is it a showerhead and screen mounted within the bath itself.
4   Do you prefer your toilet to be in the bathroom itself, or in a separate cubicle?
5   How is the space going to be heated? Are you going to install a tower rail? If so, what type and size, and how will it be connected to the hot-water system and electrics?
6   What's your water pressure? If fancy showerheads and taps are your thing, you may need to consider installing a pump if the pressure is low (see opposite).

Once you have made these decisions, you are in a position to begin planning the layout of the space.

GETTING STARTED

Before you start designing the layout of your bathroom space, make sure that you have a plan of the room available, and that it's blown up to a good scale. You will be making very important design decisions, so draw in the walls and the position of your doors on your gridded paper. There are standard templates for all bathroom sanitary ware on the Internet, or they can be traced from the manufacturer's catalogue. It's incredibly important that you have these templates for your bath, sink, shower and toilet, in order to rearrange them to scale in the space and discover the best layout.

Take a look at the some of the layouts that can be achieved in a standard-sized bathroom space. Most of the options have disadvantages and advantages, so experiment until you find the perfect one.

Bathroom layouts

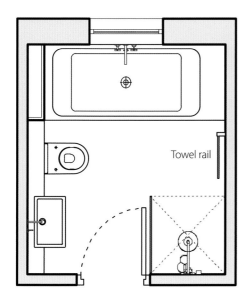

Towel rail

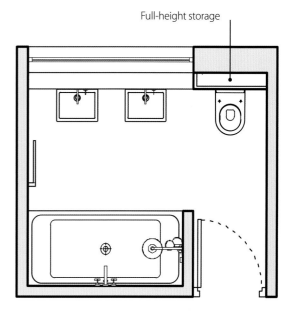

Full-height storage

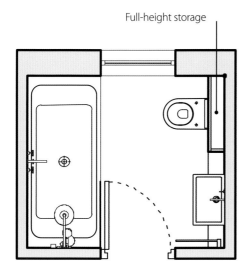

Full-height storage

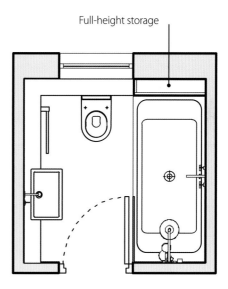

Full-height storage

En-suite shower rooms

Even if you live in the smallest apartment, it is always important to try to squeeze in an en-suite shower room. Over the past 20 years, en-suites have become increasingly popular – to the point that it seems quite unusual to walk into a master bedroom in any kind of property and not see one. En-suites are a great way of having your very own private space for morning and evening ablutions, leaving the family bathroom for kids or guests.

If you have a larger home – and can afford the space – it's definitely worth installing a full en-suite bathroom, rather than simply a shower. This is super-luxury, where you can completely pamper yourself in your own domain – without being hassled by others (particularly the very little kind of others). In smaller properties, an en-suite shower room is more than sufficient and it doesn't necessarily need to be a large luxurious space. Unlike a bathroom, where you might spend an awful lot of time relaxing in the tub, a shower room needs to be functional, because you'll be in and out of there quickly.

Having said that, even the smallest en-suite can be beautifully detailed and finished with lovely materials; it's just the scale and the size of the room that need to be functional.

Wet rooms

There's a new trend afoot! More and more common in bathroom or shower-room design is the wet room – a simple space with a showerhead installed, in which every wall and floor surface is waterproofed in either tiles or rubber-flooring systems, with a drain in the centre. Wet rooms are fantastic because the principle of bathing is returned to the most simple level. They are easy to clean, seriously modern-looking and fun to manoeuvre!

What is incredibly important is that the quality of the build is absolutely perfect – and that all of the floors are laid to sufficient falls for the water can drain away properly. Poor design or bad-quality build will soon mean that you will spring a leak. This is an absolute disaster, as the majority of the fittings will have to be ripped out and replaced in order to find the source of the leak.

When I design a wet room I always try to provide a second layer of waterproofing beneath the tiled or rubber surface; if water manages to get through one layer, it certainly won't get through the next. This may seem like over-design, but – believe me – it isn't!

What I love most about wet rooms is the fact that they are an incredibly efficient use of space. Even the smallest wet room, cluttered with all sorts of fixtures and finishes, can feel like a spacious room. And kids absolutely love them because they don't have to worry about getting water everywhere – it already is!

opposite A stylish and functional wet room.

above You don't need a huge amount of space to create an en-suite. They can be incredibly efficiently designed to give you everything you need without losing lots of space from your bedroom.

above There are a number of clever ways of hiding your en-suite, and using mirrored doors is both effective in making the room feel bigger and useful.

left It can feel like a real luxury to have a full en-suite shower room - treat yourself!

Bathroom lighting

All electrics need an electrician
You'll need to be aware that building regulations have changed for electrical installations. They now state that the halcyon days of DIY electrics being undertaken by untrained people are over. You must use a fully qualified electrician to carry out any installation.

Lighting becomes incredibly important when you are trying to create a tranquil and serene atmosphere in your bathroom – particularly when your tubs are in use in the darker hours. Getting the lighting design element right, which sets the correct mood for your bathroom, allows bathtime to become a real treat at the end of a long day.

In the old days, you would find a pendant light in the middle of the room – or, even worse, a long white fluorescent tube that would give the most awful quality of sterile light and flicker terribly when you turned it on. Thankfully, things have moved on; light fittings and bulbs of all shapes and sizes can now be selected to create the right atmosphere for you.

Bathroom safety

It may be stating the obvious, but remember that water and electrics don't really go that well together. This is the main reason why there should never be any sockets in a bathroom or shower-room space, apart from special low-voltage sockets placed at high level for shavers.

For our own safety, lights have been developed with an IP (instrument protection) rating. The IP rating is simply two numbers: the first ranges from 0 to 6 and indicates the level of protection against solid objects; in other words, '0' is a fitting that offers no protection at all, and '6' is a fitting that can be highly protected against things as minute as dust.

The second number ranges from 0 to 8, and indicates the ability of the light fitting to be protected against liquids. Again, '0' offers no protection whatsoever, '2' will protect against rain dripping vertically, '4' can withstand water splashed from all directions – all the way up to '8' which allows total immersion in water for a long period of time. For this one, the depth of the water must be specified.

This may all sound horribly complicated, but it's worth taking note of these figures. *All* lights within a bathroom or shower room *must* be IP rated to a certain standard, to be protected from direct splashing of water, and also high levels of steam. Your electrician will take responsibility for this, and make sure you have the right fitting for the job, but if you are out there sourcing your own products, you'll need to bear this carefully in mind!

Getting the lighting right in your bathroom

1. Make sure that all lights can be dimmed, and that you have the flexibility to turn the lighting level up and down for *all* of the lights on an individual circuit. This means you can create the right lighting atmosphere to suit your mood.

2. In shower areas, try to specify a combined downlight with an extractor fan. These are units where the extractor fan forms part of the lighting installation, which avoids having an unsightly mechanical extractor grill somewhere else in the room.

3. Avoid putting downlights over your bathtub. It drives me mad when people do this! When you are lying in the bath, the last thing you want to do is look up into a huge amount of glare, with direct light shining in your face. It is most definitely not conducive to a relaxed atmosphere.

4. Try to provide lights to the side of mirrors – or within mirrored wall units. An equal balance of light across the face is helpful for women applying make-up, and can do no harm when blokes are shaving.

5. If you have a bathroom or shower room within a loft space, recessed downlights can look unsightly within the sloping roof. Consider installing elegant wall lights instead.

6. Bathrooms provide a great opportunity to explore decorative light, such as fibre-optic or coloured lighting fixtures. Make sure these are IP rated.

7. Feature lighting can be used to make the architecture more exciting. For example, a bathtub that is slightly raised off the main floor level, on its own plinth and deck, could have lighting hidden beneath so that the bathtub looks like it's floating. There are also interesting lighting tricks you can use to create amazing details that will bring the quality of the architecture to life. Try and design in recesses or small alcoves, into which candles can be placed. These are great around the bathtub, if you are a bit of a romantic. If you are a little more practical, then reassure yourself that candles around the bath provide extra light for reading in the tub.

8. If you are lucky enough to have incredibly high ceilings in your bathroom, consider installing wall lights – in particular, up-lighters that will enhance the sense of space.

9. If you have storage cupboards or vanity units, install lighting within the unit itself, which will come on automatically when you open the door. This will make it a lot easier to find the shampoo!

above Task lighting above or either side of your bathroom mirror is essential.

Bathroom design features

There are so many ways of creating interesting features within a bathroom. Whether you are aiming to design the ultimate romantic setting, a practical, easy-to-clean room for the teenagers in your family, or something fun for the kids, there is plenty you can do to make your bathroom truly special.

I always like family bathrooms to be as child friendly as possible, and that means making them accessible. This can present some problems! For example, it can be impractical to put in a low-level sink for kids, particularly since they grow so quickly. My solution is to design in a fixed raised deck, or some clever, movable steps, so that children can easily raise themselves up to sink and mirror level. Similarly, walk-in showers or wet rooms are great for kids, as showering in the bath won't work when your kids have to scramble in and out. Ultimately, your children need to feel that they are in a bathroom space suited to them, rather than using something that is simply not practical. If they feel involved in their space, you might just get them in there to wash!

right A simple bathroom is transformed into something truly stylish by clever lighting, elegant sanitaryware and a colourful worktop.

opposite It may not always be practical, but I'd love to have a view like this from my bathroom!

Technology

Developments in modern technology mean that you can have a lot of fun integrating gadgets into bathroom designs. Here are just a few of my personal favourites.

1 Heated mirrors. This may sound like a bit of a gimmick, but they are a fantastic way to provide additional levels of comfort and warmth in the space. Towel rails are quite often draped with damp towels, and unable to emit much heat into the room. A heated mirror is quite a trendy way to produce some additional heat and avoid the need for unsightly radiators.

2 Integrated TV mirrors. Now these are seriously cool. With a flick of a switch, the mirror in your bathroom can turn into a TV. OK, OK, you are probably asking: *Just how many TVs do we need in one house?* You might be right. But I still think it's a fantastic idea to catch up on the day's news or watch a bit of sport while you take a bath. Just think, you never need to miss a goal!

3 Integrated bathroom speakers. Imagine lying in the bath with a few scented candles burning away … How good would it be to have some gentle, ambient music to put you in that chilled mood? Gone are the days when you'd have a basic radio that is constantly damaged by dripping water when your wet hands fumble to change the station. Technology has moved on so much you can change your music by remote control or (and we are talking extreme here) by voice-activation.

4 Intelligent home systems. In a nutshell, this means that you can now buy a bathtub whose taps can be turned on or off automatically; you can set the amount of water you want in the tub, as well as its temperature. All of this can be done in a matter of seconds via your iPhone, while you are driving back from work in your car. How cool is that, if you are running late for a night out? Your own bathtub set to the perfect level, at the perfect temperature to suit you.

below Not for everyone, but you can now integrate a TV into your bathroom wall!

Designer sanitary ware

About 25 years ago, a bath was bath and a sink was a sink. Both had familiar shapes in standard white, with fairly standard taps and fittings. Of course, you go could go plum or avocado, but the look of the products was pretty much the same. How things have changed! Now, product designers all over the world are producing the most unusual styles of sinks, taps, baths and toilets. The range of materials and designs is phenomenal. Just take a standard bathtub: you can now buy one in simple white plastic, ceramic, metal, wood or marble. They can be nearly any size or style, and some of the greatest product designers in the world – like Philippe Starck – are striving to find the balance between extravagant *stylish* design and major comfort.

above There are so many amazing designs that whatever budget you have, you will be able to create something really special.

Bathroom storage

We have a lot of stuff and if it's all on display at the same time, our bathrooms will look a complete mess. The obvious solution is built-in storage, which allows you to integrate the sink, toilet, bathtub and shower in a very neat and considered way, making the best use of the space.

A bathroom is planned with very fixed points of servicing; in other words, when you've got your layout right, you'll have very specific positions for the sinks, bath, toilet, shower and towel rail. In some ways, it's quite similar to your kitchen, where your key appliances have to fit into the right location, and you fit your storage around them.

In your bathroom, you can expect much the same, with storage organised around the fixtures and fittings; however, there is one main difference! Kitchens tend to be rather larger than bathrooms, and you'll need to be incredibly inventive to design in as much usable and easily accessible storage as possible. Gone are the days when our sole bathroom 'equipment' consisted of a tube of toothpaste, a toothbrush, a bar of soap and the odd razor. We are a generation obsessed by products, with everything from cleansers, moisturisers, gels, waxes and body scrubs to bath and aromatherapy oils, mouthwash and fake tan vying for space with the essentials. The modern 21st-century bathroom is starting to look like a chemist!

WHAT DO YOU ACTUALLY NEED?

Start by making a list of all of your storage needs – in other words, consider what you really need to store. Be ruthless with yourself about what's actually important to you. You'll need to analyse the way you use your bathroom now, and assess what is successful and what isn't working. Then ask yourself a few simple but testing questions:

1 How long have your products actually been sitting in your bathroom cabinet? I can guarantee you that there's stuff in there that you've never used for years, including half-empty pots of products that are well past their use-by dates. These can be quite unhygienic, so have a mass clear-out.

2 Do you have any existing shelves or ledges that are very useful? If so, what do you use them for and do you need more? What would be their ideal position?

3 Are there any products or items, such as towels, that you actually like to have on view? And which items would you prefer to be hidden away?

4 If, like me, you have kids, there is normally a Noah's ark level of plastic animals floating around in the bath at about 7pm. Where is the best place to keep all this stuff?

5 Are you a bit of a traditionalist, and like to have a separate airing cupboard to store your bath and hand towels?

6 If you're considering having a wet room (and assuming you are making this choice because your room is particularly small), how can you protect all your stuff from splashing water?

The answers to these questions will guide you towards the type of storage – and how much of it – you'll need. You'll need to decide whether you want it to be open, closed or a combination of both, and what its purpose will be.

Most families are unique and have their own idiosyncrasies, so you'll undoubtedly have your own answers to these questions. The point is that you need to answer them clearly in order to form your own design brief.

above A three-in-one screen, mirror and storage unit.

opposite Integrated storage is the most efficient way of using your bathroom space and the void underneath the sinks is usually the first place to look.

The best storage solutions for your bathroom

1 Design a full-length vanity unit that is sturdy enough to support your sinks, integrate all drainage, hide your toilet system and provide ample storage space beneath, for towels or cosmetics.

2 If there are any narrow spaces remaining when you've defined the position of your sanitaryware, build full-height cupboards to make the most of the narrow recess.

3 Select wall-hung toilets and sinks rather than those on pedestals; it's much more difficult to build in storage when your sanitary ware is on a pedestal.

4 Create an area of open shelving for everyday products and accessories, to ensure that they are within easy reach.

5 Try to create a separate area to store bath towels and linen, as conditions within the bathroom itself may be damp and steamy. You can keep the flannels and towels you need for daily use hanging on the towel rails.

6 Keep soap on a designed wire rack and keep your toothbrushes in a wall-mounted toothbrush holder; having either of them sitting in a container half-full with water is unhygienic and uses up valuable space on your counter top.

7 Use as much available wall space as possible for wall cabinets that provide storage; choose mirrored surfaces that help to make your space look bigger.

8 Don't go overboard on the storage, though. Your bathroom can start to feel claustrophobic if every surface has been used to the max.

9 Make sure that you specify a towel rail large enough to be able to heat all of your family towels.

10 Buy storage containers in whatever style suits your bathroom, such as plastic, metal or straw baskets, to organise your stuff. These can be easily accessed from open shelves.

The golden rule to remember is that fully integrated storage within small bathroom spaces is the best way to maximise the amount of storage you have, reduce the level of clutter and create a style of architecture that is elegant, clean and simple.

opposite A variety of built-in bathroom storage options.

below Stand-alone storage units are useful as long as clutter is kept to a minimum (IKEA).

Bathroom finishes and materials

The look, standard and quality of the finishes on the materials you'll use in your bathroom all come down to personal taste and the budget you have available. I am sometimes astonished by the amount of money some that clients spend on their bathrooms. If you go for absolutely top-quality materials, taps, showerheads, tiles and sanitary-ware, a single bathroom space can run into tens of thousands of pounds – or much, much more. However, with more products coming onto the market and a greater number of competitive companies fighting for your business, there are lots of ways to get a great look, on even the most affordable budget.

Here's what I think works really well in a bathroom, as well as a few ideas of what you need to avoid:

Vanity tops Over the last ten years I have seen many vanity units and tops made out of MDF; this surface simply cannot live up to the daily exposure of splashing water. Any vanity top has to be incredibly durable and hard-wearing, using stone or tile on the surface. Think about what you'd use in your kitchen, and choose something similar. Corian is a great option here.

Flooring Timber flooring can work very well in bathrooms if – and only if – it's properly sealed and maintained. If you take the long view, however, there's no doubt that a few years of constant exposure to water is going to make it look very tired. If you do want to use timber alongside under-floor heating, make sure you specify an engineered board, to avoid splitting and cracking. Tiled floors – in stone, ceramic, marble or travertine – are perfect for bathrooms and can improve with age.

Glass This is a fantastic material to use in your bathrooms, for shower screens, sinks or vanity worktops. It looks great, but you need to be fairly disciplined to keep it clean.

Stainless steel I've seen bathrooms where the bathtub and all the sinks are formed from stainless steel. This can provide quite a cold and harsh look that borders on being industrial rather than domestic, but it can be done.

- Consider having your sinks created from the same material that you select for your tiles. For example, in my own bathroom, the sinks were specially made from blocks of travertine to match the travertine tiles on the floors and walls.

Timber sanitary ware Unless they are constantly maintained with sealant, wax or oil, sinks or bathtubs made out of solid timber tend to look pretty awful after a couple of years. You need to be a very disciplined person to keep look looking good.

Mosaic tiles I am a big fan of mosaic tiles, as they come in a huge variety of designs, colours and shapes. Mosaic tiles that are made from coloured glass have a beautiful shimmering effect and work really well in bathrooms. They are also really easy to lay – even for a DIY novice. I always prefer my mosaic tiles to be in quite a bright, vivid or bold colour – it stops a bathroom from taking itself too seriously. You can also lay them in patterns – an animal ark to match your kids' bathtime collection may be a fun place to start in the family bathroom!

Rubber Rubber is an incredibly good, waterproof material and it can be used as one huge single sheet – in order to waterproof the floor of a bathroom properly – or laid as rubber tiles. These are bonded to the surface beneath and are a very cost-effective way of waterproofing a bathroom. I always think rubber flooring looks great in kids' bathrooms or en-suites – and even better in the brightest, boldest colours.

Ironmongery With any bathroom it's very important to be consistent with the ironmongery – in other words, any metal finishes, such as door handles, locks, shower-screen brackets, dressing-gown hooks, toilet-brush holders, soap trays and taps. You need to decide upon a style and a finish and stick with it. Mixing up chrome and satin finishes, in different metals, just looks like an inconsistent mess.

If you use large, thin tiles for your bathroom floor – such as large sections of travertine flooring that may only be 10mm thick – they'll need to be laid on a mesh sub-base to give the material adequate strength. Laid traditionally, those large sections of travertine will crack. Always make sure you speak to the tile or stone manufacturer to find out the exact requirements for laying the material. Many have to be bonded to a solid sub-base, which is a concrete or screed floor, or a plywood or screwed-down plywood sheet. If you want your flooring to last, you need to get this right.

The affordable bathroom

The key to designing and specifying an affordable bathroom is to make the space as efficient as possible to avoid wasting any space, and to select affordable materials that are incredibly hard-wearing and long-lasting. You'll also have to be pretty disciplined, ensuring that the space is cleaned regularly to avoid any build-up of dirt and grime. This may sound like an obvious one, but regular maintenance really is the key to making an affordable bathroom look good for more than just a couple of years.

The following products and materials are at the affordable end of the scale. When you bring them together, they can really make your bathroom look great.

above You don't need to spend a fortune on taps. Fittings like these will do the job just as well.

opposite A colourful, functional and above all affordable bathroom.

Simple sanitary ware Avoid anything over-designed. Quite often the simplest shapes in white are the cheapest options for your bath, sink and toilet. They may not be bursting with style, but their simplicity means that they can make a statement in a minimalist kind of way. I like them.

Taps Choose those from the budget end of the sanitary range. Topping your simple sink and tub with something fancy will just look odd and cost you money you don't need to spend.

Soften your water Install a water softener to soften all of the hard water that comes into your property. Even expensive taps and showerheads clog up very quickly with limescale build-up. A water softener will ensure that your budget fittings have a longer lifespan. The other benefit is that it will stop streaky limescale from building up on shower screens and doors.

Rubber flooring This is incredibly economical and durable, and it always looks fantastic – particularly if you go for the studded tile. A bright, bold, colourful studded rubber tile that has a level of detail is much more interesting than a flat sheet of lino. It's also incredibly easy to clean and never streaks.

Extractors Make sure you install a very good mechanical extractor system. One of the main reasons why affordable bathrooms look tired very quickly is because the finishes become damaged by the high level of moisture in the air. The faster you can get this moist air out of the bathroom, the better.

Mosaic tiling This is a fantastic and affordable way to tile the walls of a budget bathroom. Like the studded rubber flooring, mosaic tiles have a level of interest and detailing that makes them look a bit more interesting than flatter tile varieties.

Ceramic tiling If your budget is tight, then forget about fancy marble and stone finishes; there is absolutely nothing wrong with a decent-quality ceramic tile. Make sure you select a strong grout that

compliments the colour and style of the tile. For example, light tiles with dark grout looks terrible. If you select a grout that is similar to the tile, it creates an elegant, uniform effect. If you pick a grey ceramic tile, pick a grey grout.

Be brave with paint colours Coloured paint is no more expensive than a tin of white paint, so why not be a bit adventurous and go for an interesting colour to give a unique feel to your space. This may sound obvious, but check that it's suitable for bathrooms. The fastest way to ruin your brand-new finish is to use the wrong paint; it will peel and discolour within months.

Ironmongery, fixtures and storage baskets Pay a visit to some home-improvement stores such as IKEA; the range of affordable gear to kit out your bathroom is amazing. This genuinely brilliant, affordable will make an enormous difference to the look of your bathroom without breaking the bank. Once again, choose a theme and stick to it. Too many colours and metals in a small room will cheapen the overall look.

Candles and flowers A bit girlie, you might think, but there is no doubt that walking into a bathroom that has been scented by beautiful candles and one or two nice flowers in mini-vases on the vanity top really do give the space a nicer feel. There's no reason why you can't dress your bathroom with a bit of luxury and style.

With such an amazing range of affordable materials and products on the market, and a little bit of creative thinking, there is simply no reason why you can't create a great-looking bathroom on a tight budget. Go simple, stylish and consistent, with splashes of colour to create an individual look, and you'll have a masterpiece on your hands.

top Bold paint can add real style to your bathroom.

above An example of an elegantly themed bathroom.

Bathroom ecology

'When the well is dry, we know the worth of water.' Benjamin Franklin

The amount of water that we individually use in the UK is phenomenal. On average, only about 3 percent of the water that enters your home is actually used for drinking, and each of us uses almost 144 litres of water every single day. Take a peek at the box opposite for a few examples of how we use water in Britain.

Because it is so convenient for us to turn on a tap and have water instantly at our disposal, we take it for granted. And because of this, we are using far, far too much of it. This over-use of water means that we are not only putting a huge amount of pressure on the environment, but we are wasting huge amounts of our own money to pay ever-increasing water bills. Add to this the energy expended cleaning up this water for re-use and finding new sources, and we have a pretty disastrous situation on our hands.

There's also the issue of hot water. Reducing the amount you use can not only make a massive reduction in your heating bills, but it will lower the expenditure of energy necessary to make and keep it hot.

So what can we do to reduce our water usage?

1. Turn off the water while you brush your teeth. You will have heard this a million times before, but there is no harm in being reminded.
2. Turn off the water while you wash your hands. You don't need to leave the water running while you rub in the soap.
3. Take showers rather than baths. This simple measure will save approximately 45 litres of hot water a go.
4. Consider purchasing a low-flush toilet, which requires less water.
5. There are some great water-saving ideas making their way into product design. I recently saw a combined toilet and sink unit where the water drained from the sink automatically filled the toilet system alongside. So you are using waste water that you used for washing your face to flush your loo. Brilliant recycling ideas like this are inventive and make a real difference.
6. If you are super-green, consider installing a rain-harvesting system. Let's face it: we have more than enough of this stuff in the UK.

It has been estimated that up to 75 percent of all indoor water use comes from the bathroom and that the toilet alone accounts for over 25 percent of total water usage in the average home. Change old habits and find ways to conserve water every day. Don't allow water waste to continue.

Water use in Britain today

- 1 litre – brushing your teeth
- 6 litres – flushing the toilet
- 9 litres – washing your hands and face
- 35 litres – taking a shower
- 80 litres – having a bath

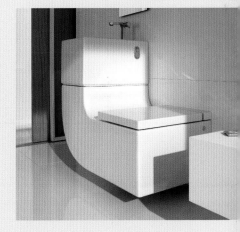

above This combined toilet and sink reduces water wastage by using the used sink water to flush the loo. An ingenious piece of design.

The ideal bathroom

The ideal family-bathroom layout really depends upon the scale and proportion of the room you have – and the way that you enter it. Bathroom space that is long and thin – as opposed to one that is wide and deep – will have both advantages and disadvantages. The secret is to get the layout right, to make best use of the space.

Bathrooms have more constraints than any other room in the house, not only because they tend to be small rooms with a lot to fit into them, but also because there may be issues with your existing drainage system, not to mention personal requirements. For this reason, every single bathroom layout is unique. The best way to choose the layout that is right for you is to consider all of the elements we discussed earlier in this section, but also to look at some great family bathrooms that really work.

Here's one layout that works incredibly well.
1 As you walk through the bathroom door, the window is aligned perfectly – straight ahead of you – providing a lovely view out.
2 The loo is located in the corner of the space against the external wall, as close to the soil-vent pipe as possible. This makes it much cheaper and easier to install.
3 There are two sinks – one for him and one for her – built onto an integrated vanity unit. This vanity unit is a box-out that can hide all the hot- and cold-water feeds, waste pipes and the toilet system. This creates a very clean and simple design.
4 A good-sized family shower (90cm by 90cm), alongside a large bath (180cm by 80cm) will meet the needs of most families.
5 The towel rail is tucked neatly behind the door swing – or a low-level towel rail could be located beneath the bathroom window.
6 To make the space feel substantially wider and larger, there is a full-width and full-height mirror mounted on the wall above the toilet and sinks. This makes the bathroom feel twice as wide, with all the reflections bouncing around the space.

What makes this bathroom incredibly efficient is that both the sinks and the loo are fitted to the vanity unit on one side, with a very simple drainage run to the soil-vent pipe. Having the door opening into the centre of the space makes it architecturally welcoming, because you get a view straight out of the window. And having the bath and shower next to each other makes all of the hot- and cold-water feeds incredibly simple to install. This, for me, is the ideal family-bathroom layout.

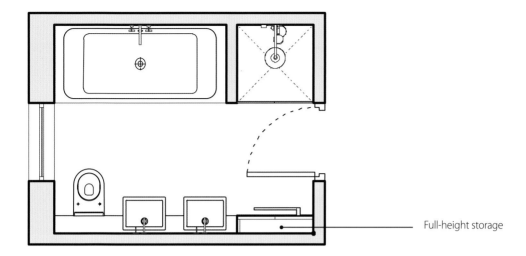

Full-height storage

The ideal bathroom and en-suite need:

- Great water pressure. Most good-quality sanitaryware fittings require around 3 bar of water pressure. To have an invigorating shower in the morning is a fantastic start to the day and you are only going to get this with top-quality pressure. Ideally, you'd like to achieve this without a noisy pump.

- I always specify underfloor heating in every shower room or bathroom. If you have underfloor heating in the rest of the house, then this water-based system is by far the best. It's more efficient and cheaper to run. However, unless you are doing a major refurbishment project, it's always difficult to install an underfloor system throughout your home, as it requires lifting all of the floorboards and coverings. If you can do it, great, but if you can't afford to go that far, then you may just have to be satisfied with radiators throughout the rest of the property and underfloor heating in the bathroom. If you are going for isolated areas of underfloor heating, it's cheaper to install the electric-mat system rather than the water-based pipe system. The electric mat is easier to install, but slightly more expensive to run.

- Make sure you have a very efficient, pressurised hot-water cylinder. The larger the cylinder, the better, if you want to avoid a drain on the amount of hot water you have at your disposal – particularly if you have a number of bathrooms or showers in your home. It's really important to install a pressurised system so that you don't get that awful drop in pressure – and terrifying drop in water temperature – when you are in the shower and someone turns on a tap elsewhere in the house.

- When positioning your bathrooms and shower rooms throughout your property, try to locate them in a similar zone – where areas

above An elegant bathroom with separate walk-in shower.

opposite A simple yet functional shower room.

that need drainage on the first floor are positioned close to or over the top of rooms that require drainage on the ground floor. By clustering bathrooms, shower rooms, utility rooms, and toilets in a similar zone – irrespective of what level they are on – your drainage system and your hot/cold water supply will be much easier to design and build. This will save you loads of money on your budget as well as being easier to maintain in the long run. What's more, grouping them together means that your plumber can provide a number of services saving you a lot of money on your budget. By grouping all of these rooms together means your plumber can provide service risers all the way through the house with access panels to make it easier to carry out any necessary maintenance.

- Try to avoid bathroom spaces that are awkwardly shaped or badly proportioned. Ensuring that they are as square or rectangular as possible will make your design more efficient. Chamfered corners or bizarre angles will make your bathroom hard to plan, and it will probably date sooner rather than later.

- Maybe I'm just too British, but I *hate* bidets. They are a complete waste of time and space. I know the Europeans love them, but when I go into any bathroom in a British home and find a bidet, it tends to be used for nothing more than storing magazines for bathroom reading.

- I think it is always better to have a walk-in shower than something integrated into your bath with a shower screen. Obviously, this is only possible if you have the available space, but shower screens over bathtubs – whether fixed or hinged – are always awkward.

- Shower curtains should be banned. Yes, they may be cheap, but the idea is that you replace them as soon as they begin to look slightly grimy. That is why they are *cheap* – they are effectively disposable. The problem is, of course, that we never *do* throw them out, and they always seem to make themselves at home for longer than they should. So you get that awful brown-stained line across the bottom of the curtain that is, frankly, disgusting. Worse than that, your entire shower experience becomes a wrestling match with a sheet of cheap plastic. Changing air pressure when you turn on the shower means that the shower curtain automatically sticks to your backside. This is not the kind of experience you want to have first thing in the morning, when you are trying to have a nice shower. Ban shower curtains and install good glass shower screens.

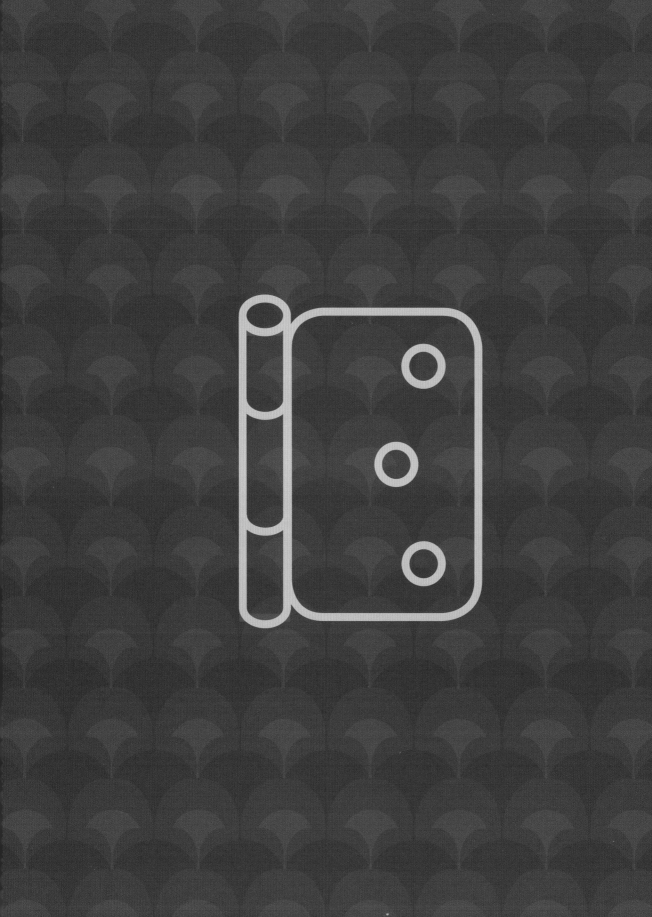

Section 6

Resources

'The space within becomes the reality of the building.'

Frank Lloyd Wright

Now for the nitty-gritty details. Using your imagination, assessing the needs and lifestyle of your family and exploring the huge multitude of options there are for refurbishing, renovating, restoring or reconfiguring your house can be great fun, and the end result can literally transform your life.

It is, however, equally important to enter any project with your eyes firmly open. With a bit of luck, you'll be in a position to hire plenty of experts who know what they are doing and will get the job done efficiently and to your specifications. But this doesn't mean that you can sit back and wait to see the final product. This is your home, and you will need to be actively involved at every step along the way.

Ideas are one thing, putting them into practice is quite another. You'll need to understand the process of a build, the experts involved in making your dreams a reality and the whole planning process. You'll have to get to grips with costing your project and keeping tabs on your budget, and you'll also need to grasp the key terminology that everyone in the building trade uses. If you don't know what's going on, you'll soon be lost, and your project will spiral out of control.

This may all sound dead boring – particularly if you are paying out wads of cash for someone else to do the work – but understanding the basics is essential for your building proposal to become a successful reality.

Finding the experts

The building game is no different from team sports. If everyone understands the job they have to do, where they have to be and when, and they are constantly communicating and 'in sync' with each other, then you're on to a winner. It is impossible to deliver a successful refurbishment project without the right winning team.

It's a team game

When we use the word 'experts' in the building industry, people often think we are talking about the professionals, such as the architect and the project manager. I don't agree with this at all. Everyone you employ to be involved in the project, from your plumber, electrician and roofer to your chippy, brickie, plasterer and decorator, should be regarded as an expert, as their experience and knowledge is invaluable. As an architect, my designs are nothing more than paper architecture until they are physically realised by the craftsmen on site.

So who do you need? This really depends upon the scale of the project and what it is you are actually doing. The team is also determined by your budget – the lower the budget, the smaller the team. In order to keep your costs to a minimum, you need a very focused group of people who know exactly what they have been appointed to do, and are able to work well with you and with each other.

With so many different trades involved, all with very different jobs to do, that take varying lengths of time, good communication is vital. First and foremost, they just need to be nice people who turn up when they say they will – and really take care and pride in their work. The priority of the building team is to do a good job, on time and on budget. Sometimes that is easier said than done. Ultimately, however, the most important thing you need when appointing *anyone* to work on your home is trust. If, for any reason, you don't trust someone, then don't give them the job. It's as simple as that.

Putting together the right team

The truth is that anyone can set up as a builder, so you need to know that you are getting the right person for the job. This means doing your homework! Personal recommendation is the very best method of finding someone who is going to get the job done to your specifications. Good builders pride themselves on their reputation, and if they've been recommended to you they'll want to be sure that they live up to expectations. There is no point in plucking a random company out of the Yellow Pages; you need to know what and whom you will be dealing with.

If you don't know anyone who has had building work done recently, there are a few other options. The first is to look at impartial sites where people list the tradesmen that they recommend, and give details of how that builder operated. One such site is www.mybuilder.com.

Another great way to find the tradesmen you need is to talk to the staff at your local builders' merchant. These guys work with the trade on a daily basis, and have plenty of inside knowledge of who operates in your local area – and how good they are. Like many things in life, it's about who you know.

Trade Associations will also be able to put you in touch with qualified members. See the list of useful websites for a list of some of the key organisations in the UK.

Finally, your architect or project manager may be able to provide details of tradesmen with whom they've worked with in the past – and also steer you clear of builders who aren't up to the job. There is a good network within the trade, and builders work regularly with other experts in the field. Your plumber may be able to suggest a great plasterer, and your decorator may know just the right guy to get your new electrics done.

When to ask more questions

If you've been given recommendations for tradesmen, it's important to do a little research and take a close look at projects that they've completed. This means paying a visit to previous renovations or rebuilds, and looking at the finish. Talk to previous clients and see how they feel a few months or even years down the line. You want a finished project that is going to wear well, so make sure that something that looks fantastic when it is completed *stays* fantastic when even in everyday use.

Watch out for builders who seem too good to be true! If they can start 'immediately', you want to know why. They may be a large company with additional resources available – which is great news for you – but you need to make sure that they aren't scratching around for work. Even in the midst of a recession, most professional builders with exemplary standards are busy. Unless a big project has just fallen through, most good builders are booked up well in advance. The second thing to look for is a hugely optimistic quote that comes in much lower than the others you've received. It has to be said that you get what you pay for in the building trade, and cheap labour isn't necessarily a good thing.

Cheapest isn't always best and if they have underpriced the job, they will find ways of clawing their money back throughout the project – with phrases like 'we didn't allow for that' or 'we seem to have found another problem'. Similarly, you may find that the quote or estimate doesn't cover everything you'd expect, so go through it with a fine-tooth comb and make sure that the nitty-gritty details are included. One or two surprises on a project are inevitable when you refurbish an existing building, but too many send your stress levels through the leaking roof and add a huge burden to the budget.

Your project manager may put together your team, making the job that much easier for you; however, if you are planning to manage your own project, it's worth researching how the various experts work, and what their job normally entails. If it's a complicated project and you have no project-management experience, please don't attempt to do it. It will only cost you more money in the long run.

The idea is that a good project manager makes the build more efficient and actually saves you money. You can even shadow them so that you gain more experience yourself – which will certainly help you on future projects. In fact, even if you aren't managing the team, it's in your interest to know who is doing what on the build.

Masters of the trade

Let's look at the main tradesmen who will form your team. You may need all of them, or just a few, depending on the size of your project.

Groundworkers These are often organised by a foreman and are responsible for the heavy physical work on your project, such as digging up the ground for new foundations or electrics and pipes, or getting your garden space ready for work to begin.

Labourers These are the boys who put their hands to any manual work, cleaning up, lifting gear, loading and unloading, and making tea! They are good guys who like a bit of banter and can often lift the spirits on site.

Bricklayers These are the guys who get the shell of your building in place, creating walls and cladding any exterior with brick or interiors in concrete blockwork. As their name suggests, they do the majority of the actual building work, sometimes in conjunction with a carpenter. In the trade, these builders are known as 'brickies'.

Carpenters These workers are responsible for working with wood, including building timber frames, suspended timber floors, roof trusses and frames, and installing doors and windows. They'll also be responsible for completing most of the 'first fix' work (see page 370), which basically means the first stage of the build. You can expect carpenters to create staircases and window boards, and they may go on to do things such as install kitchen units and fitted wardrobes. Carpenters are known as 'chippies', and I can't think of very many projects where you won't need at least one!

Roofers Once the structure of the build is in place, the roofer will deal with the surface of the roof and usually the flashing and guttering as well.

Electricians These are highly qualified tradesmen who will become involved once the structure of the build is complete. In a nutshell, they deal with all of the wiring and will work closely with the carpenters to be sure they have access to the project before the plasterboard has been fitted. Wiring will need to run throughout your whole house before any decorative work is undertaken, including tiling and plastering. Your electrician will make connections to all of your switches and install light fittings, too. Doing electrical work yourself is now a no-go area. If you aren't certified, you aren't allowed to do it.

Plumbers Your plumbers will also need access to the build before the plasterboard stage and even before some of the flooring is installed, as they'll lay the pipework for your water supply and central heating system, and sort out waste piping. They'll work on your kitchen and bathroom, and probably bring any necessary pipework up to the house. Some plumbers will install taps, sinks and bathroom fittings, too. Make sure you establish early on who is doing what, as there can be some crossover between the trades. Check that your plumber is actually certified to do the specific work you are asking him to do. Some are only certified to do particular jobs.

Plasterers Once the electrics have been sorted, and the walls are fully boarded, your plasterer will skim the walls and possibly the ceilings to give them a smooth finish. They'll also make good any areas around sockets or other fittings that may be uneven as a result of earlier work. A good plasterer is worth his weight in gold.

Specialist joiners These are, in effect, specialist carpenters who may be required to fit cupboards, build staircases or lay wooden floors. They are highly skilled and can usually create bespoke woodwork, such as doors and even skirting boards.

Tilers Whether you are tiling walls, floors or even the worktop in your kitchen, these are obviously the guys to call. They've got the necessary skills to cut and shape tiles for any room in your house.

Decorators When you reach the final stage of your project, call the decorators who will prepare the walls, paint, wallpaper and create the finish you want throughout the house. Poor decoration can spoil a good building project, so get the best you can afford.

Other experts Some manufacturers will supply their own contractors or tradesmen to install kitchens, specialist windows, carpets, conservatories or bathroom fittings, and these can be worked into the schedule for your build.

LOOKING AFTER YOUR BUILDERS

As soon as you begin working with tradesmen, you will be establishing a very important relationship – a relationship that needs to be nurtured. The most successful projects are based on good communication, and a belief that you are all working towards the same outcome. You'll need to be scrupulously reliable if you expect your builders to be. That means paying regular visits to the site, being available when your builders have queries or problems, and taking an interest in your team as people. This is so important! It's your project and you need to make all of the right decisions at the right time to drive it forward.

Drop in with tea and snacks from time to time, or set up a hot drinks station on the build and keep it stocked up. This may sound trivial, but your team will appreciate the effort you make to set up great conditions. If you take on the lead management role on site, try and take the guys for a few drinks on the odd Friday after work. Its good for morale and gets you involved in the banter at the same time – all good fun!

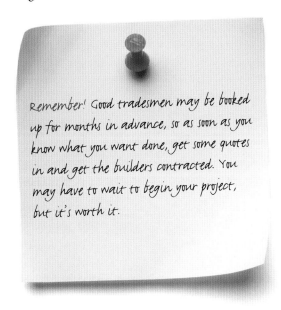

Remember! Good tradesmen may be booked up for months in advance, so as soon as you know what you want done, get some quotes in and get the builders contracted. You may have to wait to begin your project, but it's worth it.

The build process

Home renovation projects are set up in the same way, regardless of the work you are planning to do. The reason for this is that each tradesman will become involved at a particular time so that the project can progress in an orderly fashion. For example, you don't want your plasterer turning up before your electrician has finished sorting out the sockets, and you won't want your joiner to fit your gorgeous bespoke wardrobes until the plastering has been done.

This is one reason why it's important to schedule your build carefully at the outset, to be sure that the experts you need are available at the right time. If one aspect of the build runs later than expected, you can end up losing your 'slot' with the appropriate tradesman and be forced to wait until he becomes available to do the job. Again, communication is crucial. If things are running late, you'll need to be the first to know. Keeping everyone abreast of the schedule and any changes to it can make everything work much more smoothly.

It's a linear process

If this is your first project, you might find the build process a bit mind-boggling. It is effectively a very linear series of sequences that must be carefully organised and coordinated, and one thing follows the next in a fairly strict order. Any delays caused by one task – either through over-ambitious programming, bad weather, guys not turning up when they say they will, or clients changing their mind – can have an enormous (and dare I say it: catastrophic) impact on the success of the project.

After your pricing/costing document (see pages 380-1 and 383-385), your project programme really does become *the* most important piece of paper on the build. It has to be carefully monitored and adjusted every single day. Labour, materials and the delivery of all products have to be cleverly organised to make the build as simple, efficient and cost-effective as possible.

One terrible and very costly example of clients changing their minds on one of my projects involved a decision to install under-floor heating when we were a long way into the build. So, out went the traditional radiators – as well as the schedule and their budget. We made it *very* clear at the costing stage that if they changed their mind about this particular element of the build, it would have a terrible impact on progress. They said they wouldn't make any changes, as they wanted to go for the most affordable option. But they did!

Of course as a client it's your prerogative to change your mind. However, if you do so, you must fully understand the implications. On this project, it wasn't just a case of paying a little more for under-floor heating, which definitely came in above the cost of radiators, we also had to take into account the change in floor material, the delays caused by changing this, and the fact that all of the other tradesmen couldn't work efficiently on site while all the under-floor heating pipework was being laid. In fact, many chose to go home until this part of the work was fully complete.

The delays were terrible, and the increased costs were enormous. The client paid up, but it was a massive waste of time, effort and resources. If only they had made the decision at the outset of the project. What's the message here? Make your decisions and stick to them!

Breaking it down

The first step at the outset of any project is to break down everything that needs to be done to achieve the finished project. Next, work out who will be responsible. This can seem like a pretty time-consuming operation, but it's an important one. You'll need to get this up on a big board with a timeline, so that you know who is doing what at any stage of the job. Break everything down into smaller projects, and then get them down in order of importance before you decide what should be undertaken first.

Sometimes the tradesmen you need may not be available exactly when you would ideally like their services, so you may need to make some adjustments to the usual order of things. But remember: big jobs need to be done first! This means that big structural work such as foundations, walls, roofs, insulation, brickwork, doors and glazing need to be done first. Damp-proof courses and any underpinning should also be given first priority.

First things first!
- Foundations
- Walls
- Roofs
- Insulation
- Brickwork
- Doors
- Underpinning
- Damp-proof coursing

FIRST FIX

You may have heard your builders refer to 'first fix' and 'second fix', and these are effectively stages of a build. In the first fix, carpenters, builders and joiners get the walls up, while plumbers and electricians get the basic wiring and pipework sorted. For example, your plumber will put in the boiler and lay all the pipes, and your electrician will get the wiring right all over the house, through the walls and the floors. It's important to get these jobs done now because they are undertaken in the structure of the property; you'll be putting plasterboard, floors and ceilings in on top. Once this is done, your plasterers can move in and skim the walls.

The first fix is probably the most complicated to co-ordinate. A good project manager can ensure that carpenters and builders work together with electricians and plumbers, making sure that all the elements of the build are done efficiently. If you are managing the build, you'll need to keep a close eye on what is being done, and carefully schedule your tradesmen so that they turn up at the right time.

SECOND FIX

Once you've got those walls plastered, you've entered the 'second fix'. Ideally, all the main work has now been done. At this stage, the light switches and sockets are installed, the fixtures in your bathroom, utility room and kitchen are sorted by your plumber, and he'll also connect the radiators and anything else that affects your heating and water supply. After this, the final stages of decoration can go ahead, which means installing and finishing bathroom and kitchens.

If money is tight, you need to prioritise your first fix. It's a lot more expensive to get the structural work done in fits and starts; when you've got the tradesmen on site, it's a good idea to get it all done. You can, however, delay the second fix in some rooms if necessary; you don't need so many tradesmen at this stage, and it's more of a connection job than anything more major.

SNAGGING

Snagging is a term used to describe minor errors or defects, which will need to be corrected by the builder. At the end of the project, it's your responsibility (or your project manager or architect, if you have one) to check everything over with a fine-tooth comb to ensure that you are happy with the finishes – and literally anything else. This doesn't mean that you can suddenly decide that your sink is in the wrong place; it simply means that everything has been completed to agreed specifications. The contractor is obliged to put these problems right if they do not meet the standards required for the job.

DEFECT LIABILITY PERIOD

After the snagging has been completed, there should be an agreed 'defects liability period'. This can be as little as six months or as long as a few years. A small portion of the budget is retained by the client (maybe 2.5 percent) so that if any problems do occur within the agreed period, the contractor has to come and put them right. When the defects liability period is over, and any defective work has been corrected, you then need to pay the balance of the retention. The most common problem during this period is cracking which can occur in plasterwork affecting decorative finishes, as materials dry out over a longer period of time.

The planning process

The planning process is as much fun as sticking pins in yourself. It's as hard to understand as Chaucer and it's as difficult to navigate as the maze at Hampton Court. I'm serious. The planning process in the UK needs a radical overhaul to make it simple, efficient, and logical with a little bit of common sense thrown in for good measure. I've been praying for this since I entered the world of architecture at the age of 16, but the planning gods refuse to answer my prayers and make our lives easier. I completely understand that if there was a planning 'free-for-all', with no laws or constraints, then who knows what state our towns and villages would be in, but the level of control has gone too far and it is never clear what the planners actually want. There is confusion between style, taste and the letter of the law in planning policy. You can follow the policy like a studious pupil, ticking every planning box imaginable, but it will still go to the planning committee and an annoying member with no design or planning expertise could say 'I just don't like it'. Your scheme could be thrown out on the basis of one person's opinion, costing you time and often a lot of money in fees. It drives me nuts!

The basic principal is that if you are making any significant aesthetic change to the outside of your building (changing window positions or opening up new doorways to the front of your house) adding any additional space (porches, extensions, conservatories, or dormer windows) or if you are making any change of use to the inside of the building (dividing your house into two separate flats) then you will need some form of planning permission granted by your local council.

The planning process is a game. If you try and fight the game aggressively and without clever tactics you will never win. You need to understand the laws of the game and use them to your advantage to push your proposals through. Think like a chess player, a politician, a diplomat, a peacekeeper and military strategist to win the planning war. Employ a good architect and even a planning consultant to beef up your battalion.

Planning laws have changed a great deal in the last few years, and you can now make significant alterations to your home without the need for planning permission. This is called 'permitted development'. You still need to make an application for your permitted development rights, but it is a quicker process and does not need to go to public consultation; so, in effect, no one can object to what you are doing as long as your proposals are within the local permitted development rules (see page 372).

Having said that, there are still many renovation projects that need permission from either your local council or, if you live in a conservation area or on a private estate, the board, management committee or residents' association. Always, always check that the changes you propose are acceptable well before you begin the build. Finding out that you needed permission *after* the build has been completed is not only illegal but can be a complete nightmare, and it's possible that you'll have to tear the whole thing down and begin again from scratch.

Your architect should be able to advise you on what permissions will be required, and who you need to contact in order to get them. In some cases, they'll fill out the forms for you, too – something that makes them worth their weight in gold!

Planners have a responsibility to ensure that every element of your proposed build is suitable for the character of your house and the area, and that it doesn't infringe on the privacy of your neighbours, the outdoor space, light and even parking. There are additional levels of control when your home is a listed building, or if it is situated in a Green Belt or conservation area. In this case, planners will also be looking at how your renovated property will appear from the street, including your choice of cladding, windows and conversions to the loft area that may affect the appearance of the roof.

Permitted development

In October 2008 the planning laws were relaxed (slightly) so that for certain changes you would only need to apply for 'permitted development rights'. These range from extensions and conservatories, to loft conversions, fitting solar panels, roof alterations, patios and driveways. The idea is that under permitted development, as long as the size or volume of anything you propose is under the maximum required size (an extension has to be less that 10 percent of the overall area of your house or less than 50 cubic metres in volume) then the local council have absolutely no control over what you build and what it looks like.

Permitted development rights are based on general planning permission that has been granted by parliament, and not your local authority. Remember, though, that the permitted development rights that apply to houses don't apply to flats, maisonettes or other buildings. You'll need to talk to your local authority about what's permitted in these cases.

You will need planning permission if you're building an extension:
- that will be closer to any kind of public access (for example, roads and footpaths) than the nearest part of the original house – unless there will be at least 20 metres between your extension and the road
- that will cover more than half the area of land around the original house
- that is taller than the highest part of the roof of the original house
- that has any part more than 4 metres high within 2 metres of your property's boundary
- that increases the volume of the original house by more than 15 percent or 70 cubic metres (whichever is greater)
- that comes within 5 metres of another building belonging to your house
- that seriously overshadows a neighbour's window that has been there for 20 years or more. In which case, you may face objections
- that's in a conservation area or it is a listed building (see pages 373-374)

You may also need planning permission if you're planning a loft conversion:
- that includes a dormer window or roof extension that would extend beyond the plane of the existing roof slope and is facing a road
- that will make some part of the house higher than the highest part of the existing roof
- that will add more than 40 cubic metres to the volume of a terraced house or more than 50 cubic metres to any kind of other house
- that increases the volume of the original terraced house by more than 10 percent or 50 cubic metres (whichever is greater), or by more than 15 percent or 70 cubic metres (whichever is greater) for any other type of house

Otherwise, you can make changes to your property inside, including moving walls, installing new bathrooms, changing your kitchen and altering flooring and other fixtures and fittings. Any significant internal changes will still require 'Building Control Approval', though. Building control is completely separate from the local planning department and its their job to monitor the standards of the building work to ensure it complies fully with things like disabled access, fire safety and insulation standards.

You still need to make an application to your local authority for permitted development work, but the planning fee is less than the usual 'full planning application fee' and takes less time. You should get a decision in four to six weeks, depending on how busy your planning officer is. You need to fill out a form, and, in some cases, the application may not need any architectural drawings.

I have to stress the fact that you should *always* ask if permission is required, even if you are pretty sure that your changes fall within the permitted development brief. Some councils have peculiar views on the ruling, and you just never know … it isn't worth the risk!

In some areas of the country, known generally as 'designated areas', permitted development rights are more restricted. If you live in a conservation area, a National Park, an Area of Outstanding Natural Beauty or the Norfolk or Suffolk Broads, you will need to apply for planning permission for certain types of work which do not need an application in other areas. There are also different requirements if the property is a listed building.

Full planning

If you want to make any changes or build any structure onto your house that is larger than the allowable permitted development size then you need to make a 'full planning application'. This will require a full set of existing and proposed architectural drawings, an ordinance survey map, a design and access statement, and a cheque from you to pay the planning fee (see below). This process should take eight to 12 weeks, but it often takes a lot longer!

Full planning means that your design goes to public consultation in your local area to allow people to voice their opinions; the planner will make a site visit and will recommend the project for approval or refusal. If it is a simple application, the planner will make the decision independently under what is called 'delegated powers', which means they do not need to consult the councillors within the local authority. If your scheme has many objections or is contentious in any way then the planner will refer the project to the monthly planning-committee meeting for the councillors to decide. This is a public meeting and you can attend if you wish. You can even book yourself in to make a three-minute speech (very accurately timed by the chair of the meeting!) to the councillors to hopefully push your project through.

Full planning permission grants permission for *all* aspects of your proposed build, although there may be some conditions attached. These will vary according to the council or estate's individual terms and ideologies, but they can include things like ensuring that certain materials are used, trees being planted or kept in place, and the colour or finish of external materials. In most cases, one significant condition is that the

development has to be commenced within three years of permission being granted. So while it's important to get the permission process started as early as you can, don't jump the gun if you aren't going to be making the changes in the near future!

Full planning applications:
What you need
• Full set of existing architectural plans
• Full set of proposed architectural plans
• Ordinance survey map
• Design and access statement
• Your chequebook!

Conservation areas

If your home is in a conservation area, you'll have extra hoops to jump through. In general, areas that include important examples of our social, cultural or aesthetic history are safeguarded from 'indiscriminate' change. This means that the buildings have to be protected, as well as their surroundings and the general environment, so that the character is not diminished.

Don't be too worried if your home falls into this category. Although councils have made a commitment to protect and preserve your area, they are aware that communities do change over time – and, in fact, must in order to remain vital and prosperous. What they are looking for is sympathetic development. So they may have particular conditions in terms of scale, design, materials and space between buildings. There may also be issues with trees, demolition and even satellite dishes! Your application will be more detailed than it would be for the usual planning permission, and you'll have to provide details and examples of materials and colours, as well as a design statement.

Listed buildings

When buildings are 'listed' they are placed on statutory lists of buildings or 'special architectural or historic interest'. Listed buildings may or may not fall within a conservation area, but they will require special permission. There are three grades of listed buildings, which show their relative importance. These are:

- Grade I buildings: buildings of 'exceptional interest'
- Grade II* buildings: particularly important buildings of *more* than special interest
- Grade II buildings: these warrant 'every effort' to preserve them.

If you aren't sure whether your building is listed, or, if it is, what grade it is, contact your local authority, who can let you know.

Making alterations to listed buildings requires special, sensitive planning within quite strict guidelines. It's worth talking to your local council before you make an application, to work out the boundaries within which your project will need to fall. You'll need to provide:

- an assessment of the impact of the works on the significance of what they call 'the asset' – in other words, the special features of the building that make it of interest to the authorities.
- a statement of justification, explaining why the works are necessary or desirable.
- an archaeological assessment or field evaluation and a mitigation strategy where important archaeological remains exist.
- a structural report by an engineer familiar with heritage assets, which identifies defects and proposes remedies.

Don't panic. Listed buildings are not intended to be preserved in their original state forever, and as long as your proposals are sympathetic, you are in with a good chance of making the changes you want. You will need to get listed building consent (usually from your local planning authority in the usual way, although sometimes from the Secretary of State), and be rigorous about sticking to the terms of the permission. You can be sure that someone will come round to check, both during the build and after. This may all sound a bit daunting, but your architect and surveyor can give you a hand when you need it.

To find information on your local Planning Authority go to:

www.planningportal.gov.uk

and enter your postcode.

How to get planning permission

Phone your local council's planning department to see if you need to apply. It's also worth asking up front whether there are likely to be any problems with your application, what sorts of things are likely to be rejected, and how you can amend your proposal to get the permission you need. In fact, your local authority may be able to offer (possibly for a fee) pre-application discussions before a formal application is submitted in order to guide you through the process. This can minimise delays later in processing the application. You can even call into your local department to meet the 'duty officer', who can also advise you. Take in photographs of your property and an idea of your proposals and head over there when it suits you. You may have to sit there and wait to speak to someone, but it's well worth doing before you commit to any further work.

You will be sent an application form, which should be returned to them with the correct fee, a plan of the site, and a copy of the drawings and plans that show what you wish to do to the property. From here, your application will be placed on a Planning Register at the council's offices, where anyone who is interested can inspect it.

Your application will be considered by the relevant panel, and you can expect an answer within about eight weeks. If you don't hear from them, don't hesitate to chase them up! If your application is refused, ask the planning department if changing your plans might make a difference.

APPEALING A DECISION

If your plans are rejected, you can usually submit a revised application with modified plans free of charge, within 12 months of the decision on your first application. If you decide to appeal, you must do so within three months of the councils' decision.

If you need help, you can hire a planning agent who will make the appeal for you. Your architect can also do this. Be aware, however, that this type of assistance will cost you. In most cases, appeals are made in writing, but for bigger projects you may have a 'hearing' or an 'enquiry' or, if you are in one of the councils running this pilot scheme, there may be a fasttrack appeal process. You'll need to ask your local council for details about what's on offer.

It's worth noting that about a third of all appeals overturn the original decision. If you don't get the permission you want, carefully study the inspector's report, which is included with the decision notice. This will explain the decision in some detail, and make it pretty clear what your options are!

BUILDING REGULATIONS

Just when you think you've got the permissions thing cracked, you may be surprised to learn that your development work may also need building regulations approval. This has nothing to do with planning permission and the rules are there to ensure that minimum standards on the build are upheld – in other words, your property is structurally safe, protected from fire risks, is energy efficient, and has adequate ventilation. Some building work doesn't need approval, including repairs, replacing drains, new bathrooms and new central heating, where no major structural alternations are required. Once your build has started, a building control surveyor will drop by to check that the regulations are being complied with. At the end of the works, you'll need to get a 'completion certificate'. You'll need this in the future, if and when you decide to sell your home. There are loads of clauses in the building regulations, and it's worth chatting to your surveyor, builder and/or architect about the process. They can help you draw and submit plans and obtain approvals, as well as oversee the project from a regulation point of view. Don't be tempted to skip the building regulations stage; if you fail to comply you'll be in seriously hot water!

PARTY WALLS

Party wall agreements have become one of the most important, yet bureaucratic parts of many building projects. If you don't get these in place as quickly as possible, they can enormously delay getting the project started on site. If your development plans will affect a party wall (a shared wall separating two properties) you will need a party wall agreement,. This basically states that you agree to pay for any work needed to put right damage to the party wall of your neighbour's property. Even if you aren't actually touching the party wall, any work undertaken close to it will count. It normally takes about eight weeks to get this agreement sorted.

You will have to appoint your own surveyor to act on your behalf and he or she can also act on behalf of your neighbours. However, your neighbours must agree to this and they have the right to appoint their own surveyors if they wish. But you are liable for *all* of the surveyors' fees, no matter how many are involved in the process. On an ordinary domestic project, this can run into thousands of pounds. But it is more than worth it, to keep your neighbours happy and protected!

Costing your project

Creating the house of your dreams costs money, and chances are it's going to be more than you anticipated. Some of the most difficult moments of *The Home Show* are when I ask owners for a cheque to cover the work that needs to be done. On almost every single occasion they've underestimated the costs significantly – or employed wishful thinking! That's one reason why I always have several options available. If corners have to be cut to meet a budget, it's important that they are made in the right areas. It's better, for example, not to renovate one whole room than it is to renovate them all with inferior fittings. The people I work with on *The Home Show* like to see what they can get for their money, and make a decision based on what they really want and need. This is something you can do, too, with the help of a good architect.

Personally, I prefer to get the structural and spatial changes right, as these are the most important moves in the house. You can always compromise on the specification of the finishes to bring it on budget. Finishes can be upgraded later at fairly minimal cost, whereas calling in the big guns to make major changes can cost you a lot.

When costing your project you have to keep your eye on a whole host of elements – not just the build costs themselves, but the future replacement costs of the appliances, fixtures and fittings, their running costs and the potential cost of upgrading later on, if you can't afford what you want right now. If there is one key message to consider when planning your budget, it is: *Think long term*.

Estimates, estimates, estimates

Whether you are planning to run the project yourself, employ a project manager or simply get someone on site to supervise, you will need to keep an eye on the spreadsheet and the bottom line. Most importantly, however, you will need to work out the cost of every single element of your project, from the cost of skips, surveys, bin bags, nails and tool hire to labour, fixtures and fittings, planning fees and even mortgage or loan repayments. You need to know these costs, even if someone else is looking after the project, because it's your money being spent and you need to know exactly where it's going.

ASK YOUR ARCHITECT

First and foremost, your architect or surveyor should be able to give you a ballpark figure for overall renovations. This is useful to bear in mind when working out how much you can afford to do, but remember that this is only an initial guide. With any existing building, you are bound to come across unforeseen problems. This is one reason why you'll need a contingency fund. The golden rule is that you should make all of your decisions up front – well before your builders start on site. This way they can be priced properly. If you change your mind when works have started, you'll not only slow down the whole build, but you'll take a hit on your wallet, too. Fix everything up front and make sure you have a fixed-price contract.

I can't think of very many projects that haven't run over budget to some extent. Houses have a nasty habit of throwing up unforeseen problems, such as dry rot, damp or electrical circuit issues, as the project progresses, and no expert can account for these at the outset. Unfortunately, clients tend to have an equally nasty habit of changing their minds, too! Some changes can easily be absorbed into a building contract, but it's worth remembering that changing your mind at a critical time can be seriously costly.

GATHER ESTIMATES

Next, it's estimate time. Get more than one estimate for every single aspect of your project. You may wish to employ a building firm, with a team of specialists who can deal with the whole of the build or renovation. My office provides a full design and build service. I like to think of it as something like buying a car. You like the design, you can afford the price, and in 'x' number of weeks, we can hand you the keys to the finished product, created to your specifications.

Alternatively, you may wish to hire individual

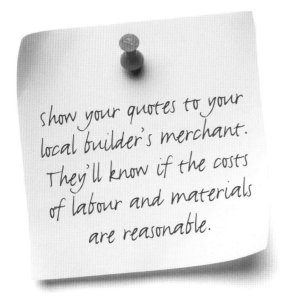

show your quotes to your local builder's merchant. They'll know if the costs of labour and materials are reasonable.

tradesmen to get the work you want done. You may ask your builder to sort out the materials and the fittings for the work, or you may wish to source them yourself. Whichever way you choose to work, get three estimates from completely different companies or experts, and do the same with the materials you are hoping to use.

Look at the fine print. If one quote seems substantially less than the others, work out why. The cheapest price is not always the best! Does it include *all* of the costs for all of the work you want done? Does it include the cost of materials? Does it include labour? Have they understood your brief and your needs as a client? Do they understand the standard and quality of finish you expect to suit your budget? Most importantly, perhaps, does it include a breakdown of a certain number of hours, or does the estimated cost get you the finished product?

Your local builder's merchant is a seriously good place to start if you want to cost the materials. In fact, even if your builders have included the cost of materials in their quote, you should check that you are getting a good deal. It may seem boring and pedantic to cost everything, but it's worth doing at the outset of the project so that you have a clear idea of what you are working with.

It's also worth showing your quote to your local builder's merchant. They'll be able to tell you

straightaway if the labour costs are usual for the area, if the costs of materials are accurate, and if the job you are proposing should come in at this price. These are the experts, so make use of them. Developing a relationship with your local builder's merchant may just be the best thing you ever do!

From estimates to quotes

An estimate is normally pretty much a 'guesstimate' on the part of your contractor, who will give you a ballpark figure of the costs involved in taking your project from beginning to end. An estimate – whether it is written or given verbally – is not legally binding, and you can count on an extra bill at the end in most cases! A quotation, however, is a definite price. It's worth getting at least two quotations, rather than estimates, and from builders who have been recommended to you. Remember that a seriously cheap quote is probably cheap for a reason; I hate to say it, but you get what you pay for!

Written quotes should itemise every single aspect of the work that needs to be done, and provide a breakdown of the costs of everything. It makes sense to set it up as a sort of 'shopping list', so you can choose exactly which items can be compromised in order to hit your budget. It may sound silly, but make sure there is a total, too, and that it includes VAT. It's amazing how many clients forget about VAT! Always check whether there are any exclusions or caveats, which might involve extra expense. Check your two quotes against each other, line by line, and see if there are any areas where there is a vast difference.

Looking at the prelims

This is something that needs mentioning. The vast majority of clients with whom I work haven't really heard of 'preliminaries', otherwise known as 'prelims'. These are normally the first thing on a contractor's pricing document, and they are comprised of the costs that need to be paid by the contractor to be able to do the job.

Not surprisingly, there will be a clear cost to finish each element of the building, such as the costs of fixtures, fittings and materials, as well as labour. In your bathroom, for example, you'd expect to pay for the tiles, the fittings and the cost of a plumber and a tiler. The prelims, however, are for all the other things that aren't actually elements of the building work itself. They include things like the contractor's insurance (very important!), health and safety, site set-up costs, skips, reserving parking bays, hoardings, building regulation fees, portaloos, parking costs, congestion charge and anything else that will come out of the contractor's pocket before he can even begin the build.

Prelims aren't cheap, so make sure you include them in your costings. In fact, on a major project they can often account for a substantial part of the build budget. As a client, these are the things for which you have to pay for, in order for the project to be completed professionally and in accordance with lots of building and insurance laws. Once you've got a quote with which you are happy, you can contract the work.

WORKING WITH ESTIMATES

Early estimates will always be approximate, but they can help you make important decisions. Once you know the likely costs, you can modify your plans to meet your budget.

Make sure you always check what is included in the estimate; although they are approximate, you need to know if something major hasn't been included, and then factor it in.

Remember that builders, architects and even surveyors can be very optimistic, and underestimate the cost significantly. Once you have an estimate that works, make sure you pin down the details so that you are both working to the same fixed cost.

It's in every tradesman's best interest to offer the best quote, so make sure you know exactly what you are paying for, and ensure that the quote isn't going to rise partway through the job.

Remember that the most common cause of rising costs is clients making changes to their plan. It's really important that you nail down exactly what you want before you get started. That might mean getting a surveyor and/or an architect on board to ensure that your plans are feasible and that you are making the best use of the space. Although this might seem like an outlay you can't really afford, trust me, you'll

Try Spon's Architects' and Builders' Price Book, it is updated every year to give you an idea of costs and cost management.

recoup the fee and more if you are able to stick to a plan that works.

The truth is that if you have never priced a project before then you need the help of a professional, whether it be an architect, quantity surveyor or your builder. On more complicated projects, a quantity surveyor's or an architect's fee will be easily repaid by the expert service that they offer.

Cost in everything! The most common mistake that people make is to take the estimate at face value, and look at the proposed cost of labour and materials alone. There is a lot more to consider (see page 00), and you just have to cost this in.

Take on board how long the project is likely to take. Projects almost always over-run, which will cost you more in many ways. For example, if you are renting somewhere to live while your home is being renovated, you are paying a loan until your mortgage can be extended, or you are paying some labourers on a day rate.

If you are managing the building project yourself and have some experience then produce a detailed schedule of all costs from material, screws and nails to any labour costs. When I was starting out I used to go in to see my local building merchants and the guys would help me price up the job based on their current material prices. It was great!

With experience you will be able to price your project on an average price per square metre of work, but you'll always find a detailed price is preferable and much easier to keep track of.

You need to have a fully fixed and accurate price before starting any work. This means turning an estimate into a quote.

CREATING A CONTRACT

Once you have agreed an estimate and a quote, it's important to create a contract with your builder. A contract makes it clear what your legal obligations are – and theirs! This is a legal document, although you can draw it up yourself without incurring any solicitor's fees. The most important elements to include are:

- the timescale (this can be broken down into stages, if required)
- the budget (this should *definitely* be broken down to indicate the costs of every element of the project; if your builder says that nails are going to cost £220, then they should)
- your builders' fees (again, if there are working with one contractor who has a number of different tradesmen working for him, break it down into the cost of the labour for each)

If you are hiring individual tradesmen, you'll need to draw up a contract for each one, including your project manager. This may seem like a time-consuming operation, and you may feel that it is unnecessary when you are working with reliable, trustworthy tradesmen, but take it from me: this is a step you simply can't afford to miss out.

Visit the Federation of Master Builders (www.fmb.org.uk) to download a free contract. You simply need to fill in the blanks.

DO I NEED A PROJECT MANAGER?

Project managers can be brilliant at securing cost-effective quotes and haggling on your behalf; they know the game, and they know the best prices. What's more, they can help to manage the project from all angles, including labour, materials and any licences or permissions you may need, and will be on hand to sort out problems practically and quickly. If you have another job, this can be a godsend. This doesn't mean that you don't have to

be on site as often as possible, or pass over all control for your budget. Keeping your eye on the bottom line at all times is essential, no matter who's running your project. Bear in mind the cost of your project manager; they'll need to be paid on a daily or weekly rate in most cases, so make sure they will add the equivalent value.

If you've never done project management before, don't try and do it yourself. It's a false economy and you will undoubtedly make some very costly mistakes. Project management is a fine art that takes a great deal of time to learn and master. If you do want to get involved, then employ an expert and work alongside them so that you can learn from him or her.

Remember that the building game is not just about raising the necessary funding to do the job; it is about managing that money properly once you have it.

Go to www.fmb.org.uk to download a free sample contract.

This is a sample chart that shows one way of keeping track of your build on a week by week basis.

	Task Name	W -3	W -2	W -1	W 1	W 2	W 3	W 4	W 5	W 6
1	Client instruction	▌								
2	Mobilisation		██	██						
3	Start on site				▌					
4	Site set up				██					
5	Strip-out				██	██				
6	Demolition					██	██			
7	Ground works/foundations						██	██		
8	Structural; brick and steel							██	██	██
9	Roofing								██	██
10	Partitioning								██	██
11	First fix electrical									
12	First fix plumbing									
13	Joinery/doors/windows etc									
14	Plastering									
15	Second fix plumbing									
16	Decoration									
17	Tiling									
18	Specialist glass									
19	Hardflooring									
20	Skirtings									
21	Second fix electrics									
22	Decoration finals									
23	Floor coverings									
24	Snagging									
25	Final clean									
26	Handover									

	W 7	W 8	W 9	W 10	W 11	W 12	W 13	W 14	W 15	W 16	W 17	W 18	W 19	W 20	W 21	W 22

Managing your money

First of all, think about where you are getting your money from, and then break it all down. Will you have a lump sum available to you, or will you rely on payments to meet the costs? The next step is to keep a detailed record of all of your payments and compare them constantly. If you are borrowing money from the bank then you may consider drawing it down in stages to suit the payment schedule from your contractor. There is no point drawing the entire sum down in one lump sum, as you will only have to pay interest on the grand total from the outset, when you may not need to.

FINANCING YOUR PROJECT

There are many ways of sourcing the appropriate funding for your project, but this depends on your personal financial situation, the type of refurbishment project you are doing and obviously the amount of money you need to do the job.

As my little Nana used to say to me: *If you can't afford it, you can't have it!* She hated taking on any debt and used to save her pennies like mad to enjoy the odd treat in life. She is right: the best way to pay for any work on your property is to save it, minimise debt and avoid any unnecessary interest charges. My Nana practically refurbished most of her little house herself with no experience whatsoever to keep the costs down.

If you need to borrow money then the most competitive way to do this is to increase your mortgage. A mortgage usually has low interest rates that can be spread over a long period of time. However, please make sure you don't over extend yourself! Being unable to repay your mortgage, falling into arrears and having your home repossessed is one of the most awful things to happen to any family. And in today's economic climate, lenders are pretty ruthless. Be incredibly safe and conservative with your borrowing.

If you need to borrow money against your credit cards or take out an expensive loan to fund the work, it's not the right time to make changes. The property market can fluctuate wildly, and you could end up pouring thousands of pounds into your home only to find that when you are forced to sell, you've made a loss. Wait until you are in a strong and comfortable financial position before making changes. I can't overstate the importance of this.

KEEPING TRACK OF YOUR MONEY

Always keep a record of all your payments and compare them to the original quotations at every single step of the way. Most builders provide breakdowns in stages, and are often paid at the end of each stage. Never, ever pay your builder a penny more than the work that has been completed to date on site. If you do, and he goes bust for any reason, you've lost your money.

You'll need to learn to operate a spreadsheet, whether you do this on your computer (a nice idea, because programs such as Excel will do the sums for you, and prevent any costly errors!) or in a traditional notebook with columns. Even if it seems insignificant, note down every cost in the appropriate column – that means everything from tea and biscuits for the builders, to the new light bulbs required. Little things have a habit of mounting up and if things become tight, you'll want to know where you are spending your money.

Keep a very tight reign on your finances. Watch every single penny, make sure you are getting good value for money by doing your research and managing your payments properly throughout the build. Get this right and you will be a very happy homeowner, get it wrong and you'll never want to do building work ever again. That would truly be a shame!

Sticking to your budget

The estimate (and, indeed, quote) you are given will be based on the materials, fixtures, fitting and finish you suggest at the outset. This is one reason why it's very important to do your research well before you get started! If you've got a top-of-the-range kitchen in mind, you'll need to be sure that you know the cost, and that it's factored in to the quote.

Sample tender from builder detailing the cost of upgrading a one-bedroom, one-bathroom, top floor flat to two-bed, two-bath with an attic conversion.

No.	Item	Description	Cost £
1	Preliminaries		
1.1		Waste clearance and hiring of skips including skip licences	1,200
1.2		Scaffolding	
		Option 1 with roof	4,000
		[Option 2 without roof	2,000]
1.3		Protection measures to minimise dust/disturbance to flat below	400
2	Demolition/strip out		
2.1		Kitchen & bathroom to include all redundant electrics and pipework, laminate floor covering throughout, stair carpet and electric cupboard	400
2.2		Remove wall between existing sitting room and bedroom	600
2.3		Remove existing ceiling for new staircase and existing roof structure	400
2.4		Remove skirting board in order to fit new hardwood floor	80
3	Structural work		
3.1		Remedial brickwork to party wall as per engineer's drawing	250
3.2		Cast padstones in concrete for steels	600
3.3		Supply and install steel beams to engineer's spec and drawings	2,500
3.4		Build up party walls to form cheeks for new roof in stock bricks	4,000
3.5		Install new suspended timber floor joists allowing for new loft ensuite drainage run	1,300
3.6		Install new roof timbers and double up existing rafters to structural engineer's spec and drawings	1,200
3.7		Adapt existing rafters to allow for 2 no. Velux roof lights	Inc in 3.6
3.8		New timber studwork for walls to loft rooms	850
3.9		Supply and fit new staircase to loft positioned over existing flight. New stairs to be fitted with newel posts, handrail and spindles	1,400
3.10		Supply and fit tongue and groove high density board to new loft room floors	500
4	Coverings and Insulation		
4.1		Install breathable membrane and roof tiles to mansard pitched roof	2,500
4.2		Felt/EPDM rubber membrane or similar to flat roof	800
4.3		Install insulation to loft rooms. Allow for Actis Tri iso Super 10 insulation below rafters to minimum build up but ensure adequate ventilation	1,800
4.4		Supply and fit lead flashings as per drawings	1,000
5	Windows		
5.1		Supply and fit 2 no. timber dormer windows to loft mansard. All windows and roof lights to provide adequate light and ventilation in accordance with National Building Regulations	900
5.2		Supply and fit 2 no. Velux roof lights	Inc in 5.1
5.3		Supply and fit 1 no. small bathroom window	Inc in 5.1

No.	Item	Description	Cost £
6	Electrics		
6.1		All power, auxiliary and lighting to new loft bedroom and en suite. Allow for standard white goods, cover plates to be decided.	800
6.2		All power, auxiliary and lighting to new open plan kitchen and sitting room , existing bathroom and small bedroom as per drawings	600
6.3		Supply and fit 5 no. spotlights in kitchen, 2 no. spots and wall light in bathroom	200
6.4		Relocate main supply and meter to above ground floor entrance	500
6.5		Supply and fit 2 no. self-contained mains operated smoke alarms must conform to BS5446 part 1	180
6.6		Supply and fit 1 no. computer socket, 1 no. telephone socket and 1 no. TV socket	150
6.7		Supply and fit 1 no. shaving socket in en suite bathroom	50
6.8		Supply and fit 2 no. underfloor electric heating mats beneath tiling of two bathrooms	320
7	Mechanical services		
7.1		Adapt existing and supply new drainage for new loft en suite, replumb existing bathroom and new kitchen. Supply and fit new gutters and downpipes to roof in black plastic	700
7.2		Supply and fit new standard combi boiler in new location in new kitchen and associated pipework	1,650
7.3		Supply and fit new pipework as per drawings to new open plan kitchen and sitting room to include all core drilling and fans	included
7.4		Supply and fit 2 no. 4 " Expelair fans to both bathrooms	300
7.5		Supply and fit 3 no. TVR controlled ouput convector radiators and 2 no. (wet) towel rails	900
7.6		Labour only to fit provided sanitaryware to both bathrooms.	1,000
8	Plasterboard/plastering		
8.1		Supply and fit plasterboard and finish skim coat to new loft rooms and to ceilings of 1st floor rubbed down ready for paint finish.	2,100
8.2		Remedial works throughout 1st floor as required rubbed down ready for paint finish	500
8.3		Replace cornices in sitting room and kitchen	300
9	Kitchen		
9.1		Labour only to fit new kitchen and appliances	1,000
10	1st & 2nd fix carpentry		
10.1		New en suite bathroom cupboard	150
10.2		New bathroom undersink cupboard	150
10.3		New bedroom cupboards and undereave storage cupboards	450
10.4		4 no. new FD30 fire-resistant doors with intumescent strips, architraves, door furniture and ironmongery	700

No.	Item	Description	Cost £
10.5		New skirting boards to sitting room, open plan kitchen and bedroom	540
10.6		Replace front door and locks	320
10.7		Dormer fascia boards to be in timber	included
11	Finishes		
11.1		Supply and fit new engineered oak hardwood floor to sitting room, open plan kitchen and 1st floor landing @ £48 per m^2	1,440
11.2		Supply underlay and carpet to new loft bedroom, 2 no. staircases, loft floor landing and small 1st floor bedroom @ 28 per m^2	1,120
11.3		Supply tiles and tiling to en suite and existing bathroom wall and floors	2,000
12	Decoration		
12.1		Allow for painting throughout. Colours to be decided	2,800
13	Communal areas		
13.1		Remove and replace flooring to include inlaid coir matting	300
		Total	47,900.00
		Total inc VAT	£56,282.50

No.	Item	Description	Cost £
2.	Client's costs for buying materials		
2.1	Sanitary ware	2 no. wash hand basins, 2 no. wc's (one with concealed cistern), 1 no. shower enclosure, tray and shower head and controls, 1 no. bath with shower attachment and glass side panel	1,900 inc VAT
2.2	Kitchen and equipment	1 no. 1400 rpm washing machine, 1 no. dishwasher, 1 no. built-in oven, 1 no. gas hob, 1 no sink and tap, 1 no 70/30 fridge freezer, cupboard carcasses, drawers and doors and wood block top	3,752
			for fitting + 1,000
		Total	6,652.00
		Total inc VAT	£7,816.10

Changes cost money! Although a few hundred pounds spent here and there 'upgrading' your original plans might not seem like much, they can add up to thousands and take you well over your budget.

When setting your budget, make sure you are getting exactly what you want, and that you know the costs of the materials and how much it will take to get them fitted. It can, for example, cost considerably more to get some worktops fitted than others, and some items may need to be custom made to fit your space or your individual requirements. Remember, too, that 'top-end' doesn't necessarily mean 'right for you'! Consider carefully your lifestyle, the way your family uses the space, and the things you use the most. If you are a whiz in the kitchen and spend your free time cooking, then you'll want the right appliances to get the job done. If you've got a house full of teenaged boys, you'll want hardwearing and durable, rather than fashionable and expensive. Spend your money at the heart of your house where it really matters to you.

You'll have to be ruthless with yourself once the work has begun, and stick to your guns. Obviously small changes can throw up better and bigger ideas, and you may be forced to alter your plans to get what you want, but the nitty-gritty details should remain the same or you'll be paying through the nose just when you least expect it.

Contingencies, and more contingencies …

There's not just a small chance that your renovation project will cost you more than you expect – it's pretty much a certainty that it will. You will need a cushion against cost over-runs, and this will be your 'contingency fund'. Builders' quotes do not cover 'unforeseens', which can be anything from unexpected subsidence, rotting timbers, electrical disasters and damp to a change in the exchange rate, which means that your delightful Italian tiles will cost much more to purchase and transport than expected. Your contingency fund covers these potential problems which will massively reduce the pressure when things go wrong, and also leave you a little leeway to make small changes.

For small projects, the golden rule is to allow a contingency of about 15 to 20 percent. In the past, 10 percent was recommended, but I feel very strongly that having a plumper cushion can definitely make things more comfortable. So if your quote comes in at £20K, then make sure you have about £24K at your disposal. That doesn't mean leaving this money to sit in the bank, but simply having access to it at the same rate when it is required.

The good news is that you'll have room to manoeuvre, money to cover the 'unforeseens', and, if you keep your money tightly controlled and impeccably costed, some money left over at the end of the project to splash out on something really special.

THE TRUE COST OF THE CHOICES YOU MAKE

While it can seem cost-effective to skimp on some items, such as finishes, appliances or even fittings, it's worth thinking about the cost of replacing them in future, and, of course, the cost of running them. If a top-end washing machine is going to cost a little more now, but save you hundreds on your electricity bills in future, it's a good investment. If purchasing a budget toilet and sink will save you money on your build costs, but cost twice as much to replace in future, you aren't making any real savings. Look at the difference between what you'd save by cutting corners, and what your replacement and running costs might be in the future, and make your decision based on that.

Allow a contingency of 15-20 per cent – it will leave you room to manoeuvre.

Thinking long term

Although you may dream of having a spacious new addition or a luxury kitchen, it may not be practical for a few reasons. First of all, are you planning to stay in your home long term? If moving is on the cards, you have to consider whether you are adding any real value to your home by making the changes you want. You may end up selling at a loss, if the changes don't increase the value of your home. It might be worth talking to an estate agent to see if that beautiful new bathroom or conservatory is money down the drain.

Secondly, even if you are planning your 'home for life', you need to consider your budget constraints. This is important. You need to plot out what's most important to you and then prioritise. Chances are you may not be able to afford to do everything at the top end, so what matters most? Where do you spend most of your time? What do you hate or love most about your present home? If you spend all of your time in your kitchen, then spend your money there. If you hate dark halls, then open things up to let in the light.

Don't be tempted to think short term. If you can't afford everything you want, then do the best you can with the parts of your house that matter most. There's no point in thinking that a budget kitchen will work in the short-term, and that you'll simply replace it in a few year's time. The cost of this will be far, far greater than just the price of the units and materials. You'll need to factor in taking out the old kitchen, potentially moving pipes and electrical sockets, the cost of the new fittings and appliances, and, of course, labour, skips and everything else. And don't forget the disruption! It may just not be worth going halfway now.

It is worth remembering that if you have the builders in now, you might as well get the most for your money, even if that means leaving some rooms until you can afford them. Having said that, if you've got an electrician on site and you know what you want to do when the funds are available, it may be more cost effective to get the sockets moved now; similarly, you may want to get the plumbing done for your dream bathroom, and get the location of the fittings right, plumping up for the best-quality

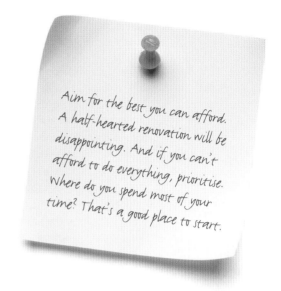

Aim for the best you can afford. A half-hearted renovation will be disappointing. And if you can't afford to do everything, prioritise. Where do you spend most of your time? That's a good place to start.

ones later on. Ideally, work should be done in one go. You'll save time, money, and they'll be less disruption if all the plumbing, all the electrical work and everything else in your home – or the part of the house you're working on – is completed as one job rather than just 'here and there'.

Aim for the best you can afford. Not only will good-quality materials, fixtures and fittings last longer, but you'll also be happier. A half-hearted renovation with compromises all over the place is never going to be satisfying, and you'll end up plotting your next refit, which you may not really be able to afford. Your home is your castle, so make sure you are happy with every decision you make.

Useful websites

APPLIANCES
www.howdens.co.uk
www.smegretro.co.uk
www.stoves.co.uk

ARCHITECTS
To find an approved local architect contact
the Royal Institute of British Architects
(www.architecture.com) or contact your
local planning department who may be able
to make recommendations.
www.architect-yourhome.com
www.clarkedesai.com

BASEMENTS
www.londonbasement.co.uk

BATHROOMS
www.agapedesign.it
www.artquitect.net
www.bathstore.com
www.bristan.com
www.cphart.co.uk
www.duravit.com
www.hudsonreed.co.uk
www.ideal-standard.co.uk
www.mirashowers.co.uk
www.plumbwell.co.uk
www.roca-uk.com
www.shadesfurniture.co.uk
www.siadaw.co.uk
www.surfacetiles.com
www.tapcentre.com

BI-FOLD DOORS
www.csg-ltd.org.uk
www.expressbifoldingdoors.co.uk
www.sunfold.com

BLINDS AND SHUTTERS
www.digetex.com
www.blindsuk.net

www.nicora.co.uk
www.shutterlyfabulous.com
www.simplyromans.co.uk

CORIAN WORKTOPS
www.corian.co.uk.

BUILDING CONTROL
www.mlm.uk.com

CARPETS AND RUGS
www.funonthefloor.com
www.knotsrugs.co.uk
www.mailorderrugs.co.uk
www.wovenground.com
www.yourfloors.co.uk

FIREPLACES
www.biofires.com
www.conmoto.com
www.cvo.co.uk
www.encompassco.com
www.thecastironfireplacecompany.co.uk

FURNITURE
 www.designclassics.co.uk
www.aram.co.uk.
www.atlanticshopping.co.uk
www.atlanticshopping.co.uk
www.bedsdirect.com
www.bonbon.co.uk
www.chesterfields.co.uk
www.desser.co.uk
www.dwell.co.uk
www.erik-jorgensen.com
www.frostdesignuk.com
www.habitat.co.uk
www.haloliving.com
www.ikea.com
www.indigofurniture.co.uk
www.jamesburleigh.co.uk
www.johnlewis.com

www.johnplanck.co.uk
www.knoll.com
www.lescouillesduchien.co.uk
www.marksandspencer.com
www.pavilionrattan.co.uk
www.scp.co.uk
www.stokke.com
www.thechair.co.uk
www.theoldcinema.co.uk
www.theorchardhomeandgifts.com
www.thewallbedworkshop.co.uk
www.trendyproduct.co.uk
www.vitra.com
www.zedsofabed.co.uk

GARAGE CONVERSIONS
www.garageconversions.com
www.garageconversionsuk.co.uk

GARDEN SHED/STUDIO
www.greenretreats.co.uk

GLASS
www.csgs.ltd.uk
www.jeld-wen.co.uk
www.londonandlocal.com
www.pilkington.com

INSULATION
www.celotex.co.uk
www.energysavingtrust.org.uk
www.kingspan.com

INTERNAL DOORS
www.enfielddoors.co.uk

IRONMONGERY AND DOOR/ DRAWER HANDLES
www.detailplus.co.uk
www.fulhambrass.com

KITCHENS
www.binova.com
www.eclecticinteriors.co.uk
www.graincreative.com
www.howdens.com

www.ikea.com
www.poggenpohl.com
www.simplehuman.com

JOINERY
www.howdens.com
www.inputwindows.co.uk

LIGHTING
homeshow.simply-scandinavian.co.uk
www.aarevalo.com
www.anglepoise.com
www.christopherhyde.com
www.flos.com
www.gblighting.co.uk
www.ilight.co.uk
www.johnlewis.com
www.lightahome.co.uk
www.lighting-direct.co.uk
www.litecraft.co.uk
www.londonlights.net
www.lutron.com
www.next.co.uk
www.originalbtc.com
www.thelightsource.co.uk

PAINT
www.johnstonespaint.com
www.rowleysdecoratormerchants.co.uk
www.thelittlegreene.com

RADIATORS
www.bhl.co.uk
www.bisque.co.uk
www.theradiatorcompany.co.uk
www.theradiatorgallery.com

RUBBER FLOORING
www.dalsouple.com

SOFT FURNISHINGS
www.brianfisher.co.uk
www.busbyfabric.com
www.coloroll.uk.com
www.harlequin.uk.com
www.johnlewis.com

www.linenhouse.com.au
www.marksandspencer.com
www.next.co.uk
www.nono.co.uk
www.thefinecottoncompany.com
www.wilmaninteriors.com

STONE
www.agandm.co.uk
www.granite-concepts.co.uk
www.stonell.com

STRUCTURAL SURVEYORS AND ENGINEERS
www.rics.org.

STUDIES
www.bonbon.co.uk
www.hammonds-uk.com
www.nevillejohnson.co.uk

TECHNOLOGY
www.apple.com
www.sonos.com

TILES
www.britishceramictile.com
www.ceramictilewarehouse.com
www.firedearth.com
www.johnson-tiles.com
www.material-lab.co.uk
www.originalstyle.com
www.toppstiles.co.uk

TIMBER FLOORING
www.urbaneliving.co.uk
www.floors2go.co.uk
www.junckers.co.uk
www.kahrs.com
www.yourfloors.co.uk

UNDER-FLOOR HEATING
 www.theunderfloorheatingstore.com

UNDERPINNING
www.asuc.org.uk.

VELUX WINDOWS AND SKYLIGHTS
www.velux.co.uk.

WALLPAPER
www.blendworth.co.uk
www.cole-and-son.com
www.harlequin.uk.com
www.scandiliving.com

WARDROBES
www.spaceslide.co.uk
www.wardrobemagic.co.uk

TIMBER FLOORING
www.urbaneliving.co.uk
www.floors2go.co.uk
www.junckers.co.uk
www.kahrs.com
www.yourfloors.co.uk

UNDER-FLOOR HEATING
www.theunderfloorheatingstore.com

UNDERPINNING
www.asuc.org.uk.

VELUX WINDOWS AND SKYLIGHTS
www.velux.co.uk.

WALLPAPER
www.blendworth.co.uk
www.cole-and-son.com
www.harlequin.uk.com
www.scandiliving.com

WARDROBES
www.spaceslide.co.uk
www.wardrobemagic.co.uk

Acknowledgements

Thanks to everyone who has helped make this book possible: a special thank you to my wife Catri for her love and support and to my kids Georgie, Emilio and Iona who make everyday the perfect day; to my Mam and Dad, and my sisters, Sam, Ava and Shirley and all of my family in the North-East and in London.

Thanks also to my business partner and close friend Bobby Desai (architectural super hero), his family, and to all of the super-talented guys at my office, Clarke:Desai, who work so hard to realise our incredible projects. Thanks especially to Owen and to my PA, Kellie, who helped deliver so much of the material you see in the book.

I will always be grateful to my publisher and the wonderful team at Weidenfeld & Nicolson, in particular Michael Dover, Jane Sturrock and writer Karen Sullivan who were not only brilliant, but somehow remained unbelievably calm throughout all the chaos. I still don't know how we did it!

Thank you to Jo McGrath (TV super hero) and our team at Tiger Aspect Productions. It's been a great years!

A special thank you to my agent Rosemary Scoular and her assistant Wendy Millyard at United Agents.

And I'd like to say thank you to everyone who reads this book. I hope, in some way, that it helps to improve the quality of ordinary homes and the lives of people across Britain.

Thanks to all!

George x

Index

Picture credits

ALAMY
230 © First Light / Alamy; 304 © Joe Fairs / Alamy; 306, 310 ; © Red Cover / Alamy.

ARCAID
239 (right) Marc Gerritsen/arcaid.co.uk (arch. Louis Liou/Very Space); 173 (both) Martine Hamilton Knight/arcaid.co.uk (arch. Bauman Lyons); 178 (bottom left and right) Gavin Jackson/arcaid.co.uk (arch. Milk Studio); 168 Gavin Jackson/arcaid.co.uk (arch. Luis Trevino); 169, 171 (centre left, centre right, bottom left), 180, 254, 255, 258-9, 262 (top), 266 Will Pryce/arcaid.co.uk (arch. Paul Archer); 166, 171 (top right) Will Pryce/arcaid.co.uk (arch. Curtis Wood).

CORBIS
302 © Abode/Beateworks/Corbis; 80 (top) © Elizabeth Whiting & Associates/Corbis; 80 (bottom) © Image Source/Corbis.

BOBBY DESAI
138

MICHAEL DOVER
162 (all)

EDIFICE
90 (bottom) Edifice/Emily Cole; 78 Edifice/Gillian Darley; 8 (bottom left and right), 79 (top), 90 (top), 98 (both), 106 (both), 112 (both) Edifice/Philippa Lewis; 8 (top left) Edifice/Kim Sayer; 79 (bottom) Edifice/Tom Thistlethwaite.

ELIZABETH WHITING & ASSOCIATES
222 Rodney Hyett/Elizabeth Whiting & Associates; 225 Di Lewis/Elizabeth Whiting & Associates.

FLOS
283 Kelvin LED lamp (designers Antonio Citterio with Toan Nguyen).

GETTY IMAGES
294 Melanie Acevedo/Getty; 218 Matthew Ward/ Dorling Kindersley/Getty.

IKEA
196 © Bjursta dining table, 215 © Rationell waste storing bins, 220 (both) © Rationell pull-out interior fitting; Rationell Variera iron holder, 232 © Besta/ Framsta TV storage combination, 291 © Effektiv storage combinations, 326 © New Komplement 5 compartment trouser hanger, 353 (both) © Lillangen washbasin cabinet combination; Antonius basic desktop unit on castors, 354 © Godmorgon/Norrviken 2 drawer washstand with Norrviken double washbasin and Grundtal legs.

MARK JOHNSON
150, 167, 174 (bottom), 177, 194-5, 212, 234, 237 (bottom), 248, 287, 289 (bottom), 293 (bottom), 296 (all), 312, 319 (both), 330 (bottom), 331, 337 (all),

ANDREW LEE
120, 334 Andrew Lee; 352 (bottom left) Andrew Lee (arch. Chrichton Wood Architects); 165 (top), 216 (both), 240, 279 Andrew Lee (arch. Dualchas); 299 Andrew Lee (arch. McKeown Alexander); 358 (bottom) Andrew Lee (arch. Morris and Steedman Associates); 199, 352 (bottom right) Andrew Lee (arch. Richard Murphy Architects); 301 Andrew Lee (arch. Rural Design); 256 Andrew Lee (arch. Studio KAP); 281 Andrew Lee (arch. Zoo Architects).

MASTERFILE
305 (right) © Red Cover / Masterfile; 305 (left) © Sheltered Images / Masterfile.

GORDON MATTA-CLARK
146 © 2010 Estate of Gordon Matta-Clark / Artists Rights Society (ARS), New York, DACS London.

NIKO (UK) LIMITED
238 Niko (UK) Limited.

JEREMY PHILLIPS
146 (bottom), 161, 196 (top), 200 (right), 204, 205 (top), 206, 207 (right), 241, 245 (bottom), 252, 268, 280, 315 (both), 320, 344 (both), 345, 347, 349, 350, 355, 358 (top), 362 Jeremy Phillips.

NIGEL RIGDEN
149, 154 (all), 157 (top), 171 (top left), 171 (bottom right), 188, 191, 201, 202, 203 (top left), 205 (bottom), 214, 239 (left), 245 (top), 246, 253, 263, 264, 270, 272-3, 282, 286, 322-3, 340, 341, 343, 348, 351, 357, 363 Nigel Rigden; **203 (bottom), 242-3** Nigel Rigden / Stan Bolt Architect; **247** Nigel Rigden / Peter Dowsett Architect; **288** Nigel Rigden / Rebecca Dyer; **207 (left)** Nigel Rigden / Chris Dyson Architects; **157 (bottom left and right)** Nigel Rigden / McLean Architects Ltd; **215 (bottom)** Nigel Rigden / Robert Seymour & Associates; **208-9, 342-3** Nigel Rigden / Western Design Architects; **8 (top right), 165 (bottom), 200 (left), 203 (top right), 346, 352 (top)** Nigel Rigden / David Wright Design.

ROBERT HARDING PICTURE LIBRARY
126 (right) Christopher Rennie / Robert Harding Picture Library.

ROCA LTD
359 W+W (Approx. £2300 RRP ex.VAT), Roca Ltd

SHADEPLUS BY TENSARC
262 (bottom) ShadePlus by tensARC

CHRIS TERRY
4

THE ART ARCHIVE
277 National Gallery London/Eileen Tweedy

TIGER ASPECT PRODUCTIONS
124, 139, 148

BONBON TRADING LTD
285 © Ulisse wall bed, **327** © LGM 02 wallbed combinations

JOHN WRIGHT
2

First published in hardback in Great Britain in 2010
by Weidenfeld & Nicolson an imprint of
the Orion Publishing Group Ltd
Orion House, 5 Upper St Martin's Lane,
London WC2H 9EA
an Hachette UK Company

10 9 8 7 6 5 4 3 2 1

Text copyright © 2010 George Clarke
Design and layout copyright © 2010
Weidenfeld & Nicolson

A CIP catalogue record for this book is available
from the British Library.

ISBN: 978-0-297-86032-7

Art directed by Natasha Webber
Designed by John Round Design
Picture research by Caroline Hotblack
Plans drawn by Owen Jones
Edited by Jane Sturrock, Karen Sullivan
Proofread by David Atkinson
Index by David Rudeforth

Printed and bound in China.

The Orion Publishing Group's policy is to use
papers that are natural, renewable and recyclable
and made from wood grown
in sustainable forests. The logging and
manufacturing processes are expected to conform
to the environmental regulations of
the country of origin.

www.orionbooks.co.uk